"Success is not final, failure is not fatal:
it is the courage to continue that counts."

—Anonymous

As you pursue this edition of The Innovative Dinosaur, *embrace the agile mindset within these pages,*
bearing in mind that it may include inadvertent errors.
In the spirit of adaptability, this book is presented in its proof-ready stage, potentially containing errors
that reflect our commitment to growth and change.

Published by Forbes Books, Charleston, South Carolina. An imprint of Advantage Media Group.
Forbes Books is a registered trademark, and the Forbes Books colophon is a trademark of Forbes Media, LLC.
Printed in the United States of America.

ISBN: 979-8-88750-673-9 (Paperback)
ISBN: 979-8-88750-674-6 (eBook)

Praise for *The Innovative Dinosaur*

"I recommend this book for all leaders who are heading toward building the enterprise of tomorrow... What I also like about the work is the way the author is telling stories through friendly visuals—he has mastered that art."

Pascal Bornet, Best-Selling Author, AI & Automation Expert, Previous Leader of AI & Automation at McKinsey

"The author has done a great job explaining the challenges faced by the traditional manufacturing sector in light of the ongoing technological disruption....This book is a great read for business managers and owners to walk them through the demands of tomorrow's landscape."

HE Mahmoud Mohieldin, Executive Director for the ME at the IMF, UN Special Envoy on Financing the 2030 Agenda

"The Innovative Dinosaur is a must read for CIOs and CTOs who are serious about transforming their ICT organization and ushering the business into the elite club of innovative digital organizations."

Mike Haddad, Former Director of Information and Communication Technologies, UNFCCC

"This book fills a gap in the current literature by collecting both the background needed for the reader and the organizational transformational process needed for the professional."

HE Ahmed Darwish, Former Chairman of Suez Canal Economic Zone, Egypt Minister of State for Administrative Development.

"In a fast moving environment, the strongest does not mean the mightiest, but the most agile and resilient and, as a matter of fact, the most suitable ecosystem....
Motaz has the unique ability to create this ecosystem, being both innovative and structured.... The Innovative Dinosaur perfectly reflects it."

Guillaume Devauchelle, Member of French National Academy of Technology, Board Member of ESIGELEC (Engineering School)

"In general, it is rare to find a book that combines both theoretical and practical approaches. The Innovative Dinosaur (TID) takes us into a complete journey.... TID is a must read book for any executive/leader who is willing to drive, not only the digitalization agenda, but a real transformation toward a more agile and innovative approach."

Ayman Hegazy, Chairman and Chief Executive Officer, Allianz Egypt

"Conveying deep gratitude to our early endorsers, your early validation and advocacy has been fundamental to our journey and vital to bringing these pages to life."

For more praises, please visit https://theinnovativedinosaur.com/endorsements/

MOTAZ AGAMAWI

Currently Partner & Chief Technology Officer, *CTO— PwC ETIC;*
Board Member, National Telecommunication Institute

Previously
Director, *Smart Service Center, Valeo Group*
Director, *Research and Innovation, Valeo Group*

Previous Non-Executive Roles:

- Member of Advisory Board, *Faculty of Engineering, American University in Cairo*
- Member of Advisory Board, *Faculty of Engineering, Zewail University*
- Member of Board of Trustees, *TIEC-Technology Innovation and Entrepreneurship Center*
- Visiting Professor of Practice, *Management of Technology, Nile University*

✉ magamawi@gmail.com ✉ motaz@enterpriseinnovationdesign.com in www.linkedin.com/in/magamawi 🌐 www.theinnovativedinosaur.com

---

11	**+390**	**+80K**	**+100**
Number of Chapters	Number of Pages	Word Count	Number of Diagrams
+20	**+50**	**+250**	**+50**
Number of Canvases and Tools	Case Studies and Examples	References & Reading Resources	Glossary

THE INNOVATIVE DINOSAUR

Motaz Agamawi's life work is about managing technologies development to the benefit of our humankind. He is a believer that technology leads to a better tomorrow when the proper technology management paradigm is applied. Motaz previously held the role of Director at Valeo Service Smart Service Center and the Head of Research and Innovation. Currently, he is Partner and Chief Technology Officer of PwC Egypt Technology and Innovation Center (ETIC) and a Board Member of the National Telecommunication Institute.

During his 20+ years of professional experience, Motaz has initiated and led the establishment of several global software research, development and delivery teams serving Fortune 500 clients and government entities. During that time, he established and led teams and projects in more than eighteen countries and forty geographical distributed entities. He also led the delivery of hundreds of projects, successful launch of tens of commercial digital products, eighty innovative proof of concepts, two hundred digital novel patent proposals and dozens of published scientific papers in the diverse field of cutting-edge digital technologies. Motaz has also led the establishment of two software global delivery centers from the ground up and was one of the leaders who participated in initiating global software delivery centers of more than three thousand engineers in both Egypt and India.

Starting his career as a software developer just after graduation, Motaz then worked as a software technology commercial professional for almost ten years. He then moved to establish his own startup in the field of semantic and sentiment analysis which was later acquired. Afterward, he moved to continue his endeavors in Sydney, Australia, in the field of AI-based chatbots. In late 2013, Motaz joined Valeo Egypt as part of the leading team and played a pivotal role in increasing the center capacity and maturity, during which he established the engineering operational excellence and expertise capabilities, built the research and innovation center and digital transformation center from the ground up. Motaz has also supported the establishment of the Valeo India software center research and innovation teams. Both Valeo Egypt and India have reached during that time more than three thousand software engineers and went through the software value chain leader with full delivery scope and responsibility. Such a path provided him with a unique perspective of seeing two sides of the coin: the entrepreneurial mix with corporate experience. Mastering both the commercial and technical management skills. Owning the startup and global multinational enterprise management complexities experience. Deep hands-on experience of the digital disruption and building mature global delivery teams from different perspectives and dynamics.

THE INNOVATIVE DINOSAUR

As part of his continuous intention to return the favor to the community, during the recent years, he held several non-executive positions with a purpose to support the academia industry collaboration:

- Member of Advisory Board, Faculty of Computer Science, American University in Cairo, the leading liberal arts university in the Middle East,
- Member of Advisory Board, Faculty of Engineering, Zewail University, a leading technology research university,
- Visiting Professor of Practice, Management of Technology & Innovation Management, Nile University, the first nonprofit university in Egypt,
- Member of Board of Trustees, TIEC- Technology Innovation and Entrepreneurship Center, a governmental entity supporting technology innovation and entrepreneurship.

THE INNOVATIVE DINCSAUR

THE
INNOVATIVE
DINOSAUR

**THE
INNOVATIVE
DINOSAUR**

IN
GRATITUDE

I believe that *The Innovative Dinosaur-TID* itself is proof of the change we are living. Being authored by a Middle Eastern technology professional who has been raised and developed while living in Egypt. Having his human experience shaped as a result of the digital revolution. *TID* for me is a means to return the favor to all who have helped me to learn and develop. It is a trial to achieve a better tomorrow. I see that I was lucky and blessed all over the different stages of my life. I am dedicating this section of the book to show my gratitude to different persons and circumstances I believe that played a major role to shape my character, personality, and experience as of today.

My human experience is the result of the globalization and information revolution. These two factors have major impacts in my formation as a person and human being as I was provided tools, accessibility and exposure which was not available for the generation before me. Such access was given to me through my different stages of development since my childhood to my professional experience. Both factors led to the formation of a global citizen who is open to the world and belonging to its values, concerns and hopes for a better future for humankind. Thanks to all the global and technological leaders who have helped to achieve what we have as of today in our world.

Another blessing was my career journey. I started as an entrepreneur working in a family business in the field of information systems for more than ten years as a technology commercialization professional, managing sales and marketing teams serving Fortune 500 customers. I then moved to the corporate world as an operation research and development manager, then went into research and innovation and then general management, during which I was always able to connect different diversified spaces. Entering the automotive industry with a clear software transformation responsibility in 2013 was a blessing. Having such responsibility in the time of disruption in such a large, mature and strategic industry was an eye opener and a source for a unique experience.

During my journey, I have met special people and interacted directly/indirectly with role models who have helped in shaping my thoughts and vision even without knowing. In the following lines, I would like to thank some of them, and I wish if I missed any, that they will forgive me:

- My first direct manager, Alaa Al-Agamawi, my father for the professional experience and mentoring all over the years which set the foundation of my professional career.
- A family member and a friend, Mike Elhadad, for helping me to discover myself and giving me the opportunity to revisit my beliefs, thoughts and perspectives.

THE
INNOVATIVE
DINOSAUR

- Wael Abouelmaaty, a unique leader and a professional manager who always pushed the limits for an inspiring vision and realization on ground. The one who achieved a unique success story for his teams and company. Someone who gave me the opportunity and needed support to turn my ideas into reality.
- Dr. Nawal ElDegwi, an entrepreneurial role model who was able to build a world class educational institute and provide a unique learning experience in Egypt. I would like to thank her for giving me such an educational experience all over my K12 and university education.
- Dr. Khairy Ali, Ahmed Farouk and all my BSc in computer science professors for the knowledge and values they seeded in me.
- Professor Tarek Khalil, for his dedication to establish Nile University and the MOT-Management of Technology MSc in Egypt. Giving me and my generation of technology professionals in Egypt the opportunity to learn and experience such concepts and principals.
- A dear friend, Mohamed Azzam, for pushing me several times to go out of the comfort zone and follow my potential.
- Hicham Arafa, a customer, a manager and a friend. Someone who believed in my capabilities, availed to me opportunities, backed me up, supported my ideas, initiatives and who was always supporting me being recognized.

- Sorina Matos, the lady behind my career recognition even without realizing the positive impact she did. In one of the darkest career moments this lady appeared as a light in a dark space, explored what I was doing, believed in its value and opened to me the doors with the appropriate sponsors. Based on her support, I am where I am in my career today.
- Guillaume Devauchelle, a godfather role model and business professional sponsor from 2016 till 2021. The person who believed in a thirty-four-year-old professional based in Cairo giving me the opportunity for global exposure and experience. Sponsoring my transformational initiatives and giving me the opportunity of global implementation.

My professional colleagues who have collaborated and engaged with me. Together we succeeded and failed Thanks for sharing the experiences, dreams and knowledge. Such collaboration was a major part of my career maturity and development.

THE
INNOVATIVE
DINOSAUR

SPECIAL DEDICATION FOR...

My parents, both Alaa Al-Agamawi and Sahar ElFandary, for everything they did and still doing over the years that is leading to whom I am as of today.

My love, life partner, friend, the mother of my two lovely angels, Nancy El-Baroudy for her continuous support, baking and for taking the ride with me in my everlasting endeavors in the past and the one to come.

My sweetheart Sara Al-Agamawi and my second brother Ahmed Mansour for being part of my life and journey.

My twin angels both Salma and Karim for every moment of love, care, joy and pride they give to me. For their support and understanding while I was writing *TID* for more than three years. Both are main contributors and backers to *TID*.

My grandfathers and grandmothers, May God bless their souls for the love, care and values they seeded in me.

My father, mother, and sister-in-law, Khaled El-Baroudy, Hala Ghatwary and Sarah El-Baroudy, for believing in me and for extending my family through the limitless love and support they always provide.

My uncles and aunts for every unique moment of love, care and joy. Both Amr Al-Agamawi, May God bless his soul, and Ahmed Elfandary for being two role models all over my life, each with his special character and perspective.

The brothers and sisters that I have chosen, my beloved cousins.

My journey mates, the ones who always understands me before I speak, who always believe in me and who are always there to help me stand after each failure and celebrate with me each success. My lifetime friends, either from school or university, as being an integrated part of my memories and for joining me in many adventures that left a trace in my soul.

ACKNOWLEDGEMENT

During the journey of designing and compiling *The Innovative Dinosaur*, I have been supported and inspired by many true family, friends, backers, volunteers and colleagues. I am dedicating this section to thank each and every one of them.

Both Lamia Abouzeid and Nancy El-Baroudy for the brainstorming we did until reaching the name of the book "The Innovative Dinosaur."

My mentor and role model, Waleed Hamza, for all his advice, support and contributions. Many many of them led to basic foundations of the core thoughts represented in this book.

My lifetime friend, Mahmoud Rozaka for all his direct and indirect contributions for this book to come to light and his belief in me.

Ghada Sobhy, *The Innovative Dinosaur* professional final version text and content editing, proof reading and rephrasing.

Elle Kurancid, *The Innovative Dinosaur* professional book editor for the amazing job and efforts that she exerted.

Iram Shahzadi, *The Innovative Dinosaur* creative director and graphics designer for the dedication, efforts and creative designs.

Joel Bonete, the designer of the first logo of *TID* for his creative contribution.

Zaheer Hussain, *The Innovative Dinosaur* art work designer, who adjusted the book size and generated the ebook epub version, for his dedication and continued support.

Nada Oreiba, for her voluntarily, self-initiated, skilled meticulous review and thoughtful insights. Her impactful and lasting contribution left footprints. Both Rana Alaa and Omar Zayed for the volunteer effort to design and launch *The Innovative Dinosaur* beta website.

Abdelrahman Yassin, for his voluntarily support to compile the graphic design of the innovation canvases and tools.

Hoda El-Hawary, for her voluntarily support to conduct the proof reading and editing for the early versions of innovation frameworks.

Islam Sayed, for his support in the brainstorming sessions for *The Innovative Dinosaur* design themes and his support to design *The Innovative Dinosaur* second logo.

Special thanks for both Mohamed Tariq for his contribution to the design of the Enterprise team's inventiveness distribution canvas and for Ahmed Elqadi for his contribution for the design of the Enterprise Innovation Initiatives Interactive Design canvas. Also, for there brainware contribution during the several brainstorming and ideation sessions we have spent together.

During the different phases I was supported by the feedback and validation of many friends, colleagues and family through either the voting held to choose the cover and back designs or the discussions related to the internal design reader experience. Such support was always valuable and appreciated.

THE
INNOVATIVE
DINƐSAUR

THE INNOVATIVE DINOSAUR @ A GLANCE

When the "digital disruptors" of today's revolution first reached traditional industries, these newly arrived disruptors relied upon the traditional players, the longtime holders of knowledge on existing manufacturing capabilities and capacities. Digital disruptors are going to knock the value chain down a level. Though, upholding the perceived value profitability through new business models and revenue streams, while leaving the heavy lifting to the existing traditional players alone. The challenge for these weight-bearing players is not simply existential: it is more about profitability and the preservation of their preferred place in the value chain.

Traditional enterprises, especially the manufacturing variety, are the indispensable drivers of economic development and technological advancement. The productivity of non-manufacturing enterprises is positively correlated with the growth of manufacturing enterprises. Advancements in the manufacturing sector are having a direct impact on the technological advancements of other sectors. The capabilities of both service- and digital-based enterprises are completely dependent upon the produced goods coming from the manufacturing sector. Thus, preserving the traditional enterprises placed within the value chain is one of the most pressing challenges that we will explore together.

By learning how to identify and analyze the elements that constitute the different types of enterprises, we can help ensure that your organization will surf through the digital disruption journey safely and effectively. The objective here is not to determine the winning or superior type of organization; it's about defining the disruptions and redefining our businesses. To be deemed a digital enterprise, numerous organizational aspects—including leadership, business models, processes, methods, tools, team structures, governance mechanisms, and more—must be studied in detail.

The Innovative Dinosaur is designed to take us through a detailed and tailored journey of establishing, analyzing, and ultimately understanding the defining or rising digital disruptors of today.

This book features case studies on the major industries that faced them over the last twenty to thirty years and a series of deep dives into the nature of software when it intersects with traditional forces. After, a clear and concise picture of comparison between digital and traditional enterprises is depicted in terminology and illustrations.

Then we will propose new and/or improved frameworks, methods, and tools that can help an enterprise overcome the unpredictable yet game-changing chasm that is digital disruption.

THE
INNOVATIVE
DINOSAUR

WHY THE INNOVATIVE DINOSAUR?

The Innovative Dinosaur is dedicated to knowledge-sharing and the best practices related to an enterprise's digital transformation, in combination with an emphasis on fostering creative innovation capabilities. This includes frameworks, methodologies, tools, resources, and an introduction to the core concepts and techniques of digital transformation, innovation management, disruption forecasting and management, ideas management, and enterprise culture.

Today, we need a more structured, methodological, and practically-proven understanding of digital and innovation-geared organizations — ones that leverage their differentiation factors, set proper competencies into motion, accurately identify and effectively communicate their value proposition and most importantly, cultivate an internal and external culture of mutual benefit within and around their enterprise. Organizations that are unified and motivated, creating value for their shareholders, team members, and communities through cutting-edge and well-established knowledge, competitive solutions and services, and competent teams.

Based on over two decades of research and professional experience, this book unpacks six strategies for overcoming the digital disruption chasm:

ϵ Assess the Enterprise's Digital and Creative Readiness
ϵ Enterprise Management of Technology, Explored
ϵ Cultivate the Innovation Organization
ϵ Manage the Idea Funnel
ϵ Enterprise Workforce 3.0, Explored
ϵ Amplify Collaborative Power

THE INNOVATIVE DINOSAUR

INTRODUCTION

Our world is changing, our industries are changing, and we are changing as well. The rapid-fire technological advancements of today are transforming societies worldwide, disrupting or reinventing many of the ingrained norms and fundamental systems that we have come to know over the past two centuries. The speed of change is locked in acceleration, and our abilities to identify, understand, and act towards change must adapt accordingly — or we risk being left behind.

In being aware that change is constant, and that we must be prepared to face times of uncertainty and disruption.

It becomes clear that an enterprise's existence — survival and longevity — is based on its ability to adapt to change, though it's easier said than done. Across the history of humanity, disruption-driven change was the central reason for the disappearance of civilizations, races, professions, and specific social structures, and the rise of others. Today, we are on the middle of a major transition which will have an impact which is not less than the momentous forces behind the first and second industrial revolutions.

Walls are failing and falling between industries as disruption emerges from every corner and industry dynamics evolve beyond recognition. Large traditional organizations are operating in the widening shadows of unparalleled challenges and dilemmas between maintaining the successful working model of yesterday and adapting to the changes of today and tomorrow. Organizations can overcome technological disruption, but most will likely struggle when the disruption targets overall market dynamics, business models, revenue models, and common or traditional ways of doing business. As the struggles mount, these organizations face a chasm: tradition versus disruption. The ability of organizations to grasp the magnitude of change while seizing the willingness to apply the needed transformations — in a phrase, informed versatility — may become the determining factor as to whether they will transcend the chasm or not. When digital disruption targets a specific industry, the patterns of disruption manifest. Industries of all types and sizes have had to grapple with major changes and disruptions over these decades of information and communication revolution.

THE INNOVATIVE DINOSAUR

Today's products and solutions are composed of a combination of mechanical components, electronics, sensors, actuators, and software. Together, they are designed and assembled to deliver a specific use case and to achieve a desired business model objective. We can find them in a range of systems and components with various levels of complexity. This complex architecture of diversified domains has been integrated into many everyday devices. Although of the recent introduction of software components compared to other elements, its contribution into today's products and solutions is increasingly dramatically. Software, communication, and internet connectivity are major building blocks in this era of digital disruption. Additionally, software platforms and technologies are the key contributors to the desired business and revenue models of today. In many cases, the advancement of a specific industry business model is contingent on the maturity and capabilities of the software element. The ability of a given organization to deeply understand its differences and needs while being immersed— perhaps by force of circumstance — in the digitalization journey is a defining factor for the building of proper change management strategy and staying competitive in the business landscape.

A business organization can be defined as *a structured body of people that is guided by leaders whose methods of evaluating different team members and decisions are translated into processes.* Organization values are revealed in those processes, and organizational culture is shaped by these values; what an organization can and cannot achieve is perhaps defined by its culture. Identifying and understanding the elements that constitute the output or result of the leaders' daily actions and decisions is key, as the business takes on its vision for how work can and should be done, and in this digital age, it is of utmost importance for the organization to surf the digital disruption journey safely and effectively. The objective is not to determine the winning or superior type of organization, but rather to ascertain that producing cutting-edge technologies does not make a manufacturer a digital- or technology-based organization. Furthermore, the implementation of such technologies, like the Cloud, data science, and Chatbot, does not mean that the organization is digitally transformed. To be deemed a digital enterprise, many organizational aspects— including processes, methods, tools, and governance mechanisms—must be addressed and thoroughly explored.

Digital disruption is always accompanied by a standardization of the product architecture and underlying technologies. Standard architecture leads to standard hardware through driver interfaces, more standard communication protocols, and thus standard software development tools and languages. Standardization broadens the horizon for increasing the software portion of the product.

The boundary-pushing software experts truly know how to build user-centric products, offering users features and capabilities that were previously unavailable. This creates a space for the cultivation of an ecosystem of partners around a product or industry. This ecosystem is usually part of the offered user experience (UX), and it utilizes existing technologies or platforms, but through a new use case, which leads to additional user satisfaction with a new revenue model.

Digital disruption usually triggers new business and revenue models. Zooming in, digital players bring new tools and dynamics to this new frontier, ones that are completely different from the traditional ones. These players follow perceived-value pricing strategies regardless of the cost. Meanwhile traditional organizations usually follow the cost-plus strategy. Revenue models often extend beyond asset sales and, in most cases, contain a continuous revenue stream based on subscription services, upsell gadgets, or software updates. It is important to assess the true intentions of these digital players as they enter this new frontier.

In most cases, they see and seize the new opportunities at hand and frontiers ahead, while the existing traditional players sit back.

Profitability structure is crucial in this landscape. By design, digital players achieve high profitability and exponential stock growth and valuations. They are focused on perceived-value pricing and taking risks in new frontiers on radical innovations, but they do not invest in building factories and large industrial operations. Consumer behavior trends are evolving, from expectations, needs, to demands. The diffusion of digital services vis-à-vis the changes in consumer behavior directly and indirectly impacts not only customer expectations and needs, but also their willingness to pay, their buying cycles, and their priorities. Today's consumers are searching for the same experience offered by their smartphones and social media networks everywhere, on and off the screen and the web.

When a digital disruption reaches a new technological frontier, it unsurprisingly joins forces with a related wave of startups. Standardization, along with new dynamics and technology architecture, leads to a lower entry barrier and thus a vista of an opportunity-packed future that attracts startups. Investors and venture capitalists play the role of catalyst, pushing the technological hype curve toward the said future-facing vista. This trend intensifies the game for well-established traditional players as the competition pool expands.

THE INNOVATIVE DINOSAUR

Another important aspect that requires careful consideration is how fundamental business and economic models are shifting and therein directly impacting how businesses are managed and investments are made. The contemporary iteration of the sharing economy is a digital platform-driven peer-to-peer (P2P) socio-economic model that emphasizes access over ownership and flexibility over convention, with respect to the buying and selling of goods and services. For thousands of years, the marketplace and capital have constituted our main commercial economic systems. The marketplace was a physically defined space with boundaries, where sellers wait and buyers approach. Capital was key, too, as sellers often had a scarcity of capital investment, limiting their growth and operations. At the same time, the size of available capital impacted the seller's ability to buy or rent a specific store area and/or the amounts of goods offered to consumers within this area. The concept of the digitalized sharing economy has recast both components. It has expanded the size of the physical marketplace; in most cases this either minimizes or eliminates the impact of needed capital — for example, why do you need capital to have a fleet of taxis when you can utilize the investments of others? Our current digitally-driven sharing economy is designed to support the idea of utilizing unused and underused resources owned by others.

The concept of scarcity of resources, upon which most economic rules are based, is also transforming. In the past, we've constructed our business models with an implicit and/or explicit consideration for the concept. Internet bandwidth, for instance, was once scarce and expensive for the vast majority, but recent technological developments related to optimizing operating systems to consume bandwidth wisely and efficiently are increasingly leveling the surfing field. Google and Netflix are prime examples of companies that have significantly capitalized on such optimizations, pushing their customers to consume bandwidth with an added price tag.

These methods are marching industry standards and business models into previously uncharted gray areas. If we take a further look, capital itself isn't far behind. Our higher metric applied to efficiency innovation.

Investment needs to be revised. With the availability of surplus cash and easier access to it, investing in more radical innovation has a potential for higher future valuation. This is why "user first" strategies are gaining exceptional momentum in the business world, from Amazon to Facebook, and Uber to Airbnb.

The idea of building an ecosystem around a specific product or platform is not new, but it has become increasingly prevalent over the past ten to fifteen years. The business model of hardware and software producers Apple and Google is king in the tech industry, also known as "Big Tech," along with Facebook and Amazon. By availing one's technologies to a group of partners who can then build applications and offer different use models, a win-win for all appears within reach. Today, traditional industries face the challenge of meeting user expectations and needs. Many are now calling for the same widely-connected experience for their contemporary users. As user sophistication soars, they seek out the same mobile, tablet, or smart TV experience in their cars, refrigerators, and other appliances. Further afield, the diffusion and success of the crowd sourcing model in our digital age has laid the foundation for a new set of expectations for service providers and users alike; the impact of this game-changing model exceeds the original purpose of the business domain. As of today, the success of this model is one of the main catalysts for global freelancer and digital nomad cultures as well as the top-down acceptance of remote teamwork.

When the "digital disruptors" of today's revolution first reached traditional industries, these newly arrived disruptors relied on the traditional players, the longtime holders of knowledge on existing manufacturing capabilities and capacities. Digital disruptors are going to knock the value chain down a level, though, upholding the perceived value profitability through new business models and revenue streams, while leaving the heavy lifting to the existing traditional players alone. The challenge for these weight-bearing players is not simply existential. It is more about profitability and the preservation of their preferred place in the value chain. Countless traditional industries are facing a heavy wave of change. The automotive industry, the telecommunication industry, the banking and general financial sector, shipment and logistics, media and content production, building automation, and even the space industry. Another set of industries that are facing a less aggressive wave of change — for now — includes pharmaceuticals, medical devices, sports, tobacco, and even digital gaming.

The Innovative Dinosaur is dedicated to knowledge-sharing and the best practices related to an enterprise's digital transformation, in combination with an emphasis on fostering creative innovation capabilities. This includes frameworks, methodologies, tools, resources, and an introduction to the core concepts and techniques of digital transformation, innovation management, disruption forecasting and management, ideas management, and enterprise culture.

THE INNOVATIVE DINOSAUR

Today, we need a more structured, methodological, and practically-proven understanding of digital and innovation-geared organizations — ones that leverage their differentiation factors, set proper competencies into motion, accurately identify and effectively communicate their value proposition, and, most importantly, cultivate an internal and external culture of mutual benefit within and around their enterprise. Organizations that are unified and motivated, create value for their shareholders, team members, and communities through cutting-edge and well-established knowledge, competitive solutions and services, and competent teams. Our mission is to empower individuals and enterprises through sharing our in-depth take on the best practices and case studies for a structured digital transformation and innovation management framework and approach. Large enterprises must be more lean, agile, dynamic, and collaborative than ever, while Startups and small organizations must be more structured, methodological, and competitive without losing agility and passion.

The Innovative Dinosaur is designed to take us through a detailed and tailored journey of establishing, analyzing, and ultimately understanding the defining or rising digital disruptors of today, featuring case studies on the major industries that faced them over the last twenty to thirty years, and a series of deep dives into the nature of software when it intersects with traditional forces. After a clear and concise picture of comparison between digital and traditional enterprises is depicted in terminology and illustrations, then we will embark on propose new and/or improved frameworks, methods, and tools that can help an enterprise overcome the unpredictable yet game-changing chasm that is digital disruption.

Based on over two decades of research and professional experience, this book unpacks six strategies for overcoming the digital disruption chasm:

- Assess the Enterprise's Digital and Creative Readiness
- Enterprise Management of Technology, Explored
- Cultivate the Innovation Organization
- Manage the Idea Funnel
- Enterprise Workforce 3.0, Explored
- Amplify Collaborative Power

For **Assessing the Enterprise Digital and Creative Readiness**, we must combine three different audits. The **Pre-Audit Business Definition Questions** is a predefined set of questions, and answering them will help to define the business, understand its nature, and guide the audit accordingly. The **Enterprise Digital Readiness** is a quick audit for helping the organization understand where it stands in comparison to a digital enterprise. For the **Enterprise Innovation Audit**, the objective is to provide companies with an overview of their strengths and weaknesses with respect to technical innovation management, thus enabling them to highlight the areas that they should examine in greater depth.

The combination of the three audit types offers a 360-degree-type view of an enterprise's digital and innovation readiness. Based on the audit results enterprise strategy teams, top management will be able to identify gaps, set desired improvements and objectives, and ultimately design the appropriate transformation strategies. Such strategies will be translated into actionable initiatives and product portfolio management approaches, all of which are covered in the chapters of this book.

We explore the **Elements of Enterprise Management of Technology,** and its main role in gaining insight into the value of certain technologies for the organization, and fortify the firm against its marketplace competitors by applying and/or producing the best innovative solutions in the game. Technological breakthroughs present new frontiers and vistas for industrial development and economic growth. When we talk about technology, we mean "technology innovation." Innovation is the adoption of invention and the process by which invention is introduced to markets through the commercialization. Markets (buyers) may embrace or ignore the innovation. Regardless, by diffusing the innovation, the wealth creation process is initiated. Against that backdrop, we not only discuss the main points of difference between the management of technology and the management of business administration paradigms, we also set forth a common understanding for the terms "technology" and "innovation" and identify the main elements that govern an innovative digital enterprise.

We propose a set of frameworks, techniques, methods, and tools for **Building the Innovation Organization**. The organization's true competencies are represented in the knowledge, know-how, and experiences of its own team. Accordingly, the enterprise innovation culture should empower, activate, motivate, educate, and engage team members in the enterprise innovation activities. Where do we begin: the human desirability angle, the technical feasibility angle, or the business viability angle? If the end goal of the enterprise's activities is to achieve a commercially successful and competitive offering, then to do so we must devise strategies that lead to different internal and external initiatives and programs. The proposed frameworks, methods, and tools in this book were designed to ensure that our strategies and initiatives are integrated to achieve our targets and objectives.

After addressing key challenges and best practices, we discuss **Managing the Idea Funnel**. Ideas are the beating heart of products and services. The end goal is to have superior or, at the very least, competitive products and services that yield a high economic return. One of the most challenging tasks of any innovation management or new product development management team is to increase the success rate of ideas-turned-products that have a high economic impact and reward for the organization. The cost of innovation failure directly affects the overall efficiency and impact of the enterprise's innovation performance. The core concept behind the idea funnel is "fail fast, win fast," or the minimization of final innovation failure costs as much as possible. Idea funnel life cycle management comes into focus, as ideas management and its associated success rate are among the main challenges of the enterprise's internal innovation management.

We (re)trace the different models, success stories, and methods for **Establishing the Enterprise Workforce 3.0**, mapping out the context for building global development centers and related explorations of concepts, challenges, and opportunities for remote team management through discussing three models with their different levels of complexity. We begin with the work-from-home policy that is offered by many organizations, and that was heavily utilized during the COVID-19 pandemic, along with explorations of the global distributed team's management challenges, the full remote workforce model, and the crowd sourcing labor model. For small and medium enterprises, new working models are offering a magic solution for the workforce elastic capacity, giving options for professional services and deliveries with bare-minimum commitment. For larger enterprise, these models can be perceived as both an opportunity and a threat.

THE
INNOVATIVE
DINOSAUR

Large enterprise can reach the necessary means, including the methods and processes needed to integrate those models within the overall organization operational model. The enterprise will benefit from the workforce elastic capacity, tapping into the global talent pool, and even more competitive costing structure. On the other side, the enterprise must recognize that an inability to integrate with such models will negatively impact the overall competitiveness of the enterprise.

Finally, we propose a range of techniques and strategies for Fostering the Enterprise Collaborative Power. If designing a business is a challenging marathon, then building an ecosystem is a fairly complex journey to reach the top of Mount Everest. What makes the process of designing an ecosystem complex is the required holistic system perspective that goes beyond designing the value creation of each stakeholder and considers the value distribution for various players. Solving the chicken-and-egg problem of creating and attracting a critical mass of partners and customers in a scalable and defendable model while meeting the needs and expectations of each one is a heavy lifting process. Our focus is on setting the proper organization strategy to create and/or participate in an ecosystem while covering the different strategies, challenges, opportunities, and product design aspects necessary for achieving an ecosystem-ready product.

THE BASECAMP

Before we start our journey with *The Innovative Dinosaur*, we need to establish the three different types of enterprises. The first type is the industrial or manufacturing, the second is the service-based, and the third is the digital-based.

From the late eighteenth century to the mid-nineteenth century, western economies identified industrial activities as the main driver of economic growth and prosperity. In the beginning, the economies of Europe, Great Britain, North America, and Japan constituted only 27% of manufacturing production, and in the early nineteenth century, they reached 90% of the world's manufacturing economy. Accordingly, the west's economies saw significant growth compared to the rest of the world.

After the Second World War, the globe witnessed another major shift: one that was mainly derived from the ability of the developed nations to steer policies toward its strategic economic objectives and promote the industrialization paradigm to other countries. Then, we started to see the rise and diffusion of outsourcing, accompanied by the shift of the basic parts in the manufacturing value chain to less developed nations.

At that time, the service-based industry was seeing the exponential growth. This industry had gained the necessary momentum to become an integral component of economic growth, focusing on the more complex and sophisticated parts of the value chain and thus on higher profitability. At the time of writing, the service sector represents more than 70% of the global economy. With the diffusion of communication and information technology, the service sector has gained greater competitive capabilities and thereby higher perceived value.

In recent years, we have witnessed the rise of digital-based organizations, which are utilizing the current landscape of technological advancement for their benefit, leading to higher value creation for all stakeholders and disrupting various frontiers along the way.

To fully grasp the above-described landscape, we must first unpack the core differences between the three central forces at play: the traditional manufacturing or industrial enterprise, the service-based enterprise, and the digital-based enterprise. Traditional manufacturers are concerned with tangible resources, like raw material and produced goods, while service- and digital-based organizations prioritize intangible resources, from knowledge to skills.

THE
INNOVATIVE
DINOSAUR

The nature of their output is different. For instance, goods produced by manufacturing enterprises are tangible, while the delivery experience and human transaction in service-based enterprises are intangible. Moreover, in the manufacturing realm, production is easily separated from consumption. In contrast, production and consumption in the service industry are inseparable, as they require an interaction between clients and service providers during the service production process — and the nature of this interaction is leading to a major paradigm shift within their different organizational aspects, also leading to another sharp contrast with the manufacturing enterprise, which is based on standardization and mass production.

When information and communication technology (ICT) passes through the maturity phase with high diffusion, affordability, and ease of use, another wave of change emerges. This emergence is leading to the rise of a new type of enterprise: the digital-based enterprise, which utilizes the technologies of today and tomorrow to offer a range of products and services that were not yet available yesterday. Such enterprises are employing the power of data to predict user behavior, needs, and wants, shaping the future demand pattern. They capitalize on ICT capabilities to offer new, future-facing business models, even within the traditional asset sales industries. Further, they offer target customers a fresh user experience while also achieving a faster time-to-market through implementing different lean, agile, and user-centric operational methodologies. On top of that, they are simultaneously building on advanced communication channels, platforms, and techniques, particularly when approaching their target customer base.

Service-based and digital-based enterprises are perceived as having a greater economic impact than the manufacturing enterprises. This perception comes into sharp focus when we take a look at the stock market valuation, or even the profitability of the new digital enterprises in comparison to the established manufacturing ones. The evolution towards more user-centric product design and experience is impacting the production system, thus triggering a dramatic change in the way enterprises are structured and managed.

This change is exerting influence on all the aspects of the enterprises of today, from their leadership style and process design to their methods and tools implementation, and team's competency building and structuring. The new enterprise model is geared more towards an enterprise that includes continuous learning opportunities and adapts to change quickly, efficiently, and creatively. Here, the ideal scenario would be an enterprise that can identify disruption and apply the needed transformation quickly, and even disrupt the status quo by changing the way things are done to capture the highest economical returns.

THE
INNOVATIVE
DINOSAUR

To be able to achieve this, the enterprise needs to be capable of storing, sharing, and processing new information through knowledge management practices. In this era, the most complex challenge for organizations is creating an environment in which it can accumulate knowledge quickly and effectively in a cost-efficient manner. They must reach beyond their usual boundaries to interact, cooperate, and join forces with different stakeholders, including customers, suppliers, local communities, consultants, academia, competitors, and more.

Team members, once perceived in the traditional manufacturing organizations as resources alone, are becoming identified as talents. The role of workers' "teams" in manufacturing enterprises as operators on machines is completely different from a service- and digital-based perspective. In contrast, service- and digital-based enterprises view people as autonomous beings who have the knowledge and competencies to create, collaborate, evaluate, and take action or make decisions.

The economic value of service and digital enterprises is built around services in general, regardless of the product, whereas traditional manufacturing enterprises see economic value as revolving around something to be produced and sold. Thus, the value creation of manufacturing enterprises is designed around activities of processing a set of static resources to make them valuable, and they believe that efficiency is the key principle. The customers of such organizations are perceived as isolated entities, and product design is always within the boundaries of the enterprise.

The complete opposite is true for the core belief of service- and digital-based enterprises: they perceive value as a co-creation activity conducted with customers and other partners. In short, customers are cast as a supportive resource — and such intangible resources are capable of creating value. Moreover, efficiency is one of the goals to be achieved through effectiveness and not the key principle. All of this signals a dramatic shift in leadership mindset, practices, and capabilities, essentially the prerequisites for today's enterprise leaders.

THE
INNOVATIVE
DINOSAUR

We are not debating the importance of the manufacturing enterprise, but rather, on the contrary, we are stressing on the necessity of transforming traditional practices to leverage their value creation against the value perceived and acquired by today's digital-based enterprises. Regardless of this contrast in perceived value, we cannot deny that manufacturing is the core economic driver of the technological and economical advancements that we are all living, at varied degrees of access, right now. If Google's economic value is perceived higher than corresponding manufacturing entities, then we need to consider the huge amount of tangible infrastructural components that are supporting its operation. Uber is another example. Upon going deeper, it is clear that without the physical vehicle and mobility products availed through the traditional automotive industry, such value would not be captured.

Other precedents like solar power, electric car batteries, satellite internet, new mobility, vaccination, and more, also depend on the manufacturing industry's R&D and economy of scale. And so, manufacturing is still an undeniable driver of economic development and technological advancement. The productivity of non-manufacturing enterprises is positively correlated with the growth of manufacturing enterprise, and technological advancements in the manufacturing sector have a direct impact on the technological advancement of other sectors. This web of vital entanglement also concerns the capabilities of both service- and digital-based enterprises, as they rely on the produced goods coming from the manufacturing sector.

In this book, the Innovative Dinosaur highlights the concepts, processes, methods, and tools that are essential for leveraging traditional manufacturing enterprises to be able to perceive the economic value of digital enterprises. To achieve such an objective, many organizational aspects must be transformed. In the coming chapters, our journey will involve identifying and addressing these aspects.

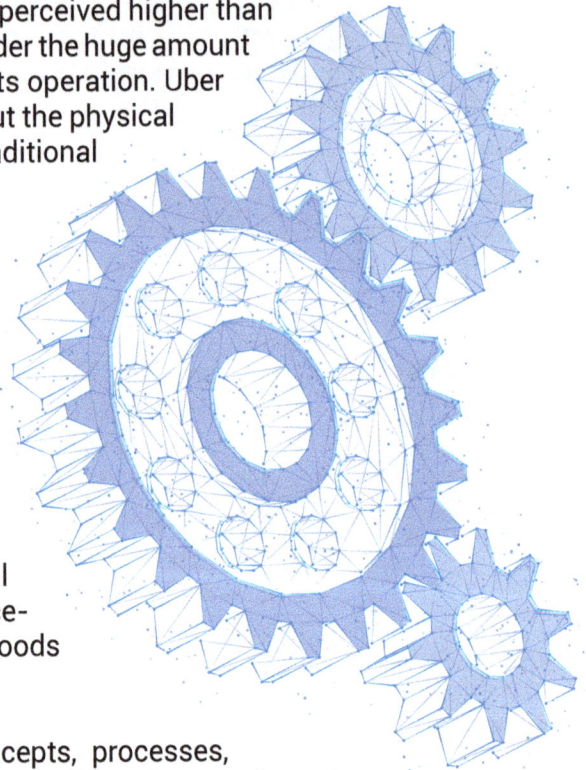

CHAPTER 1:
DISRUPTION GAINS MOMENTUM

Industry is changing. And we are changing, too. The rapid-fire technological advancements of today are changing societies worldwide, disrupting or reinventing many of the ingrained norms and fundamental systems that we have come to know over the past two centuries. We are in the midst of a sweeping transition that will forever change the socio-economic systems that have long structured and defined our days.

> **This impact will one day be tantamount to the momentous forces behind the first and second industrial revolutions. Technological and entrepreneurial developments, like social media and startups, will go down in history, too.**

Within the coming decade, at least, the world that we know — **or think we know** — will not be the same, perhaps even unrecognizable for some.

In this chapter, we will **dig into a selection of technological mega trends, particularly their striking impact on the ways in which we live today and are projected to in the near future.**

THE INNOVATIVE DINOSAUR

CHAPTER ONE SECTIONS:

- ∈ Our world is changing
- ∈ Globalization
- ∈ Global Integration
- ∈ Millennials in the Workplace
- ∈ Employment Model 3.0
- ∈ Rise of Collaboration
- ∈ Entrepreneurship Model
- ∈ Industry 4.0
- ∈ Decentralization
- ∈ Exaggerated Consumerism
- ∈ The Shift Gains Momentum
- ∈ Change as Opportunity and Challenge

CHAPTER ONE LIST OF TOOLS, DIAGRAMS, AND ILLUSTRATIONS

1. TID Illustration: Factors changing our today's world
2. TID Illustration: Globalization
3. TID Illustration: Global Integration
4. TID Illustration: Millennials in Workplace
5. TID Illustration: Employment Model
6. TID Illustration: Rise of Collaboration
7. TID Illustration: Entrepreneurship Model
8. TID Illustration: Industry 4.0
9. TID Illustration: Decentralization
10. TID Illustration: Exaggerated Consumerism
11. TID Illustration: Shift Gains Momentum
12. TID Illustration: Change opportunity or Challenge?

THE INNOVATIVE DINOSAUR

CHAPTER ONE LIST OF REFERENCES & EXTRA READINGS

1. Industry 4.0, t and f online
2. The New Age of Insurance, insuranceireland.eu
3. Work 3.0, Change in working model, techcrunch
4. The world 2050, shift in economic powers, PwC,
5. World Economic Forum, Brief History of Globalization
6. How Emerging Market and Reshaping Globalization, carnegie endowment
7. Crowdfunding is disrupting VC, forbes
8. Sharing Economy — A Symbol of the Rise of Consumerism
9. Block chain and Social Implication, richtopia
10. UNCTAD, United Nations Conference on Trade and Development, Framework for Science, Technology and Innovation Policy Review, Geneva, 2019
11. UN Global Observatory of Science, Technology and Innovation Policy Instruments (GO-SPIN), Open Access Platform
12. UNESCO Innovation Data
13. UNESCO Science Report, Toward 2030 Executive Summary
14. Adopt science, technology and innovation strategies as integral elements of national sustainable development strategies,
15. Beyond the Horizons, EU future STI with example
16. Future Skills, EU center for vocational training, Europa.eu
17. Nokia Corporate Strategy Critique, December 2011, by Motaz Agamawi
18. Mobile Industry Technology Forecast, January 2012, by Motaz Agamawi

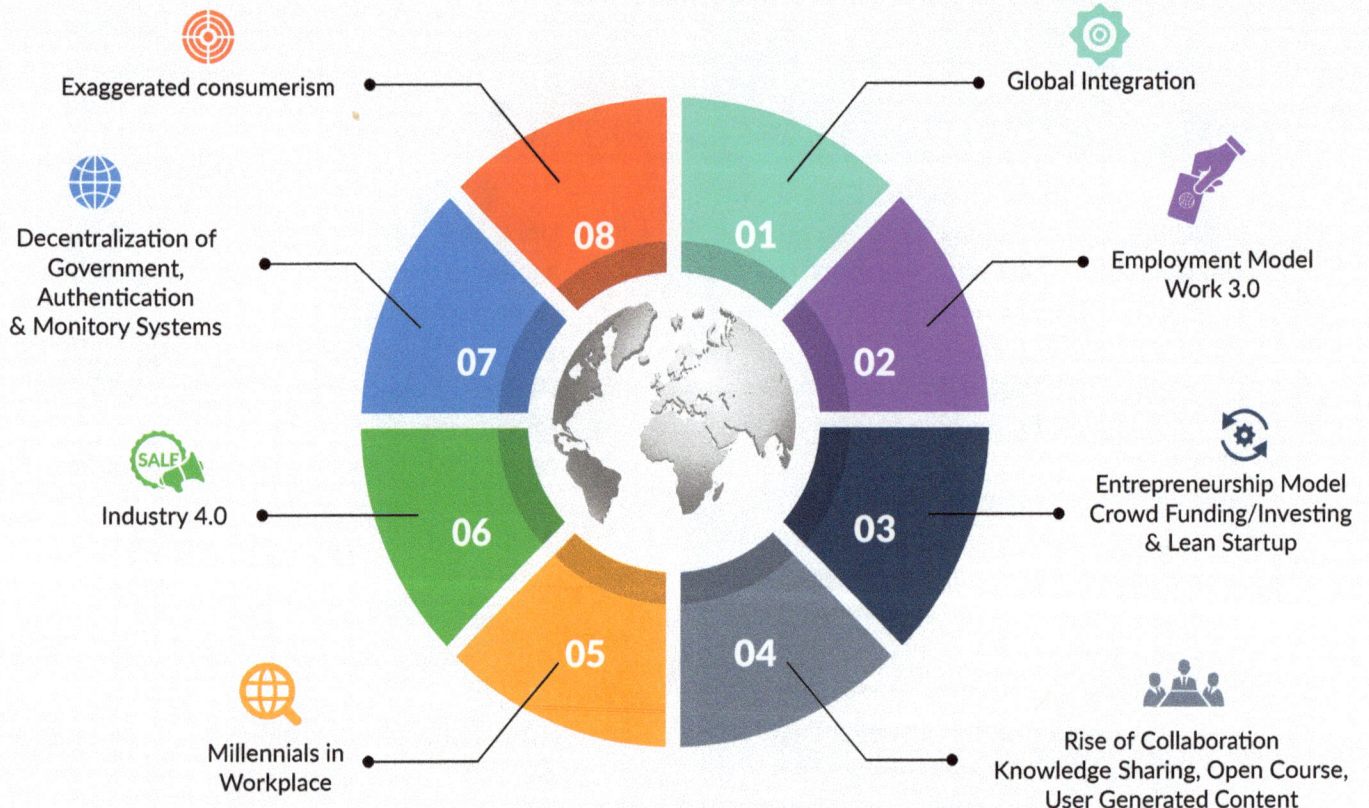

Exaggerated consumerism

Decentralization of
Government,
Authentication
& Monitory Systems

Industry 4.0

Millennials in
Workplace

Global Integration

Employment Model
Work 3.0

Entrepreneurship Model
Crowd Funding/Investing
& Lean Startup

Rise of Collaboration
Knowledge Sharing, Open Course,
User Generated Content

01 02 03 04 05 06 07 08

TECHNOLOGICAL FACTORS IMPACTING OUR WORLD AS OF DECEMBER 2017

THE
INNOVATIVE
DINOSAUR

OUR WORLD IS CHANGING

Industry is changing. And we are changing, too. The rapid-fire technological advancements of today are changing societies worldwide, disrupting or reinventing many of the ingrained norms and fundamental systems that we have come to know over the past two centuries. In fact, we are of a sweeping transition that will forever change the socio-economic systems that have long structured and defined our days.

THIS IMPACT WILL ONE DAY BE TANTAMOUNT TO THE MOMENTOUS FORCES BEHIND THE FIRST AND SECOND INDUSTRIAL REVOLUTIONS.

Within the coming decade, at least, the world that you know — or think you know — will not be the same, perhaps even unrecognizable for some. This chapter digs into a couple of technological mega trends, particularly their striking impact on the ways in which we live today and are projected to in the near future.

Global integration is impacting enterprises of all sizes, individuals of all nationalities, and countries of all wealth rankings. The employment model is approaching 'employment 3.0.' At the same time, the entrepreneurship finance model is evolving. With the support of online crowdfunding investment campaigns, lean startups, among other ground-breaking methods. The unprecedented rise of collaboration regardless of time and place, along with project-based learning and the 'unschooling' movement, is powered by knowledge- sharing platforms, user-generated content, open course initiative, online training, and education portals. *The very concept* of industrialization is facing an inflection point through the industry 4.0 movement. The decentralization of government, as well as monitory and authentication bodies, through block-chain, virtual currency, financial technology or 'fintech,' and other rapid-paced movements. Exaggerated consumerism, on the other hand, is in its last days owing to the proliferation of resource-sharing portals and, in turn, their influence on the buyer's decision-making process and their life cycle behaviors. Digital technology is in its golden days as smartphones, tablets, IoT gadgets, drones, robots, and an unimaginable range of autonomous machines and social platforms inspire change and new visions of the future.

THE INNOVATIVE DINOSAUR

GLOBALIZATION

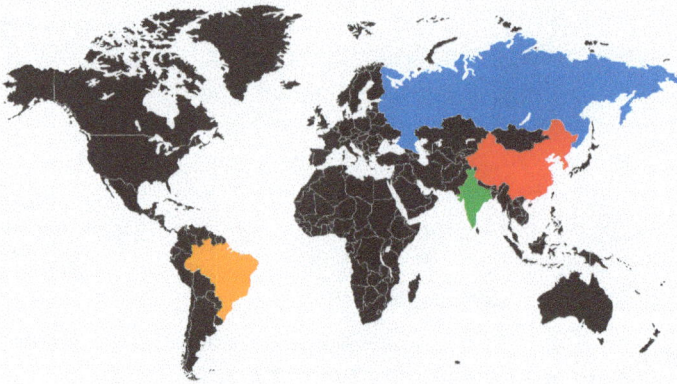

Increase of production capacity,
Capabilities and competitive cost structure

Younger population, increase
in education and income level

ECONOMIC POWER SHIFT

50%

BRIC Countries
50% of the Global GDP

BUSINESS ARE PUSHED TO INCREASE GLOBAL FOOTPRINT
in research, production, commercial

Increasing Business Complexity

NEW DEMAND STRUCTURE
Emerging Economies are gaining each day more
global market share in all industries.

More Local/Global Competition

Designed by: Motaz Agamawi
www.theinnovativedinosaur.com

THE
INNOVATIVE
DINOSAUR

GLOBALIZATION

The change started with local manufacturing and the tasks of the so-called 'lower rungs' of the value chain, as call centers for basic business operations were outsourced to low-cost destinations. Novel employment opportunities surged and, in time, saturated underdeveloped economies, helping their workforces reach high-production capacities, greater capabilities, and cost-efficient structures for increased competitiveness.

With younger populations and efficient education systems, income levels have risen. Today, the BRIC countries (Brazil, Russia, India, and China), for example, account for just under half of global GDP, but they're forecasted to achieve that milestone by 2030. In addition to representing a major contribution in product, those countries have hit a high percentage of the global demand market structure. As a result, businesses are moved to expand global operations, production scales, and their research footprints, all of which add complexity to the pre-existing model.

GLOBAL INTEGRATION

RISING OF GLOBAL CITIZENSHIP

Sharing the Same Needs, Values, Interest & Concerns

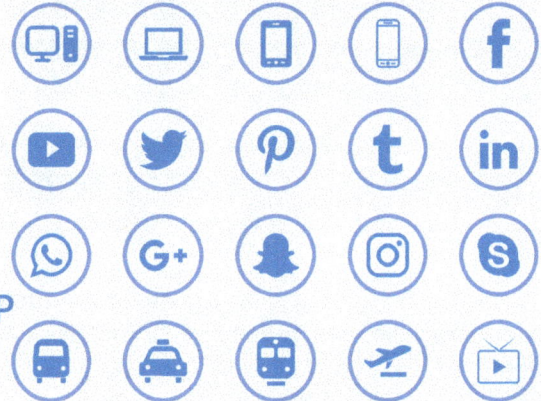

GLOBALLY CONNECTED COMMUNITIES

GLOBAL SENSE OF BELONGING

INCREASED THE DEMAND FOR MORE WESTERN LIFESTYLE

Expansion Opportunity for Corporates & Individuals

MORE GLOBAL AWARENESS & EXPECTATIONS

Increasing Pressure on both local Companies & Governments

Designed by: Motaz Agamawi
www.theinnovativedinosaur.com

THE INNOVATIVE DINOSAUR

GLOBAL INTEGRATION

In parallel to globalization, significant shifts have occurred in our world, from the information and communication technology revolutions to the ascent of global media and brands. These combined factors and forces have given shape, form, and life to globally-connected communities and global citizens — or those who hold a worldview that values shared needs, values, interests, concerns, expectations, and even dilemmas more than any human-made geographical and political dividing lines.

Western lifestyles and socio-economic systems are now seen, felt, and experienced globally, which has helped corporations in the expansion of their global strategies for product development, talent acquisition, and a single global operational experience. Against this backdrop, heightened global awareness and standards have and continue to set off pressure campaigns calling for local companies and governments to respect and uphold globally minded principles and practices.

THE
INNOVATIVE
DINOSAUR

🌐 MILLENNIALS IN WORKPLACE

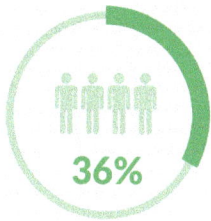

36%

Workforce in 2014

75%

Workforce in 2025

92%

92% believe success should be measured by more than profit

15%

15% are already managers

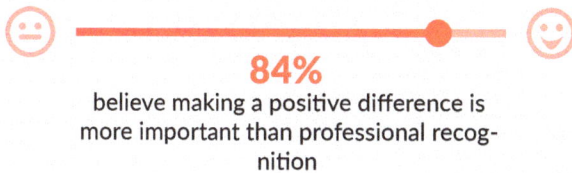

84%

believe making a positive difference is more important than professional recognition

80%

80% prefer on spot recognition over formal reviews

Source: http://barkley.s3.amazonaws.com/barkleyus/AmericanMillennials.pdf

THE INNOVATIVE DINOSAUR
WHAT IF DINOSAURS WERE INNOVATIVE

Designed by: Motaz Agamawi
www.theinnovativedinosaur.com

THE INNOVATIVE DINOSAUR

WORKPLACE PERCEPTIONS THAT MILLENNIALS NEED TO RISE ABOVE

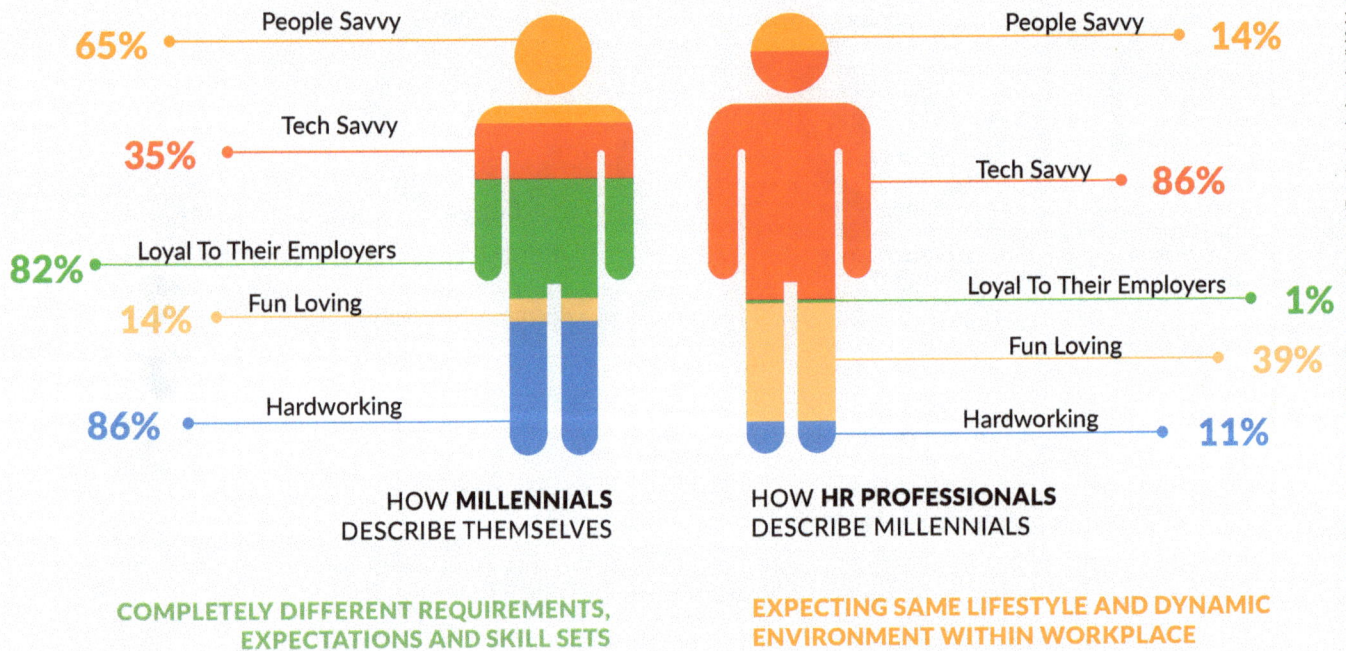

65% People Savvy

35% Tech Savvy

82% Loyal To Their Employers

14% Fun Loving

86% Hardworking

People Savvy 14%

Tech Savvy 86%

Loyal To Their Employers 1%

Fun Loving 39%

Hardworking 11%

HOW **MILLENNIALS** DESCRIBE THEMSELVES

HOW **HR PROFESSIONALS** DESCRIBE MILLENNIALS

COMPLETELY DIFFERENT REQUIREMENTS, EXPECTATIONS AND SKILL SETS

EXPECTING SAME LIFESTYLE AND DYNAMIC ENVIRONMENT WITHIN WORKPLACE

Source: A Beyond.com survey of 6,361 job seekers and veteran HR professionals, from April 12-May 9,2013

Designed by: Motaz Agamawi
www.theinnovativedinosaur.com

THE INNOVATIVE DINOSAUR

MILLENNIALS IN THE WORKPLACE

'Employee 3.0' of today is vastly different from their veteran colleagues and predecessors. They have a set of skills, requirements, and expectations born of a globalized world — and it is up to companies to use them effectively.

The general attitudes of young people — Generation X, Generation Y (aka Millennials), and Generation Z — especially towards their professional challenges and presence within their organizations, are now globally connected, influenced, and even empowered in ways that once exceeded their older colleagues' imaginations. One of the well-known values of these generations includes: work for the sake of a deeper purpose, which often translates to turning a life's passion or mission into a profitable business. They value flexibility and versatility, and so they expect their work environment to not only accommodate but also mirror their lifestyles and habits. They will often settle into a 'network of teams' model with ease — hierarchical organizational structures, less so, due to a lack of emphasis on interconnectedness. They are receptive to a leadership that is appreciative —

not exploitative – of their willingness to take on challenges while still fulfilling their responsibilities. In order to unlock the full potential of this twenty-first-century employee 3.0, it is advisable that we first review and then modify or reinvent our workplace principles and practices with this generational shift front and center. Now, more than ever before, young people are being raised and/or educated in a globalized world, or in an unexampled global integration phase. By 2025, Millennials will likely represent more than seventy-five percent of the global workforce. And they are expecting some variation of the above-described dynamic, integration-friendly environment at their present and future workplaces. The ability of organizations and current management teams to understand the needs and values of these employees 3.0 is crucial for the establishment of the competitive, even trailblazing, enterprise of today.

**THE
INNOVATIVE
DINOSAUR**

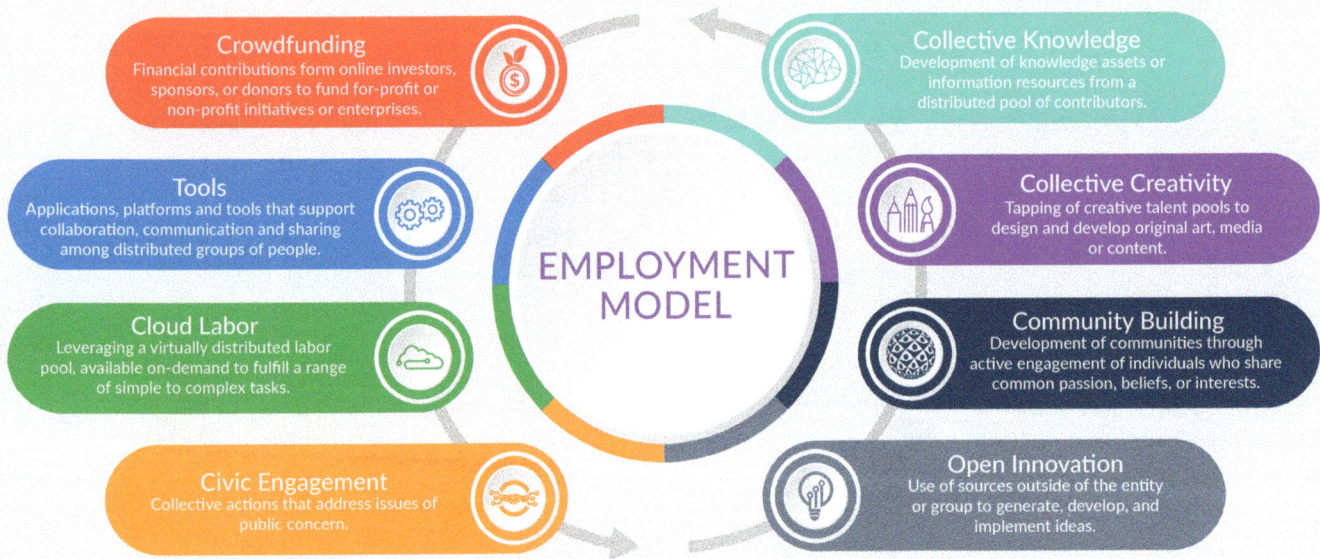

EMPLOYMENT MODEL WORK 3.0

Crowdfunding
Financial contributions form online investors, sponsors, or donors to fund for-profit or non-profit initiatives or enterprises.

Tools
Applications, platforms and tools that support collaboration, communication and sharing among distributed groups of people.

Cloud Labor
Leveraging a virtually distributed labor pool, available on-demand to fulfill a range of simple to complex tasks.

Civic Engagement
Collective actions that address issues of public concern.

EMPLOYMENT MODEL

Collective Knowledge
Development of knowledge assets or information resources from a distributed pool of contributors.

Collective Creativity
Tapping of creative talent pools to design and develop original art, media or content.

Community Building
Development of communities through active engagement of individuals who share common passion, beliefs, or interests.

Open Innovation
Use of sources outside of the entity or group to generate, develop, and implement ideas.

Source: http: barkley.s3.amazonaws.com/barkleyus/AmericanMillennials.pdf

WORK 3.0

Opportunities are by far beyond local markets and are more Global

For both individuals and businesses

FREEDOM TO CHOOSE, WHAT, WHEN, WHERE, HOW & WHO?

THE INNOVATIVE DINOSAUR

EMPLOYMENT MODEL 3.0

Then we have 'work 3.0' — our latest employment model, which is bolstered by powerful and efficient crowdsourcing platforms, business models, and ecosystems. Crowdsourcing is not only for basic tasks, but it can also help us tackle the most complex assignments. We have Upwork for programming crowdsourcing, and 99designs for graphics and creative work, both of which innocentive.com for innovation challenges.

And we have the rise of global virtual organizations, like Crossover, with one-hundred percent remote work options. Last year, I launched an online open-call competition for a logo design (as seen on the cover of this book). We received more than fifty designs from creatives worldwide in less than five working days, with the freedom to choose from diverse submissions, and with just one hundred and thirty dollars to offer. The opportunities of today exceed local market systems. Competent professionals have the freedom to choose the tasks and trajectories that suit their vision or lifestyle. Corporations have a wider choice or supply with respect to minimum overhead and commitment. Talent pools and demand rules are undergoing a democratization or sorts within more competitive environments.

THE
INNOVATIVE
DINOSAUR

RISE OF COLLABORATION FACTOR

RISE OF COLLABORATION

THERE ARE
1.4 BILLION
STUDENTS ON EARTH

1.23 BILLION
students in pre-k to high school

170 MILLION
students in higher education

65.2 MILLION
EDUCATORS GLOBALLY

9.2 MILLION
faculty in higher education

56 MILLION
teachers in pre-k to high school

% of jobs requiring some **technology skills**

50% Today   77% Next Decade

MIT OCW

210 MILLION
INDIVIDUALS HAVE ACCESSED
OCW MATERIALS SINCE LAUNCH

1.3 BILLION
PAGE VIEWS SINCE LAUNCH IN 2002

MATERIALS FROM OVER
2500 COURSES

500 MILLION VISITS

MIT OCW NUMBER OF COURSES

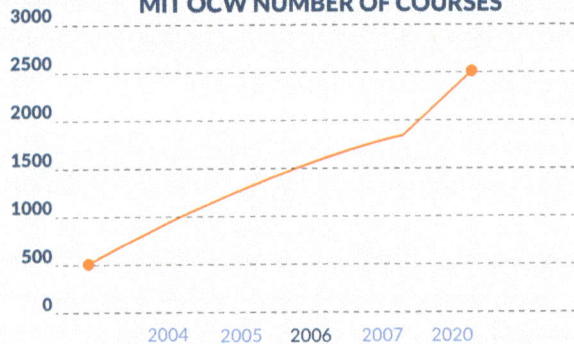

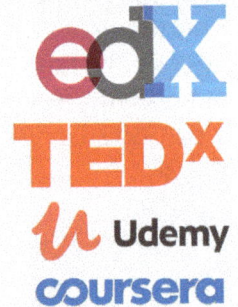

3000
2500
2000
1500
1000
500
0

2004 2005 2006 2007 2020

edX
TEDx
Udemy
coursera

THE
INNOVATIVE
DINOSAUR

RISE OF COLLABORATION

In this century, the power of bonded information has disappeared. Knowledge and information have become more accessible and affordable than ever before.

As the barriers shift, the utilization of information and knowledge is now within reach for billions of people, who can learn about any topic or discipline from the world's top experts just by having a connected device with an affordable and convenient medium. If you want to study an emerging or sophisticated topic like AI-based self-driving vehicles, just turn to Coursera or MIT Open Courseware. In the past, the major source of power for individuals, corporations, and nations alike was in the power of bonded information.

THE INNOVATIVE DINOSAUR

ENTREPRENEURSHIP MODEL

CROWDSOURCING
The Crowd Economy Defined

- Citizen Engagement
- Crowd Currencies
- Crowd Intelligence
- Peer-to-Peer Lending/ Commerce
- Open Innovation
- Equity Based Crowdfunding
- Mass Collaboration
- Non-Equity Based Crowdfunding
- Online Communities
- Sharing Economy
- Crowd Tasks & Creativity
- Customer Co-Creation
- Social Business
- Crowd Causes

https://crowdsourcingweek.com/14-parts-of-the-crowd-economy-landscape-innovation-technology/

THE INNOVATIVE DINOSAUR

ENTREPRENEURSHIP MODEL

The risks associated with financing early-stage startups has long limited the number of new startups. Today, through crowdfunding, crowd investing, and peer-to-peer lending, this risk is distributed over a larger number of micro-finance transactions.

These new methods are increasing the efficiency and strategic alternatives for the lifecycle of the finance deal flow, giving investors and venture capitalists wider options for potential exit strategies. Such disruptions in the value chain are decreasing the investment risk, thus increasing the number of financed ideas that end up seeing the light of day and entering the marketplace. Inevitably, increased competition applies pressure and poses threats for existing players.

Opening a new venue for financing early-stage phase entrepreneurs	Decreasing the angel investors and venture capitals bargaining power during early stage	Provide wider alternatives for early-stage entrepreneurs	Provide more exit strategy options	Increase pressure over medium and large size enterprises

THE INNOVATIVE DINESAUR

INDUSTRY 4.0

4th Industrial Revolution: The Age of Cyber Physical Systems (CPS)

In 2013, the Industry 4.0 concept was officially presented (GTAI 2014)

3rd Industrial Revolution: The Information Age

Introduction of electronic and ICT systems for automation

In 2005, the concept of industrial information integration based on emerging new ICT was officially presented (Xu 2011)

2nd Industrial Revolution: The Age of Electricity

Introduction of mass production utilizing electrical power

1st Industrial Revolution: The Age of Steam

Introduction of mechanical manufacturing systems utilizing water and steam power

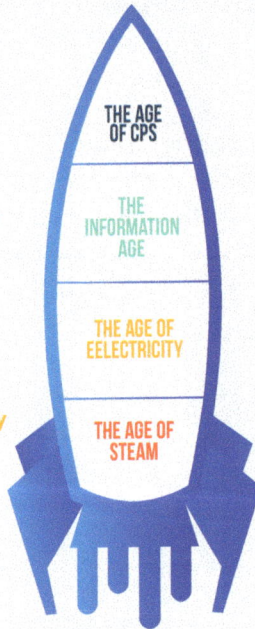

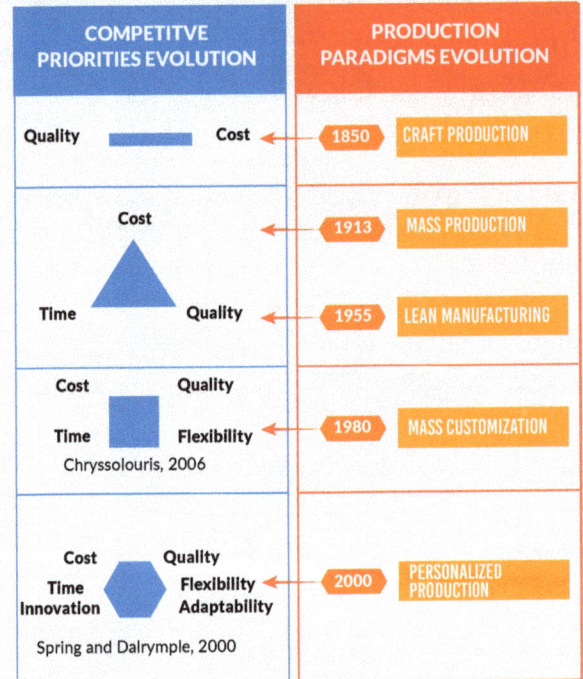

https://edisciplinas.usp.br/pluginfile.php/5824789/mod_resource/content/1/Industria%204.0%20CIMM%20PMR%203301.pdf

THE AGE OF CPS

THE INFORMATION AGE

THE AGE OF EELECTRICITY

THE AGE OF STEAM

COMPETITVE PRIORITIES EVOLUTION

Quality	Cost

Cost

Time — Quality

Cost — Quality

Time — Flexibility

Chryssolouris, 2006

Cost — Quality

Time — Flexibility

Innovation — Adaptability

Spring and Dalrymple, 2000

PRODUCTION PARADIGMS EVOLUTION

Year	Paradigm
1850	CRAFT PRODUCTION
1913	MASS PRODUCTION
1955	LEAN MANUFACTURING
1980	MASS CUSTOMIZATION
2000	PERSONALIZED PRODUCTION

https://www.researchgate.net/figure/Evolution-of-Production-Paradigms-Manufacturing-Networks-and-Competitive-Priorities_fig1_282150223

FROM CRAFT, TO MASS PRODUCTION, TO PERSONALIZED PRODUCTION, TO MASS PERSONALIZED PRODUCTION

FROM STEAM, TO ELECTRICITY, TO INFORMATION, TO CYBER PHYSICAL SYSTEMS

FROM HAND MADE, TO MACHINES, TO ROBOTICS, TO RECONFIGURABLE PRODUCTION SYSTEMS

THE INNOVATIVE DINOSAUR

INDUSTRY 4.0

Advancements in the manufacturing and industrial sectors have been quite astronomical in recent decades. At the same time, we are in the middle of a critical recalibration of the very concept of industry: it's not only about mass production and increasing quality and output, but now it also concerns enhancing cost structures and decreasing delivery times.

What we are seeing today is a kind of contradictory yet revolutionary hybrid — a personalized mass production. Companies may maintain mass production advantages alongside a complete customized production per each customer's needs and values.

All of this is supported by pioneering digital and technological advancements, including connected devices, IoT, robotics, and reconfigurable production systems.

THE
INNOVATIVE
DINOSAUR

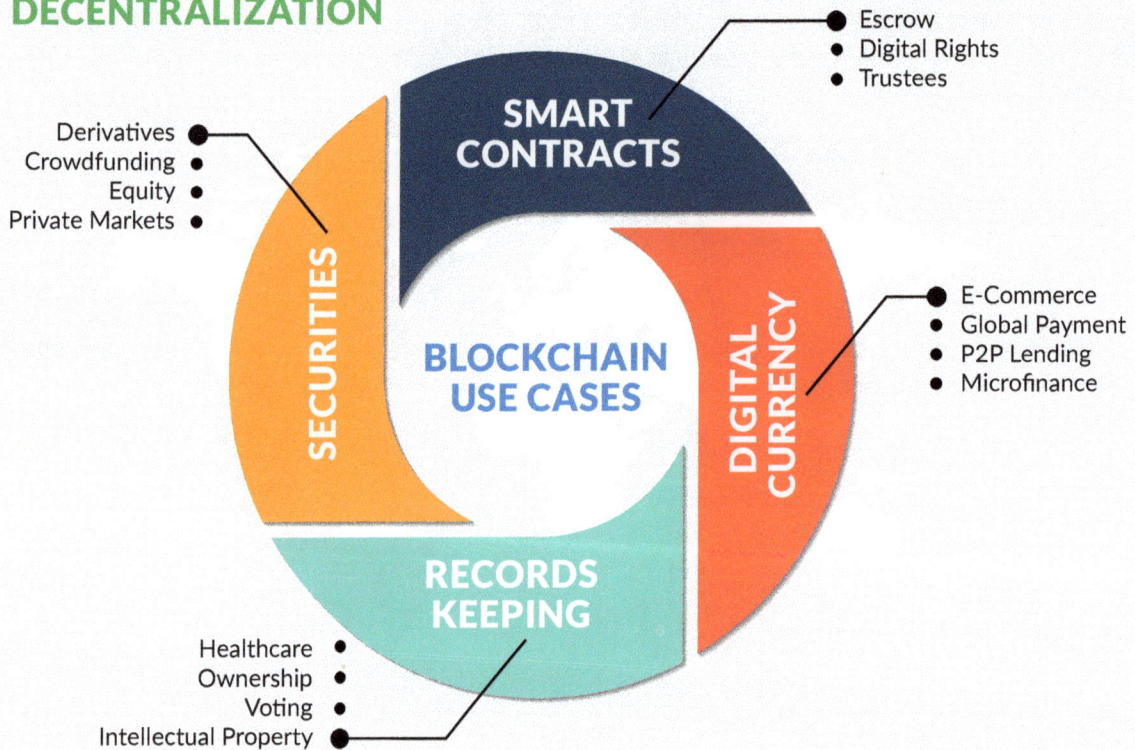

DECENTRALIZATION

SMART CONTRACTS

- Escrow
- Digital Rights
- Trustees

Derivatives
Crowdfunding
Equity
Private Markets

SECURITIES

BLOCKCHAIN USE CASES

DIGITAL CURRENCY

- E-Commerce
- Global Payment
- P2P Lending
- Microfinance

RECORDS KEEPING

Healthcare
Ownership
Voting
Intellectual Property

Designed by: Motaz Agamawi
www.theinnovativedinosaur.com

THE INNOVATIVE DINOSAUR

DECENTRALIZATION

Blockchain technology is changing our understanding of authentication while impacting the value of centralization for different stakeholders.

It goes beyond banking or virtual currency, weaving itself into the fabric of daily life, from transportation, financial to agricultural sectors. Meanwhile, smart contracts, records management, and the concept of governmental authentication are changing, too.

EXAGGERATED CONSUMERISM

"The growing Collaborative economy is a peer-based movement that empowers individuals to get what they need from each other.

From crowdfunding new projects, to peer-based money lending, to people sharing physical goods, the collaborative movement stretches across many aspects of our business."

- The sharing economy is set to reach **$335 BILLION BY 2025**
- **Companies working in the sharing economies will grow by 2,133% IN 12 YEARS**
- Crowdfunding will grow by **$196.36 BILLION** between 2021 and 2025
- **28% OF USERS** are willing to share their electronics
- China's sharing economy is expected to grow **10-15% IN 2021**
- Peer-to-peer lending and crowdfunding will grow at a **63% CAGR**
- Online staffing will grow at a **CAGR of 37%**
- Accommodation, ride sharing, and content streaming are all set to grow at a double-digit pace
- The car-sharing market volume is set to reach **$14.8 BILLION BY 2025**
- The global ride sharing market is set for a **50% ANNUAL RISE IN 2021**
- Music and video streaming will swell at a **CAGR OF 17%**

Source: Vladimir Mirkovic www.transartdesign.com /

Designed by: Motaz Agamawi
www.theinnovativedinosaur.com

THE
INNOVATIVE
DINOSAUR

EXAGGERATED CONSUMERISM

The sharing or peer-to-peer economy is booming as more and more individuals move away from traditional socio-economic systems. Worldwide, each day, an estimated one hundred and fifty thousand Uber trips take place, one hundred and forty thousand people stay in Airbnb rooms, and fifty-five funding goals on Kickstarter are met. How, we may ask ourselves and one another, is all of this impacting the sectors' traditional players, like taxi fleets and tourism companies, overall?

What advancements and setbacks are traditional workforces and citizenries facing amid this sharing economy boom?

Designed by: Motaz Agamawi
www.theinnovativedinosaur.com

THE
INNOVATIVE
DINOSAUR

THE SHIFT GAINS MOMENTUM

Four generations predominate today's world: The Baby Boomers, Generation X, Generation Y (aka Millennials), and Generation Z. At the same time, the digital age is dramatically transforming the ways in which these generational cohorts interact with one another in their collective and respective environments, both on- and offline. Their definitions and perspectives unite and divide them, while many remain either in constant flux or out of touch. In this uncertain yet exciting socio-cultural moment, the current practice of enterprise innovation is perhaps best described as having ever-evolving momentum.

- Year after year, longtime definitions and models of competition continue to shift,
- from industry boundaries to platforms and ecosystems,
- single-purpose products to connected multi-purpose ones, separate user,
- and producer roles to co-creation,
- and traditional to sharing economies.

The speed of these shifts in our era of digital revolution — dynamics, standards, and norms, all recast in years, not centuries — is impacting everyday social and economic structures worldwide. This impact will one day be tantamount to the momentous forces behind the first and second industrial revolutions. Technological and entrepreneurial developments, like social media and startups, will go down in history, too.

Empowered as Never Before

Challenged to Stand within the Crowd

INDIVIDUAL

More Global Outreach

Faster Cycle of Disruption

CORPORATE

More Alternatives to Address Chronic Problems

Challenging Global Competitiveness Positioning

COUNTRY

Designed by: Motaz Agamawi
www.theinnovativedinosaur.com

THE INNOVATIVE DINOSAUR

CHANGE AS OPPORTUNITY AND CHALLENGE

Never before in human history have everyday people been this empowered. However, they — we — must concurrently overcome ever-mounting challenges as competitiveness is no longer a matter of choice and values but longevity. Corporations are now seeking global outreach, with larger target demand to be captured in addition to more competitive operational structures that are based on global footprints.

Many have fallen between industries as competition is ubiquitous — and with exceptionally fast disruption cycles. And countries are now either initiating or replicating efficient and effective alternatives to address and solve crucial chronicle problems. The greater the global competitive landscape, for instance, the more local talent there is to keep, foreign investments to attract, and local global citizens to satisfy.

I will leave you with a single question to contemplate:
how may we seize the advantages of today's technology-driven socio-economic moments and movements, while simultaneously mitigating their associated challenges? The following chapters will guide us to the answer(s).

CHAPTER 2:
THE CHASM BETWEEN TRADITION AND TRANSFORMATION

Walls are failing and falling between industries as disruption emerges from every corner. Industry dynamics evolve beyond recognition. The leaders of yesterday are not the same as the ones of today and the leaders of tomorrow are not yet known. Large organizations are operating in the widening shadows of unparalleled challenges. Dilemmas between maintaining the successful working model of yesterday and adapting to the changes of today and tomorrow.

Organizations can overcome technological disruption, but most will likely struggle when the disruption targets overall market dynamics, business, and revenue models, and common or traditional ways of doing business. As the struggles mount, these organizations face a chasm between tradition and disruption. The ability of organizations to grasp the magnitude of change while seizing the willingness to apply the needed transformations — in a phrase, *informed versatility* — may become the determining factor as to whether they will transcend the chasm or not.

When digital disruption targets a specific industry, we begin to observe patterns of disruption. Industries of all types and sizes have had to grapple with major changes and disruptions over these decades of information and communication revolution.

In this chapter, we will:
- ∈ Analyze the past to learn from various organizations operating in different industries that have faced digital disruption.
- ∈ Exploring how current business models are impacting industry dynamics while anticipating the probable digital disruptions to come.
- ∈ Concluding with the main elements of the digital disruption pattern from industry and enterprise perspectives.

**THE
INNOVATIVE
DINOSAUR**

CHAPTER TWO SECTIONS:

- Lessons Learned from Disrupted Industries
- Business Models Leading the Digital Disruption
- Examples of Industries Currently Facing Digital Disruption
- Digital Disruption Pattern
- Everyday Customers are Changing
- Industry is changing
- Startup Tsunami
- Corporate Transformation Dilemma

CHAPTER TWO LIST OF TOOLS, DIAGRAMS, AND ILLUSTRATIONS

1. Case Study Illustration: Digital Disruption – The Nokia Case
2. Case Study Illustration: Digital Disruption – The Motorola Case
3. Case Study Illustration: Digital Disruption - The IBM Case
4. Case Study Illustration: Digital Disruption - The Sony Case
5. Case Study Illustration: Digital Disruption - The Hitachi Case
6. Illustration: The sharing platform business model value chain. By Murat Uenlue
7. TID Illustration: Digital Disruption Conclusion
8. TID Illustration: Industry Chasm
9. TID Illustration: Startups Tsunami as of December 2017, Transportation Industry Sample
10. TID Illustration: Corporate Transformation Dilemma

THE INNOVATIVE DINOSAUR

CHAPTER TWO LIST OF REFERENCES & EXTRA READINGS

1. 50 Corporates Failed to Innovate, by Valuer.ai
2. Who Says Elephants Can't Dance, by Louis V. Gerstner Jr
3. Zero to One: Notes on Startups, or How to Build the Future, by Peter Thiel
4. Good to Great: Why Some Companies Make the Leap and Others Don't, by Jim Collins
5. The Innovation Paradox: The Success of Failure, the Failure of Succes, by Richard Farson and Ralph Keyes
6. Competing in the Age of AI: Strategy and Leadership When Algorithms and Networks Run the World, by Marco Iansiti, Karim R. Lakhani and others
7. Goliath's Revenge: How Established Companies Turn the Tables on Digital Disruptors, by Todd Hewlin, Scott A. Snyder and others
8. The Disruption Mindset: Why Some Organizations Transform While Others Fail by Charlene Li
9. The Sharing Economy, Forbs
10. Thinking Inside the subscription box, McKinsey
11. Commissioning in the Human Service, KPMG
12. Insurance Ecosystem, PwC
13. Trends in European clusters: results from the 2019 European panorama, trends and priority sectors reports published

THE
INNOVATIVE
DINGSAUR

MOBILE INDUSTRY – THE NOKIA CASE

Source: 50 Corporates Failed to Innovate, by Valuer.ai

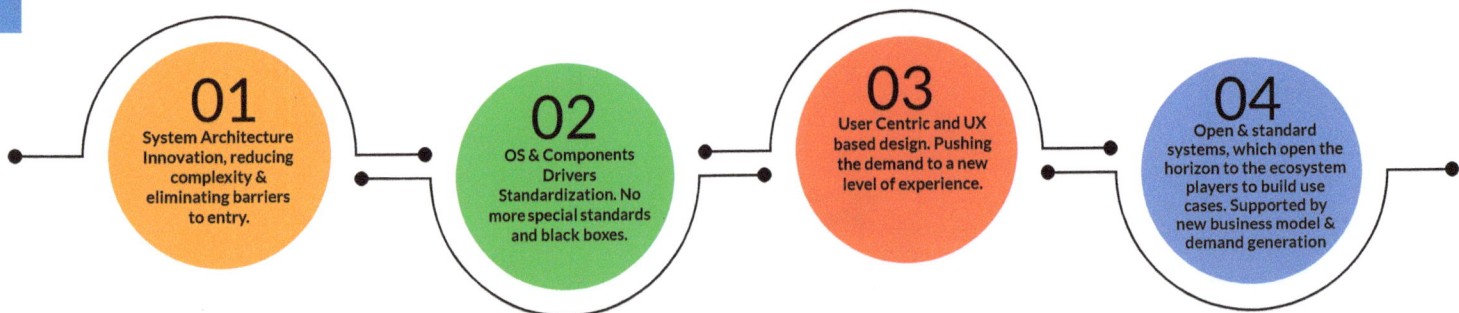

At the time of disruption, Nokia was producing more than 250 SKU with various nonstandard OS, sensors, and non-user centric UX. It was incredibly challenging for the ecosystem third party partners including application developers and content publishers to build and grow different use cases over Nokia products. The challenge was not the technology disruption, as the company had introduced the first smartphone in the mid-90s, but rather it was the industry dynamics disruption.

The digital disruption can be summarized by system architecture innovation, reducing complexity and eliminating barriers to entry, as well as OS and components drivers' standardization. No more special standards and black boxes. Only user-centric and UX-based design and pushing the demand to new heights of experience. Only open and standard systems and widening the horizon to the ecosystem players to build use cases. And, overall, the disruption is reinforced and perpetuated by new business models and generation-driven demands.

The real challenge was not the technology disruption as Nokia introduced the first smart phone in mid 90s. The real challenge was the industry dynamics disruption.

> "It wasn't just that Nokia failed to recognize the increasing importance of software, though. It also underestimated how important the transition to smartphones would be. And this was, introspect, a classic case of a company being enthralled (and, in a way, imprisoned) by its past success."
>
> *-James Surowiecki*
> *The New Yorker's*
> *Contributor*

01 System Architecture Innovation, reducing complexity & eliminating barriers to entry.

02 OS & Components Drivers Standardization. No more special standards and black boxes.

03 User Centric and UX based design. Pushing the demand to a new level of experience.

04 Open & standard systems, which open the horizon to the ecosystem players to build use cases. Supported by new business model & demand generation

THE INNOVATIVE DINOSAUR

MOBILE INDUSTRY – THE MOTOROLA CASE

"Battery lifetime was 20 mins, but that wasn't really a big problem because you couldn't hold that phone up for that long."

-Marty Cooper
Motorola's Vice President

Even though Motorola kept producing various versions of its cellphones, they failed to see that customers wanted innovation in software rather than hardware.

Essentially, Motorola didn't implement 21st century communication to its products, making it hard to compete with smartphones on the market.

In August 2011, Motorola was acquired by Google.

The real failure behind the Motorola case was the change in market dynamics, from technology's push to the market's pull. Digital disruption created a new demand level for features, capabilities, and UX. In terms of internal competency, business model, and product design perspectives, Motorola was unable to cope with the change of speed — faster, newer, smarter.

01 System Architecture Innovation, reducing complexity & eliminating barriers to entry.

03 User Centric and UX based design. Pushing the demand to a new level of experience.

02 OS & Components Drivers Standardization. No more special standards and black boxes.

04 Open & standard systems, which open the horizon to the ecosystem players to build use cases. Supported by new business model & demand generation.

Source: 50 Corporates Failed to Innovate, by Valuer.ai

THE
INNOVATIVE
DINOSAUR

PC INDUSTRY – THE IBM CASE

> "The key to success is massive failure."
> -*Thomas Watson President IBM*

IBM is one of the rare examples for enterprises which was able to overcome major down fall.

IBM Proved that an elephant can dance

In the early 1990s, IBM failed to adjust to the personal computer revolution and thus began their downfall. The company adjusted their focus back on hardware instead of software solutions.

From the late-seventies to the early-eighties, IBM ignored the PC race and refused to compete. When management realized their mistake, time was already against them. They decided to push the open standard strategy on their competition, which worked in the favor of many players, like Microsoft and Intel, but IBM was not one of them.

The digital disruption can be summarized in IBM pushing the open standard strategy even though it was not adopted by direct competition at the time. Based on this strategy, Microsoft, Intel and others established themselves as giants in the game. In time, the value shifted toward computation technology and SW experience. The open standard helped in speedily guiding the HW more toward commodity. Thus, the price competition shifted in the favor of Chinese manufacturers, to what was called the 'compatible PC.'

1 IBM pushed the open standard strategy which was not adopted by direct competition at the time.

2 Based on this strategy, Microsoft, Intel, and others have been established as giant players.

3 By time, value shifted toward computation tech and SW experience.

4 The open standard helped in speeding up the HW to be more towards a commodity. Thus, price competition was in favor of Chinese manufacturers to what was called "Compatible PC".

THE INNOVATIVE DINOSAUR

ELECTRONICS INDUSTRY – THE SONY CASE

"The bottom line is: if you want to be perceived as a creator of cool tech, you have to create cool tech. The challenge for Sony is that those examples have not been there, and they haven't been there now for a number of years."

-Steve Beck Founder of CG24

Sony didn't adopt to technological innovation such as digitalization, the shift toward software, and the growth of illegal downloadable music online. Sony actually had the technology to launch a product even better than iPod, but it never happens.

By the 90s Walkman was a must have gadget for every teen. It was the iPhone of its day. But when MP3 players we introduced to the market, the sales of the Walkman started to drop. The Walkman was killed by the MP3 players, which were later killed by smartphones

Sony owned a once-superior technology, the world's first low-cost personal stereo known as the WALKMAN. They played the game as an electronic manufacturer but later failed to play it as a true competitor in the digital market. The MP3 player, namely, the iPod, and then the smartphone, all killed this faded industry star.

The digital disruption can be summarized in the shift from HW capabilities to UX and ecosystem. The real disruption of the iPod comes from iTunes, with its IP protection for producers and affordable disruptive business model for consumers. The music industry was radically disrupted and forever changed by the advent of SW players.

01 From HW capabilities to user experience and ecosystem

02 The real disruption of iPod is coming from the iTunes with its IP protection for producers and affordable disruptive business model for consumers

03 The music industry was disrupted and changed by the SW players

Source: 50 Corporates Failed to Innovate, by Valuer.ai

THE
INNOVATIVE
DINOSAUR

ELECTRONICS INDUSTRY – THE HITACHI CASE

Source: 50 Corporates Failed to Innovate, by Valuer.ai

"The electronics industry isn't what it used to be. Time was when gadget makers could inspire lust in certain segments of consumer, charge high price and come away with healthy profits.

These days, the electronics industry find itself dealing with a different kinds of Japanese consumer, one who cares about price and only price. As a result, the industry is fallen into a fragile situation."

-Hiroaki Nakanishi, Hitachi Chairman

The electronics industry has changed, where consumers don't have a high of desire for their high price products. The digital revolution not only changed the way electronic gadget work, but also, they changed the way they are manufactured.

"Look at Apple, they make iPods and iPhone. Apple makes at least 50% profit margins on those. People say iPhones are made in China, but maybe only 3% of the value of an iPhone stays in China. So, it's hard to become rich today on the scale of just manufacturing- you have to do a lot more"

-Gerhard Fasolt, an economist

Digital disruption shifts, even inverts, customer perception. As the UX of SW was perceived to be of higher value, HW manufacturing became a commodity with less profitability.

The digital disruption can be summarized in the drastic changes in the electronic manufacturing value chain and customer perception — which is becoming increasingly aware of UX, ecosystem, and supported business models. The electronic manufacturing share of wallet is decreasing dramatically, thus impacting profitability and the means to compete.

| Electronic manufacturing value chain and customer perception is drastically changing. | Customer perception for UX, Ecosystem and supported business model is increasing. | Electronic manufacturing share of wallet is decreasing dramatically which impacts profitability and means to compete. |

THE INNOVATIVE DINOSAUR

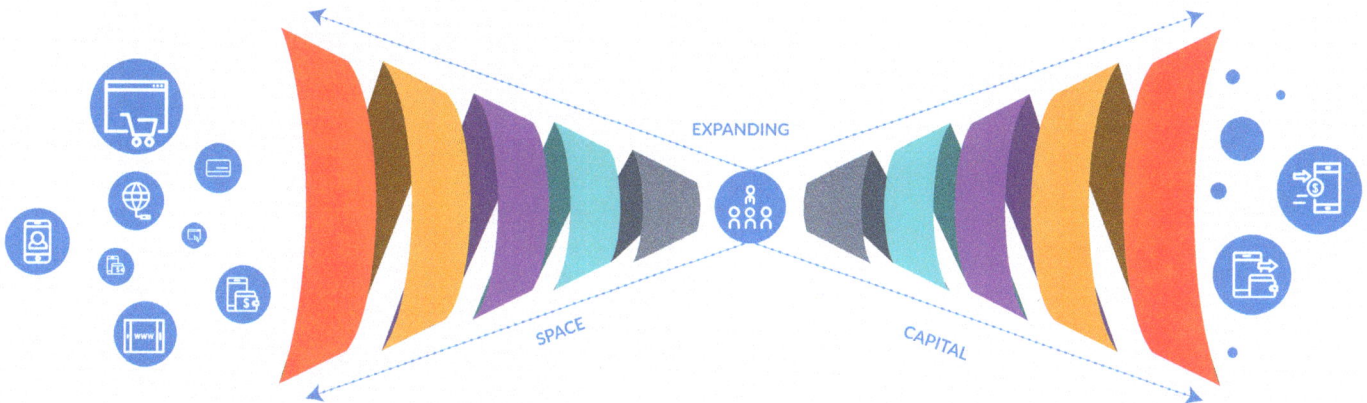

EXPANDING

SPACE

CAPITAL

VIRTUAL MARKET ← PHYSICAL MARKET

MARKETPLACE IS NO LONGER WHERE
YOU GO, IT'S WHEREVER YOU ARE

SCARCITY OF CAPITAL → DIGITAL SHARING ECONOMY

TODAY, THE LARGEST FLEET OPERATOR IN THE
WORLD DOES NOT OWN A SINGLE CAR.

Source: 50 Corporates Failed to Innovate, by Valuer.ai

Designed by: Motaz Agamawi
www.theinnovativedinosaur.com

THE
INNOVATIVE
DINOSAUR

BUSINESS MODELS LEADING THE DIGITAL DISRUPTION

SHARING ECONOMY

The contemporary iteration of the sharing economy is a digital platform-driven peer-to-peer (P2P) socio-economic model. That emphasizes access over ownership and flexibility over convention with respect to the buying and selling of goods and services. Peer-to-peer transactions, like home and apartment rentals, are nothing new. The internet, along with the advancement of digital platforms, have helped facilitate the global spread of the concept. Empowering everyday consumers with user rating systems, and utilizing underused assets with fewer entry barriers.

For thousands of years, the marketplace and capital have constituted our main commercial economic systems. The marketplace was a physically defined space with boundaries, where sellers wait and buyers' approach. Capital was key, too, as sellers often had a scarcity of capital investment, limiting their growth and operations. At the same time, the size of available capital impacted sellers' ability to buy or rent a specific store area and/or the amounts of goods offered to consumers within this area. The concept of the digitalized sharing economy has recast both components. First, it has expanded the size of the physical marketplace with the rise of mobile devices and web browsers used by target customers. In essence, the marketplace is no longer where you go, it's wherever you are. In most cases this either minimizes or eliminates the impact of needed capital — for example, why do you need capital to have a fleet of taxis when you can utilize the investments of others? In recent years, Uber has taken the traditional transportation industry by storm, just as Airbnb saturated the traditional hotel market. This is the first time in human history that the largest fleet operator and accommodation provider in the world do not own a single car or room, respectively.

Our current digital sharing economy is designed to support the idea of utilizing un/underused resources owned by others while also having buyers' demand also by others. Its online platforms are based on connecting sellers or service providers who have a surplus of a specific resource with prospective buyers for a commission fee. Along with the concept of asset ownership, consumerism — particularly the buyer lifecycle that we have been designing our businesses around – is in momentous flux.

The concept of scarcity of resources, upon which most economic rules are based, is also transforming. In the past, we've constructed our business models with an implicit and/or explicit consideration for the concept. Internet bandwidth, for instance, was once scarce and expensive for the vast majority, but recent technological developments related to optimizing operating systems to consume bandwidth wisely and efficiently are increasingly leveling the surfing field. Google and Netflix are prime examples of companies that have significantly capitalized on such optimizations, pushing their customers to consume bandwidth with an added price tag. These methods are marching industry standards and business models into previously uncharted gray areas. If we take a further look, capital itself isn't far behind. In the past, capital was scarce and costly, so we carefully spent and invested it. Today, digital platforms that run on a P2P basis have opened wide the doors of accessibility and affordability for capital to flow — think, crowdfunding and crowd investing. Generally, investments on efficiency innovation have a faster ROI than radical innovation. Our higher metric applied to efficiency innovation investment needs to be revised. With the availability of surplus cash and easier access to it, investing in more radical innovation has a potential for higher future valuation. This is why 'user first' strategies are gaining exceptional momentum in the business world, from Amazon to Facebook and Uber to Airbnb. While these corporate heavyweights lost money in the early years, high valuation was gained. The many investments and other injections of capital received by those future heavyweights led to a high ROI and landing at the end. Accordingly, the priorities and matrix of innovation investment must be revised and cross-checked with different perspectives and evaluation criteria.

PRODUCT/SERVICES CATEGORIES

REVENUE MODEL

DIGITAL GAMING CONSOLES EXAMPLE

REVENUE MODEL

HW CONSOLES AT CLOSE-TO-COST PRICES

COMMISSION % FROM PUBLISHERS → ONE TIME, COMMISSION

REFERRALS & GADGET SALES → ONE TIME, ASSET SALE

IN GAME PURCHASE COMMISSION → REOCCURRING, PAY AS YOU GO

ONLINE STORE SALES COMMISSION → ONE TIME, COMMISSION

DIGITAL NETWORK SUBSCRIPTION → REOCCURRING, SUBSCRIPTION BASED

MULTI-STREAM

Designed by: Motaz Agamawi
www.theinnovativedinosaur.com

THE INNOVATIVE DINOSAUR

SUBSCRIPTION AND PAY-AS-YOU-GO

The traditional subscription model, is based on either advance or routine payments made by a customer for a specific period.

Let us now consider the game console business model. Console producers, like Sony for PlayStation and Microsoft for Xbox, sell their HW consoles at close-to-cost prices. The main profitability comes from the licenses they issue to video game publishers, which make revenue based on the consumption of the target customers. Another important revenue is various subscription packages for accessing special features or capabilities. Sony and Microsoft are minimizing the cost of ownership, while maximizing their continuous revenue stream from consumers.

In this case, normal asset sales made in one-time transactions were transformed — revolutionized — into a continuous revenue stream business model. On the other hand, the pay-as-you-go or pay-as-you-use systems are used widely in the cloud solution offering. Microsoft Azure, Amazon Web Service, and Google Cloud Platform have designed their offerings based on such a model. Consumers may subscribe with a minimum commitment and then, based on their monthly data, bandwidth or processing usage will be tabulated.

**THE
INNOVATIVE
DINOSAUR**

CUSTOMER

Increase of Customer Stickiness to Product

Faster time to market Efficient investment

Customer enjoys
- Extra features
- Capabilities
- Use cases

Better UX while using the same product

Product Acquisition

Apps, Content & Services Acquisition

Promote & fulfill

Own, Manage, & Promote

Digital Store

Use Case Ready for Commercialization

Promote

Producer

Produce

Product

API - Application Programming Interface

Building Use Cases

Partner

Owner of the product benefits from
- Extended brainpower capabilities offered
- By the partner's (application or content).
- Additional revenue stream

Upselling opportunity

Asset Sales Revenue Model +

Commission Revenue Model

Avail

Attract, Support & Manage

Partners Network benefit from:
- Utilize an existing R&D effort
- An established customer base
- Existing fulfillment capabilities

Higher probability of demand capturing

- License Revenue
- Pay As you Go Revenue
- Subscription Revenue
- In App Micro Purchases
- Revenue
- Advertisement Revenue

Revenue Sharing Model

Product can go serving beyond its original purpose
Through use cases (the example of the smart phone)

THE INNOVATIVE DINOSAUR

ECOSYSTEM COMMISSIONING

The idea of building an ecosystem around a specific product or platform is not new, but it's become increasingly prevalent over the past ten to fifteen years. Since late 1999, the main diffusion point behind the iPod was the ecosystem of music publishers. Apple was able to address music industry publishers' copyright concerns through an advanced copyright and digital right management system and then utilize digital platform capabilities by creating a modern digital store — iTunes. Through an expanse of fresh digital features in combination with the experience of iTunes, a bold modern business model and pricing strategy were introduced: consumers could now purchase a single song for less than a dollar instead of buying the full album. The parallel example of the mobile application store, which has existed since the Nokia era, sees a complete modern paradigm and approach applied by Apple and then Google. Today, we can find a variety of application genres on our smart devices' app stores.

The business model of HW and SW producers Apple and Google is king in the tech industry. By availing your technologies to a group of partners who can build applications and offer different use models, a win-win for all appears on the horizon. The producer or owner of the platform benefits from the extended brainpower and capabilities offered by the partner's network application or content. The additional revenue stream, coming from either commission or advertisement mechanisms, presents another benefit — a sort of upselling opportunity. The partner utilizes an existing R&D effort and, perhaps most importantly, an established customer base for the device or platform. The customer enjoys extra features, capabilities, and use cases while using the specific device. This co-development concept has penetrated other industries. Facebook, for example, benefits immensely from opening its platform to other application developers, which elevates use cases and usage. The IoT industry is following the same pattern, and we also have the instance of Samsung's home automation system SmartThings.

THE INNOVATIVE DINOSAUR

Alongside the development of application stores and partner ecosystems is the rising concept of the automation platform. This online platform addresses a very important challenge against the backdrop of our digital services boom: integrating different platforms, devices, gadgets, and service producers by various suppliers, all together at once, and then giving this power to the end user in a simple and straightforward experience. By way of illustration, we then start to see products like Zapier, IFTTT, and Microsoft Automate that offer a great number of pre-integrated applications. On such user-friendly interfaces, everyday users may begin to design scenarios via simple triggers and action sequences. These users are empowered to automate their own tasks by way of an easy and efficient mechanism. With just a couple of clicks, users create a full automation scenario, linking the actions of their home automation gadgets, like cameras, or the smart bill to their mobiles, either through email or SMS. Even the user navigation systems on their mobiles, like Google Maps, may be connected to their home automation system. So, upon leaving the office, for example, the system can be triggered to execute specific actions and scenarios from afar.

Today, traditional industries face the challenge of meeting user expectations and needs. Many are now pushing toward having the same connected experience for their contemporary users. As user sophistication soars, they seek out the same mobile, tablet, or smart TV experience in their cars, refrigerators, and other appliances.

THE
INNOVATIVE
DINESAUR

ORGANIZATION

CROWDSOURCING PLATFORMS

TALENT POOL

Platforms that are built to facilitate and manage relationship between service providers and customers.

The community rating of service providers and beneficiaries gives way to a sort of community reputation management framework with the potentiality for mutual benefit and trust.

Crowdsourcing platforms provide all the processes, methods, and features necessary to ensure constructive and hassle-free exchanges.

The crowdsourcing model is expected to impact the overall competitiveness of organizations.

The rise of escrow accounts to control the payment terms, execution, and management between both parties or players.

This is especially relevant when considering other complementary technologies such as the Cloud, AI, robotics, 3D printing, blockchain, and the impact that can be achieved by integrating these elements.

Designed by: Motaz Agamawi
www.theinnovativedinosaur.com

THE INNOVATIVE DINOSAUR

DIGITAL CROWD EMPOWERMENT

Crowdsourcing is based on digital platforms that empower people every day to be part of the product/ project, or service lifecycle, from initial ideation, prototyping, development, and testing to even strategic marketing and implementation. The empowering potential of such platforms may culminate in a speedy shift from the producer-user divide to co-creation. Built to facilitate and manage relations between service providers and customers. Crowdsourcing platforms provide all the processes, methods, and features necessary to ensure — ideally speaking — constructive and hassle-free exchanges. Think to the rise of escrow accounts to control the payment terms, execution, and management between both parties or players. The community rating of service providers and beneficiaries gives way to a sort of community reputation management framework with the potentiality for mutual benefit and trust. Many other mechanisms and techniques are used to ensure that these relations or exchanges are managed with utmost professional conduct and transparency.

In the beginning, the crowdsourcing business model linked suppliers to buyers, and vice versa, through a digitally secured and reliable platform. The platform producers were focusing on the commission business model, which is based on the added value created for both service producers and consumers. Service domains included the lowest part of the value chain but, in time, were based on the complexity of the platform, maturity of the service providers, and acceptance of the consumer base. Accordingly, services rose little by little within the value chain leaders, leading to the most sophisticated and advanced service types to date.

The diffusion and success of the crowdsourcing model in our digital age has laid the foundation for a new set of expectations for service providers and users alike. The impact of this game changing model exceeds the original purpose of the business domain. Today, the success of this model is one of the main catalysts for global freelancer and digital nomad cultures as well as the top-down acceptance of remote teamwork. In the beginning, specific digital-related services and tasks were offered through platforms like Upwork, 99Designs, and Fiverr. But now all types of services can be conducted through integrated platforms, from brand-name selection, graphic design, product design, development, testing, marketing, HR services, legal services, accounting, sales, logistics, and even production or manufacturing.

Crowdsourcing has ventured beyond the idea of services. In the early 2000s, we started to notice this model, with one of the early pioneers being Kickstarter. Many other companies have since followed suit, advocating, and employing the same idea of empowering entrepreneurs and creative professionals through offering early-adoption incentives for consumers pre-ordering. Crowdsourcing eventually led to the advent of crowd investment, which gives a structural managed means for individuals to participate by investing in early-stage startups, thus shifting traditional power dynamics between financial capital and small businesses.

Upon the diffusion and acceptance of the concept by providers and suppliers alike, other crowdsourcing-related services, models, and concepts started to evolve, in particular, remote teams with scale as a successful example of crossover offerings. The concept of coworking spaces on a structural global scale followed, along with e-residence permits and e - citizenship for individual freelancers and professionals who desire to launch and operate an organization overseas. Estonia's e-Residency program, for instance, extends the EU e-residence for subscribed established entities.

At this point, the major question to ask is: how may the above-described trend and models trigger off advancements and advantages for enterprises? New and/or improved business models that revolve around the concept of empowering the crowd while also benefiting from them is a potentially solid step forward in the direction of success. Our follow-up query is concerned with the ways in which enterprises may attract crowds to fuel their operations as well as guarantee the quality of service provided in return. It is considered self-destructive when an organization cannot find the proper mechanisms and means to grasp the benefits of such a disruptive operational model. The crowdsourcing model is expected to impact the overall competitiveness of organizations of all sizes in the few years to come. This is especially relevant when considering other complementary technologies such as the Cloud, AI, robotics, 3D printing, blockchain, and the impact that can be achieved by integrating these elements.

THE
INNOVATIVE
DINOSAUR

EXAMPLES OF INDUSTRIES CURRENTLY FACING DIGITAL DISRUPTION

LOGISTICS AND PARCEL DELIVERY
crowd parcel delivery, crowd shipping model, crowdsourcing delivery fleet, Last mile delivery via autonomous vehicles and drones

WHOLESALE AND IN-STORE SHOPPING
E-commerce, virtual fitting rooms and makeovers, virtual and augmented reality, Amazon Go

TELECOM AND THE INTERNET
VoIP, SpaceX's Starlink – Satellite Based Internet

CONTENT PRODUCTION AND DISTRIBUTION
Digital newspaper, books, music, movies, social media user generated content

BANKING AND FINANCE
mobile payment options, virtual wallet payments, online payment gateways, virtual currency , crowdfunding, crowd investing, crowdlending and Fintech

SPACE TRAVEL
SpaceX is aiming to revolutionize — even democratize — the space industry

TOBACCO INDUSTRY
electronic cigarettes, IQOS (Phillip Morris is both the disruptor and the disrupted)

Designed by: Motaz Agamawi
www.theinnovativedinosaur.com

THE INNOVATIVE DINOSAUR

LOGISTICS AND PARCEL DELIVERY IN THE DIGITAL ERA

The logistics and parcel delivery industry has been a mature and stable sector for since tens of years ago. Different disruptions are transforming this sector, namely, the tools, systems, and means ushered in by the digital era. We can imagine and observe how the invention of the fax machine, followed by email, has impacted this industry in terms of volume and revenue. Further afield in our imaginations and daily lives, we can see how such an impact was deepened by the diffusion of digital electronic documents and paperless offices technologies. In the near future, the diffusion of electronic signatures will lead to a widespread decline in the necessity for exchanging physical documents between individuals and entities. The future diffusion of 3D printers may diminish our need to conduct a shipment of products and prototypes as well as for the mailing of device components.

Today, crowd parcel delivery services are eating from the traditional market share of companies like FedEx, UPS, and DHL. These collaborative platforms connect shippers and receivers to conduct the traditional service of parcel delivery in a more economical, peer-to-peer fashion and form. Still, these platforms are not mature enough owing to the absence of regulatory laws, consumer trust, and business model maturity. In time, it is expected that such factors will be tackled, and such markets regulated.

The crowd shipping model, or crowdsourcing delivery fleet, was first introduced by Uber Eats and is expanding globally, giving businesses an alternative: an elastic fleet coverage with the minimum asset investment required. Moreover, the opportunity then emerges for many everyday people to utilize their existing vehicle assets on-the-go while generating extra revenue.

Last mile delivery via autonomous vehicles and drones, both supported by the trends of the megacities, constitutes a source of real disruption; meanwhile, digital delivery mechanisms using robots or semi-robotic solutions are gaining certain momentum. In the coming decade, we can expect to see around one million autonomous delivery devices operating globally.

THE INNOVATIVE DINOSAUR

WHOLESALE AND IN-STORE SHOPPING IN THE DIGITAL ERA

Over the past two decades, the wholesale industry has faced disruptions through the emergence of different online e-commerce portals and platforms, from book publishing to grocery shopping. E-commerce is not just replacing the physical outlet business model, but it is also impacting the in-store sales. The in-store buyer decision lifecycle is steered by online searches offered by popular engines like Google as well as by online advertisements and campaigns and recommendations circulating in the social network spheres. With the spread of internet bandwidth, digital devices like smartphones and tablets, in addition to laptops and desktops, create virtual marketplaces where digital e-commerce facilitates an affordable, competitive, and convenient shopping experience.

Another wave of digital solutions is also influencing the industry, further linking the virtual and physical world. The existence of affordable technologies like virtual fitting rooms and makeovers, together with the fast-spread of virtual and augmented reality technologies, we can expect another inflection point that will dramatically change in-store sales in the coming years.

If we consider the recent move of the Amazon Fresh grocery story, we can see the future of this industry. The virtual grocer giant — touted as featuring "the world's most advanced shopping technology" — is utilizing the latest technologies to create a complete digital experience for consumers. The integration of a virtual assistant AI technology, like Alexa, to help customers locate items in combination with self-checkout technologies means that "you will never have to wait in line." And then there is the integration of the online store and the physical ones, whereby customers order goods online and then pick them up from the physical store. For another future aspect, the integration of third-party online stores and physical stores expands the spectrum of probabilities for more features and an enhanced UX. Amazon Go is still in the experimentation phase, so it's too early to evaluate its above-quoted claims.

**THE
INNOVATIVE
DINOSAUR**

TELECOM AND THE INTERNET IN THE DIGITAL ERA

Just a few decades ago, mobile network operators were seen as major disruptors in the telecommunications industry. In time, this industry faced disruption with the spread of the Voice over Internet Protocol (VoIP). The rise of VoIP-based mobile applications followed, giving users the ability to conduct high quality voice calls at competitive prices. Up to now, many countries continue to protect the industry by regulating the usage of the internet for personal calls, with some of them also blocking various applications that offer such services to users. The dilemma is evident in the amount of infrastructure investments that are carried out by telecom operators, which is represented in international communication cable lines, communication stations, and even satellites. Such infrastructure is the backbone of communication technology. Simply put, without it we do not have the internet.

On the other hand, most of the telecom operators protect their profitability through the internet usage tariff. What we see today through SpaceX's Starlink project will be disruptive to traditional telecom industry players. The first-of-its-kind service will offer high-speed internet bandwidth ranging from 50 to 150 Mbps for a monthly cost of around $99 per month, with a device cost of around $499, according to unofficial information available through the beta testing. It is worth noting that mass market commercial prices are expected to be competitive. The high-performance and low- latency promised will have a great impact on the quality of service and applications to benefit from such technologies. This latency enhancement is set to be achieved through the low-Earth orbit that the satellites will live in, which is some 300 miles above our planet's surface, compared to 22,000 miles for the traditional current satellites. Starlink has secured approval for the launch of around 30,000 satellites, compared to the 2,000 satellites or so orbiting the Earth at the time of writing. Other programs will one day follow Starlink in this disruptive domain between Earth and space.

CONTENT PRODUCTION AND DISTRIBUTION IN THE DIGITAL ERA

Content digital disruption has been around since the dawn of the PC age. A major milestone first emerged when Apple decided to enter the desktop publishing game, eventually becoming an industry disruptor itself. Around the same time, Adobe positioned itself as a rising star in the game with its desktop publishing tools and technologies, from Photoshop, Illustrator, InDesign to Acrobat. The speed of development in this field accelerated in the eighties and nineties, perhaps most notably expanding from static to dynamic content and video production. The industry — and the world — were seeing and living the diffusion and fast-spread of PC technology, followed by the proliferation of the internet.

We can deduce that the major disruptive impact of these novel technologies and forces appeared after almost a quarter of advancements, and when the many rising and competing elements of the game were integrated together.

As content creation tools reached maturity and became easier to use and afford, the medium of digitalization spread from PCs to portable media players like the iPod, and then on to smartphones and tablets. With greater availability and affordability came the rise of digital awareness and the presence of an ever-expanding consumer base.

It all started with books and music digitalization. Online portals then supplanted the traditional newspaper industry. Social media platforms followed, rendering all users or consumers participants in new creation and dissemination. Today, user-generated content is increasingly dominating our networks, from social media to the internet at large. As internet bandwidth became more available and affordable than ever before, we've seen an upsurge in online video streaming, which has changed the rules of the game for the traditional film industry.

Many new business models, revenue streams, and pricing strategies have emerged within the content and media industry. Online advertising is more than a competitive edge these days – rather, it's a necessity, even for the household names. In the newspaper industry, for instance, readers will find a combination of free, add-supported content and subscriptions targeting specific interests and sections. The music industry is an early pioneer in digital distribution and then in terms of subscriptions, with third-party providers either on devices or through specialized platforms. The film industry also faces the new model of online streaming through subscription-based platforms featuring a range of options for personalization. Internet-age giants like

Netflix and Amazon, along with veteran players like Disney, are (re)writing the rules of this disrupted, ultramodern game.

The disruption of the content and media industry was an inevitable result of the digital technology revolution that we have been living in for the past three decades or so. Users are empowered, with some of them becoming creators and even competitors themselves. Their ease of use and purchase has been a crucial catalyst for such digital-era diffusion.

BANKING AND FINANCE IN THE DIGITAL ERA

An intense wave of change and disruption has caught up to the banking and finance sectors. It began just a couple years back with the introduction of mobile payment options offered by mobile network operators, followed by virtual wallet payments. Over the last decade, we have seen the striking example of PayPal and the diffusion of like services. Online payment gateways were originally designed to bridge the gap between online payment needs and the physical limitations of credit cards. Over time, online payment gateways caused a major change in the payment industry.

Some fifteen years ago, virtual currency broke into the changing game by way of Bitcoin, the world's first open source, peer-to-peer digital currency system. As of today, many top banks and financial institutions do not accept virtual currency. Instead, we are witnessing the entrance of giant technology companies in the virtual currency arena, like Facebook, which announced its plan for a digital currency under the name of 'Diem' (previously Libra). We will surely witness yet another wave of diffusion in the coming years: as digital content, services, and applications gain momentum worldwide, virtual currencies will find their way to the base of the pyramid, to consumers. With the maturation of blockchain technology, it is expected that virtual currency will capture the attention and trust of more and more industry players and everyday people and institutions while securing a mightier technological infrastructure and thus a higher and faster diffusion rate.

THE
INNOVATIVE
DINOSAUR

The means of finance is another critical aspect to be contemplated. Upon the start of the spread of technology companies and the boom in the filed the concept of the venture capitals followed by, the concept of 'angel investors' was created to fill a gap not heeded by traditional banking institutions. Based on another gap, today's crowd-powered model first picked up speed around fifteen years ago. Crowdfunding, crowd investing, and crowdlending are providing state-of-the-art means for financing ideas, early startups, and even startups in the seed stage. Even though these mechanisms will not usurp the banks, venture capitals, and IPOs — not anytime soon, at least — they are still increasing the financial options available as well as the efficiency of the deal flow. Overall, it is increasing the possibility of success for early-stage startups to be financed and, in turn, applying a greater level of pressure on more traditional business models.

Fintech is a technology that was invented to empower the so-called 'masses' through the facilitation of peer-to-peer lending and finance. This technology's digital platforms are offering a new variety of efficiency when it comes to facilitating the availability of finance. We now have a different range of fintech models, from peer-to-peer lending to credit facilities for purchasing and even social circle-based saving plans and banking. The microfinance model has found great support in such technologies and platforms. Bolstered by the power of data, along with advancements in data science, predictive analysis and forecasts, fintech platforms are gaining ground, day by day, with clear success in financial allocation and collection capabilities.

SPACE TRAVEL IN THE DIGITAL ERA

Elon Musk's trailblazing SpaceX is aiming to revolutionize — even democratize — the space industry. After decades spent in the shadow of NASA and other agencies, the industry is now being rocked by SpaceX, namely, its successful launch of the first-ever reused rocket back into space. Not to mention, Musk is also building the world's largest rocket, and NASA itself hired SpaceX as a private contractor just last year. It is too early to forecast the possibilities and dynamics that such a move can and will create, but humanity will likely benefit tremendously from the company's brave and advanced developments and vision.

**THE
INNOVATIVE
DINESAUR**

TOBACCO INDUSTRY
IN THE DIGITAL ERA

The advent of the factory-made cigarette revolutionized an age-old industry that had otherwise seen minimal disruption. However, in the last few years electronic cigarettes have led to notable diffusion in markets worldwide. Traditional tobacco companies are now facing a change in typical consumer behavior.

In recent years, longtime industry titan Phillip Morris touted its new generation of 'smoke-free' products driven by science-based innovation. The company launched its IQOS or 'heat-not-burn' product — informally known as "I Quit Ordinary Smoking" — on a shy rollout in 2014 in just a handful countries. By 2019, it was available in more than fifty countries. This product is postured as offering a "tobacco meets technology"-edge with a completely different value proposition, all in a new and improved yet familiar experience and design. Although Phillip Morris is not claiming that its product comes without risk, it still essentially positions IQOS as a lesser of the two evils and has led to disruptions in the traditional market. In this case, Phillip Morris is both the disruptor and the disrupted.

GAMING CONSOLE
IN THE DIGITAL ERA

In 2019, Google launched Stadia, its "future-facing" cloud gaming platform, which calls to mind the Netflix streaming model. Branded as a democratizing force in the gaming industry, the subscription-based platform grants access to high-resolution interactive games without the need for any special HW — only a smart device that is supported by Google Chrome, be it a mobile phone, tablet, computer or television. This new architecture innovation based on robust Google-developed cloud technologies is already disrupting the gaming industry, in particular, it's eliminating the customer's need to buy a console like PlayStation or Xbox. The success of such an initiative is completely dependent on the quality of streaming in addition to the associated UX. With ground-breaking increases in bandwidth speed, as well as in the available alternatives for bandwidth and the maturity of the technology over time, this initiative represents the future of the gaming industry. Within the coming decade, we will notice a significant change in this global industry that generates tens of billions of dollars annually.

More toward open standards rather than closed ones

Change of business model more toward the digital ones

STANDARDS

BUSINESS MODEL

ELEMENTS OF DIGITAL DISRUPTION

USER EXPERIENCE

ECOSYSTEM

Open technologies which are designed to integrate and avail its capabilities to large pool of partners to enrich the user experience through offering different use cases

Focus on user experience, and multipurpose features

MANUFACTURING

PROFITABILITY STRUCTURE

Pushing the manufacturing to a lower part of the value chain

More toward perceive value rather than cost plus. Including new revenue streams supported by different payment mechanisms

DYNAMICS

LEAN AND AGILE

FAST TIME TO MARKET

CUSTOMER CENTRIC

NEW ARCHITEC-TURAL INNOVATION

THE INNOVATIVE DINOSAUR
WHAT IF DINOSAURS WERE INNOVATIVE

Designed by: Motaz Agamawi
www.theinnovativedinosaur.com

THE INNOVATIVE DINOSAUR

DIGITAL DISRUPTION PATTERN

When digital disruption targets a specific industry, we begin to observe patterns. It is fair to say that the diffusion of the digital industry, especially the SW industry, was set into motion in the early eighties with the introduction of the PC industry, followed by today's giants Apple, Microsoft, and Intel. Until the mid-nineties, the speed of speed was normal, as computer literacy rates climbed and households and workplaces alike embraced PC culture. But, since the early years of the twenty-first century, the diffusion of the internet, followed by social media, smartphones, and many other technologies helped to increase the speed of disruption. Industries of all types and sizes have had to grapple with major changes and disruptions over these decades of information and communication revolution. After navigating an interconnected range of aspects in the first three chapters, we can summarize the digital disruption patterns as follows:

- Digital disruption is always accompanied by a standardization of the product architecture and underlying technologies. Standard architecture leads to standard HW through driver interfaces, more standard communication protocols, and thus standard software development tools and languages.
- These examples are clearly expressed in the shift between traditional mobile phones and the smartphone. Apple IOS and Google Android standardized the full stake, decoupled HW and SW, offered open standard interfaces and thus the rise of standard development frameworks and toolchains as the commonly followed in the SW development industry.
- The home automation industry, which was disrupted by the IoT, reflects the same game of standardization and open systems.
The same is happening in the automotive industry with the elimination of black-box standards by decoupling HW and SW as well as standardizing interfaces, operating systems, and communication protocols.
- While such standardization eliminates traditional barriers for new players, the competitive edge of traditional players is dulled.
- Digital disruption provides a novel UX.

ε Standardization opens the horizon to increase the SW portion of the product — and the boundary-pushing SW experts truly know how to build user-centric products, offering users features and capabilities that were previously unavailable.

ε Industries prior to digital disruption are usually driven by industrial players who determine when to offer specific new features to target user groups. Their decisions are often related to financial return calculations. Such industries are not used to discover or validate user needs, wants, and demands; rather, they decide when users will have access to new features.

ε Digital disruption is shaking this model into a more agile, iterative, and faster user-centric approach, pushing customer expectations to unprecedented heights and thus challenging traditional players.

ε The standardization gives room and space for the building of an ecosystem of partners around a product or industry. This ecosystem is usually part of the offered UX, and it utilizes existing technologies or platforms but through a new use case, which leads to additional user satisfaction and at the same time a new revenue model.

ε Today, we can see the smartphone stores of Apple, Google, and others. By offering a standard interface and development experience, these companies were able to build a huge ecosystem of SW development partners and application developers, as well as a vast network of content partners for everything from videos, books, news to music.

ε Customers are enjoying the different use cases and models for their already-purchased asset — that is, smartphones are replacing the old guard: music players, alarm clocks, electronic book readers, productivity tools (e.g., email and word processing) — to name just a few disruptions.

ε Even the supported ecosystem is expanding. Mobile producers are starting to incorporate the external environment — meaning, your smartphone can now integrate with your car through the likes of Android Auto and Apple CarPlay, and your smart TV through Samsung DeX and even the Google Chromecast gadget.

∈ The scope ecosystem integration is only widening. Based on the digital standards that we are living today, we now have automation platforms, like Zapier, IFTTT and Microsoft Automate, which grants users the ability to integrate different SW platforms, digital solutions, and gadgets. Moreover, users can successfully pursue such integration even if the producers are not offering it. The scope of multi-purpose products and platforms are on the rise, empowering more and more users along the way.

∈ Digital disruption usually triggers new business and revenue models. Digital players bring to this new frontier their tools and dynamics, which are oftentimes completely different to the traditional ones.

∈ Digital players follow perceived-value pricing strategies regardless of cost, while traditional organizations usually follow the cost-plus strategy. Revenue models often extend beyond asset sales and, in most cases, contain a continuous revenue stream based on subscription services, upsell gadgets, or SW updates.

∈ The iPad is a prime example: first you purchase an asset with a specific price and then you can subscribe to some cloud services to extend your device's capabilities. Perhaps you'll purchase a potentially more convenient gadget or visit the Apple Store or iTunes to purchase content. Your device's OS is updated free of charge during a specific period (i.e., number of years) — but after that, the updates are no longer available and thus you lose the ability to install new apps. Finally, you arrive at a crossroad that is an unavoidable facet of today's UX: either purchase a new device or continue with your now stunted one.

It is important to assess the true intentions of digital players as they enter this new frontier. In most cases, they see a different opportunity at hand than the existing traditional players do — for instance, either to sell more content or advertisements to be consumed through a new medium, or to offer an unprecedented service. Some even see the opportunity to gain more data and insights that will strengthen their position in another industry.

- In general, digital players have a different perspective when it comes to manufacturing and industrial activities. Digital disruption pushes manufacturing a rung down in the value chain. The digital players have no intention to take a position in the manufacturing sector, or to compete with traditional manufacturers. They see manufacturing as a means — not to mention, a less profitable sector — so they're typically zoomed in on the architecture, SW aspects, and business model.

- Apple does not manufacture any of its devices; rather, all manufacturing operations are instead outsourced. The iPhone and iPad are made by Apple's major manufacturing partner Foxconn, which has tens of factories and hundreds of thousands of factory operators to thank for the product in material form, but in the end has a profitability of less than nine percent annually.

- Apple is concentrating on developing the iPhone IOS and its related SW features and capabilities, the Apple cloud services, increasing vertically, horizontally the Apple Store, and the iTunes.

- Apple decided that its main competency and differentiation factor is the UX of its distinctive brand identity, achieved through novel design and advanced SW capabilities.

- Profitability structure is another key element of this game. By design, digital players achieve high profitability and exponential stock growth and valuations. They are focused on perceived-value pricing and taking risks in new frontiers on radical innovations, but they do not invest in building factories and large industrial operations.

THE INNOVATIVE DINOSAUR

EVERYDAY CUSTOMERS ARE CHANGING

Consumer behavior trends are evolving, from expectations, needs to demands. The diffusion of digital services vis-à-vis the changes in consumer behavior are directly and indirectly impacting not only customer expectations and needs, but also their willingness to pay, buying cycles, and priorities.

Today's consumers are searching for the same experience that they have on their smartphones and social media networks everywhere, on and off the screen and the web. Some of the most interesting trends are summarized as follows:

- ϵ With the spread of the smartphones came the trend of always being connected. Customers tend to be always informed. They are willing to pay more for products and services for the sake of saving time and energy. To that end, businesses today are expected to consider this need for speed and ease, and to adapt accordingly. As much as such this trend exerts added pressure at the operational level, it may also provide a new revenue stream.

- ϵ On account of these social media-driven behavioral changes, younger generations are more aware and keener to control their online image, even if it means putting the public persona ahead of the real or everyday person, embroidering fantasies on to reality.

- ϵ This demand for more personalized service features ascends alongside offerings that meet individual needs and differentiation expectations. The impact of this will differ from business to business. In a purely digital business, personalized experiences and offering differentiation may be more easily achieved than with physical products. For physical products, linking digital-user preference personalizer or configurator with the physically delivered product is expected.

- ϵ The modern consumer is becoming more and more drawn to purpose, be it of the environmental, social, or technological variety. Connecting the product and business proposition to purpose — the beating heart — is a move that significantly impacts the consumer's decision-making process. A brand's code of ethics and level of transparency is a causal factor now closely associated with consumer perceptions and thus their decisions made, or products purchased.

- ϵ The sharing economy model is profoundly altering the concept of consumerism that we have long built our businesses around. Consumers are more aware than ever before of their usage and surplus, plus they endeavor to collaborate with other consumers, complete strangers or otherwise. This new everyday consumer is the future — and that calls for a bold and informed approach to commercial, business, and operational models. This new consumerism also opens the doors to a market focused on correlated services around a given product.

- ∈ Consumers are more concerned about product disposal lifecycle management these days, in particular, how the product will be disposed of and the associated harm on the environment Communication such lifecycle management within the product offering is yet another challenge to be addressed by enterprises.

- ∈ Consumers are seeking out beautiful products that perpetuate their daily digital routines in a familiar yet improved fashion. Thoughtfully designed user-centric approaches are no longer a luxury but rather increasingly the norm.

- ∈ Payment models and efficient delivery methods that are customized to consumer availability and personalized needs have risen in the game — and now the game to them. Your business will be compared to the efficiency and quality of service offered by digital e-commerce platforms like Amazon and eBay.

- ∈ One of critical sources for potential buyers is the availability of product information online, whether it's a book, laptop, car, flight, or even medicine. Consumers are directly using online digital search engines to identify, benchmark, check ratings, and compare competing products, services, or producers. Their — our — online presence and monitoring for the online consumer-generated data are becoming a modern-day survival mechanism.

- ∈ Product privacy, cybersecurity, data protection, and secured payment are major concerns for our target users.

A vivid example of our future customers' expectations involves my nine-year-old fraternal twins. When I got them a laptop, I received some intriguing reactions — ranging from excitement to criticism — even though they were already accustomed to the smartphone and tablet. First, my son tapped the display with his fingertip to no avail, assuming it was a touchscreen. His realization frustrated him once again as he fruitlessly searched for an application store of some kind. "What is the point of owning a device without a store like Apple's or Google's," he asked me, wide-eyed and perplexed. My daughter discovered an additional perspective when she heard Cortana giving us voice assistance. "Does this Cortana have access to the laptop's microphone and camera?" she asked me, wide-eyed and perturbed. When I confirmed its access, I received an unexpected request from my daughter to uninstall the program because she wants to protect her own privacy. The key takeaway is that our next generation of young consumers only knows the digital age, and so the devices and platforms of the future will be met with a frame of reference — i.e., a list of expectations, needs, wants, and demands — that is unexampled and thus still coming into focus.

INDUSTRY IS CHANGING

Organizations can overcome technological disruption, but most will likely struggle when the disruption targets overall market dynamics, business, and revenue models, and common or traditional ways of doing business. As the struggles mount, these organizations face a chasm between tradition and disruption. The ability of organizations to grasp the magnitude of change while seizing the willingness to apply the needed transformations — in a phrase, informed versatility — may become the determining factor as to whether they will transcend the chasm or not. **Second part of the equation, the operation dynamics of the digital disruption, needs to explored in the midst of the above-described landscape:**

- The concept of being 'lean and agile' encourages teams within a given organization to either quickly or steadily develop by managing flow, reducing the amount of work in progress, and simplifying the internal processes needed to achieve a specific and/or integral task. Agility represents a push for greater autonomy and alignment, in addition to rapid development through multi-functional teams. This paradigm of management creates a distinctive organizational culture that must be supported by all the needed means, including business structures, internal processes, and the support functions' operational mode.
- The 'fast time to market' is associated with the ability of an organization to assume the fail fast–win fast approach. To achieve this, the organization must accept failure within a safe environment, namely, one that is transparent and open to criticism. It is a culture that must be implemented in all related organization processes, from team performance reviews to various monitoring and decision-making mechanisms. If we are working in a new product development domain, failure and mistakes are the first steps toward learning and success. As the Irish playwright Samuel Becket once said: "Ever tried. Ever failed. No matter. Try Again Fail again. Fail better."
- The 'customer-centric' business is built around the ability to understand and validate customers, from their expectations to their experiences. Enter, the central role of design thinking: if we need to develop functional products that are beautiful and cover the target customers' journey, then we must also put into place the necessary creative environment, tools, and budgets for our teams to do so.
- Another indispensable element of the digital disruption journey is 'new architectural innovation.' Simplification of design and standardization, for instance, are part and parcel of digital technological disruption.

**THE
INNOVATIVE
DINGSAUR**

INDUSTRY CHASM

| Walls are Falling Between Industries | Lean Processes, Agility and Fast time to markets | Technology Disruption in all frontiers | User Centric Design and User Experience |

TRADITIONAL I N D U S T R Y DIGITAL

The industry dynamics are changing. From Technological, Industrial, business model and mode of operations.

We are in the middle of an industry inflection point.

Walls are failing and falling between industries as disruption emerges from every corner and industry dynamics evolve beyond recognition. The leaders of yesterday are not the same as today's, and the leaders of tomorrow are not yet known. Large organizations are operating in the widening shadows of unparalleled challenges and dilemmas between maintaining the successful working model of yesterday and adapting to the changes of today and tomorrow.

Designed by: Motaz Agamawi
www.theinnovativedinosaur.com

THE INNOVATIVE DINOSAUR

STARTUP TSUNAMI

2016 more than **$16 Billion of investments** in transportation deals globally. **75% greater** than 2015 investments.

Faraday Future 13M Aug. 2017	**Oryx** 50M Aug. 2017	**Volocopter** 29M Aug. 2017	**drive.ai** 50M April. 2017	**Peloton** 60M April. 2017	**ARGO AI** 1 Billion
Preferred Networks 95M Aug. 2017	**Momenta** 46M, July 2018	**Nauto** 159M, July 2018	**Otonomo** 25M, April 2018	**Autotalks** 40M, June 2018	**Charge Point** 43M, June 2018

When a digital disruption reaches the new technological frontier, it unsurprisingly joins forces with a related wave of startups. Standardization, along with new dynamics and technology architecture, leads to a lower entry barrier and thus a vista of an opportunity-packed future that attracts startups. Investors and venture capitalists play the role of catalysts, pushing the technological hype curve toward the said future-facing vista. This trend intensifies the game for well-established traditional players as the competition pool begins to swell.

THE INNOVATIVE DINOSAUR

TRANSFORMATION DILEMMA

It is always the challenge of applying the corporate transformation and the steadiness of the current operations.

Large-scale enterprises, especially the ones working in the brainware industry, often include undiscovered precious elements, which is the power of team members. The real asset of all tech-based enterprises in all industries is human being: the ones who design, develop, produce, distribute, maintain, promote, and pitch products or services to prospective customers. With each project, the participating team members (re)discover and learn about a range of (im)possibilities, including how each defective part — a glitch or a bug — is still an investment in your people, how each customer visit is an experience, and how each milestone achieved signals accumulated knowledge. The challenge of applying the corporate transformation and the steadiness of the current operation is ubiquitous.

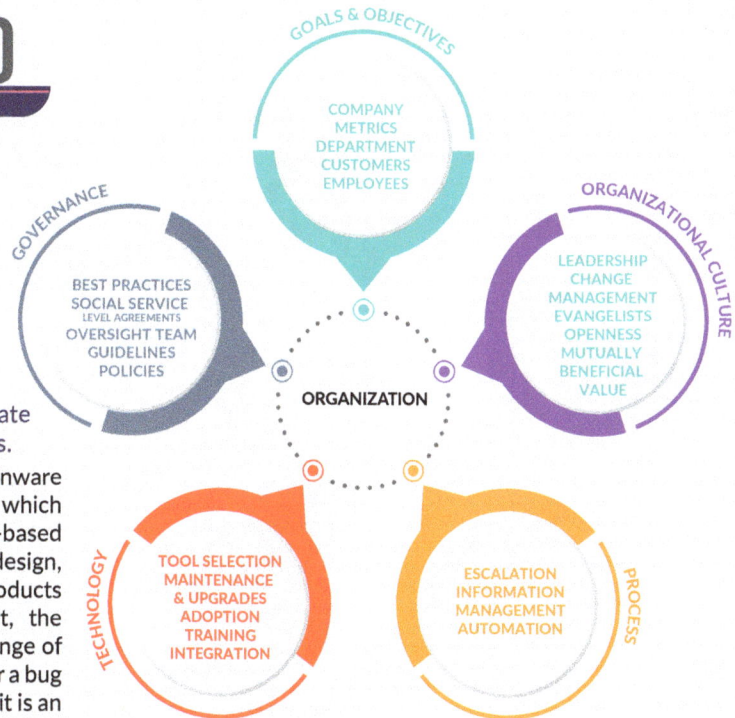

GOALS & OBJECTIVES
COMPANY
METRICS
DEPARTMENT
CUSTOMERS
EMPLOYEES

GOVERNANCE
BEST PRACTICES
SOCIAL SERVICE
LEVEL AGREEMENTS
OVERSIGHT TEAM
GUIDELINES
POLICIES

ORGANIZATIONAL CULTURE
LEADERSHIP
CHANGE
MANAGEMENT
EVANGELISTS
OPENNESS
MUTUALLY
BENEFICIAL
VALUE

ORGANIZATION

TECHNOLOGY
TOOL SELECTION
MAINTENANCE
& UPGRADES
ADOPTION
TRAINING
INTEGRATION

PROCESS
ESCALATION
INFORMATION
MANAGEMENT
AUTOMATION

Designed by: Motaz Agamawi
www.theinnovativedinosaur.com

THE INNOVATIVE DINOSAUR
WHAT IF DINOSAURS WERE INNOVATIVE!

THE INNOVATIVE DINOSAUR

CHAPTER 3:
ONCE IN A CENTURY DISRUPTION — THE AUTOMOTIVE INDUSTRY AS A DIGITAL DISRUPTION CASE STUDY

After more than a century of stability and structure, the automotive industry of today first veered toward mobility and then e-mobility. Industry dynamics are transforming, supply and value chain leaders are disrupted, and business and revenue models are undergoing an unexampled build-up phase.

New digital players are not aiming to wipe out the traditional players, since they depend upon the existing manufacturing capabilities and capacities. Digital disruptors are going to knock the value chain down a level, though, upholding the perceived value profitability through new business models and revenue streams while pushing the heavy lifting onto the shoulders of existing traditional players alone. The challenge for these weight-bearing players is not simply existential — rather, it is more about profitability and preserving their preferred place in the value chain. In response, the traditional automotive players will either surrender or fight back in this game of perception, position, and value creation. The coming days, weeks, months, or a couple of years at most, will reveal the winner of this changed and changing game.

In this chapter, we will navigate the digital disruption journey within the automotive industry. Our journey starts in the year 2012, with the introduction of Google and Tesla in the automotive industry scene. The major events that lead to disruption will be explored, along with analysis of the key shifts in the technological landscape and discussions on the "knowledge gap" concept, the "perception journey" of industry leadership, and the forecasted value chain three horizons. The automotive industry as a digital disruption case study is based on the author's perception, experiences, and anticipation of the sequence of related events. This study provides an example that incorporates many of the concepts discussed in the earlier chapters and serves as a practical and accessible analogy.

THE
INNOVATIVE
DINOSAUR

CHAPTER THREE LIST OF TOOLS, DIAGRAMS, AND ILLUSTRATIONS

1. Case Study Illustration: Automotive Digital Knowledge Gap Over Time
2. Case Study Illustration: Automotive Main Disruptive Factors
3. Case Study Illustration: Domain Controller Disruption Example
4. Case Study Illustration: Telematics & Gateways Disruption Example
5. Case Study Illustration: Automotive SW Value Chain Restructuring Example
6. Case Study Illustration: Automotive Strategic Pressure
7. Case Study Illustration: Automotive Supplier Forecasted 3 Horizons
8. TID Illustration: Leadership Mental Perception Journey toward Industry Disruption

CHAPTER THREE SECTIONS:

- The Automotive Industry
- The Collision of Traditional and New Entrants
- Industry Disruption Taking Momentum
- Disruption Forecasted Value Chain Impact
- Industry Leaders Disruption Perception Journey

THE INNOVATIVE DINOSAUR

CHAPTER THREE LIST OF REFERENCES & EXTRA READINGS

1. 5 Trends Transforming the Automotive Industry, PwC
2. Automotive Software and Electronics 2030 final, McKinsey
3. Majesco 2017 Future Trends – The Shift Gain Momentum
4. WSI, Automotive Companies Financial Analysis
5. Arm acquisition by NVIDIA
6. Mobility Innovation Map Reveals Emerging Technologies & Startups
7. Automotive Innovation Map Reveals Emerging Technologies & Startups
8. Hella Strengthening SW Competency Announcement
9. MDPI, Automotive Technology Curve
10. VW Car.Software
11. Bosch SW/Electronics restructure
12. Daimler Lab 1886
13. Bosch Startup
14. Productivity drivers in Automotive SW development, McKinsey
15. Disruptive trends that will transform the auto industry
16. Trends in European clusters: results from the 2019 European panorama, trends and priority sectors reports published
17. Consumer and industrials the future of the automotive value chain 2025, Deloitte

THE INNOVATIVE DINOSAUR

THE AUTO INDUSTRY IS FACING A MAGNITUDE OF CHANGE THAT HAS NOT BEEN SEEN IN A CENTURY

Automotive SW and E/E market with CAGR of 7% p.a. until 2030, largely driven by the power electronics, SW, and ECUs/DCUs

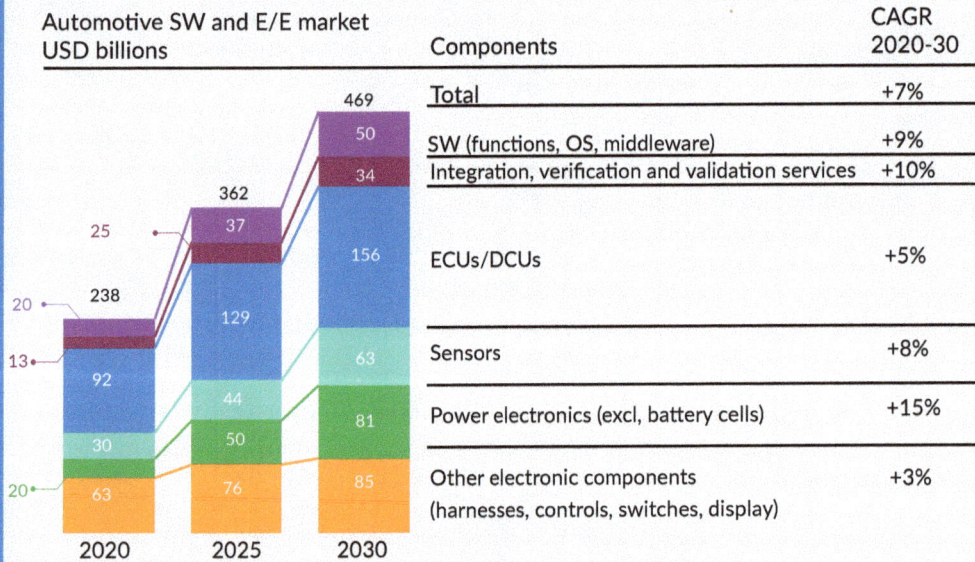

**Automotive SW and E/E market
USD billions**

2020	2025	2030
238	362	469
25	37	50
20		34
13		156
92	129	
30	44	63
20	50	81
63	76	85

Components	CAGR 2020-30
Total	+7%
SW (functions, OS, middleware)	+9%
Integration, verification and validation services	+10%
ECUs/DCUs	+5%
Sensors	+8%
Power electronics (excl, battery cells)	+15%
Other electronic components (harnesses, controls, switches, display)	+3%

Automotive Industry SW Magnitude of change

Total electronics and SW by geography in 2030	
EU	112
Chine	161
US Canada Mexico	68
Korea Japan	50
RoW	78
Total	469

Automotive sales USD billions		
2020	2025	2030
2,755	3,027	3,800
CAGR 2020-30		+3%

https://www.mckinsey.com/~/media/mckinsey/industries/automotive%20and%20assembly/our%20insights/mapping%20the%20automotive%20software%20and%20electronics%20landscape%20through%202030/automotive-software-and-electronics-2030-final.pdf

SOURCE: Mckinsey analysis: Revenue forecasts based on vehicle volumes from IHS Market, Light Vehicle Production Forecast, October 2018; pull completed on November 6, 2018

THE INNOVATIVE DINOSAUR

THE AUTOMOTIVE INDUSTRY

SOFTWARE AND ELECTRONICS WILL OUTGROW THE AUTOMOTIVE MARKET

In the next decade, the automotive industry will face a magnitude of change that has not been seen in a century. This change will be driven primarily by four mutually reinforcing trends, i.e., autonomous, connected, electric, and shared (ACES) vehicles. These will result in different user behavior and mobility preferences, shifting value pools, innovative business models, and new entrants into automotive. All of these trends are enabled by the advancement of technology in electronics and SW and thus have a substantial impact on the automotive electronics and SW market.

The automotive industry was set into motion in the late-eighteenth century. Since the introduction of the assembly line model in the beginning of the subsequent century by American industrialist Henry Ford, in combination with the proliferation of vehicle-dominant architectural design, the industry has traversed incremental innovations.

It was long considered to be mature, steady, and commodity-centric by design — that is the pedestalled technological advancements and pushes, while paying little mind to UX and user-centric design. The industry structure was typified by well-defined relationships between the different players in the value chain, with the leaders being highly respected far and wide across the game. The original equipment manufacturers (OEM) were both king and gatekeeper between motorists and the rest of the value chain stakeholders, from tiers one through three and even aftermarket stakeholders. This hierarchy was preserved from the late eighteenth century, when the horse-and-carriage model was eclipsed by combustion engines, to the early years of new disruption in roughly 2012 or 2013. The introduction of the electric motor, a movement led by Elon Musk's Tesla, has given the combustion engine its first real competitor. And then came Google's push for autonomous driving — like a self-driving vehicle, wherein AI- Artificial Intelligence is the brain behind the wheel — to reach the mass market.

Automotive Knowledge (y-axis)

Tier 1 Knowledge

For the Favor of Tier 1

New Entrance Automotive Knowledge

Time or Diffusion (x-axis)

Digital Knowledge (y-axis)

New Entrance Digital Knowledge

For the Favor of Digital Suppliers

Tier 1 Digital Knowledge

Time or Diffusion (x-axis)

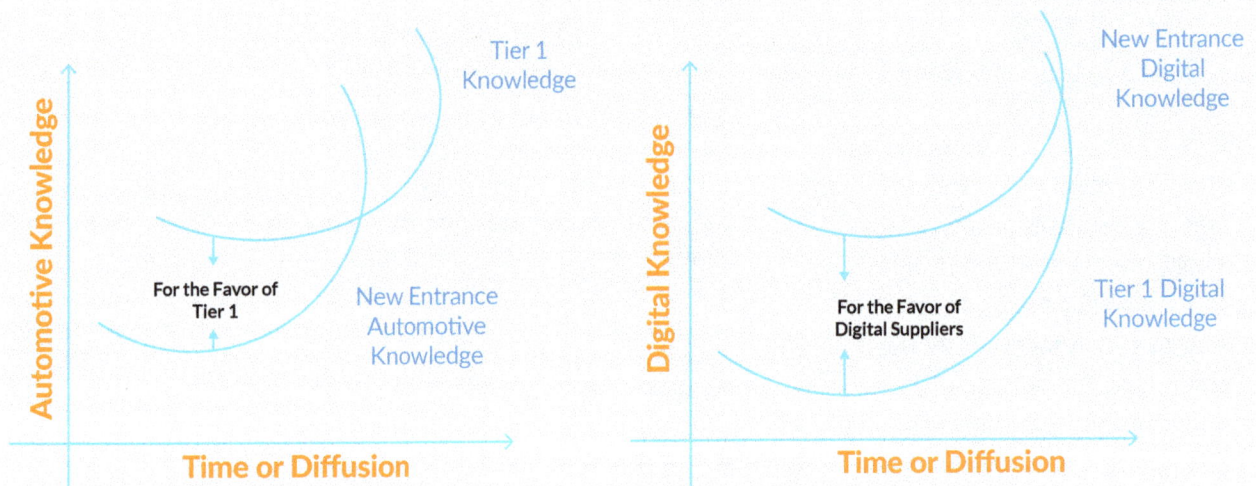

Tier 1 will defend based on the Automotive Knowledge gap and production capabilities

New Entrance will partner with Original Equiment Manufacturers - OEMs and suppliers to close the gap.

The time window available for **Tier 1** Suppliers to close the gap is very challenging.

New Entrance will benefit from the knowledge gap for his favor to **set the dominant design** and take the **market share quicker** than the expected time needed by Tier 1 to gain the needed knowledge.

THE INNOVATIVE DINOSAUR

INDUSTRY DISRUPTION TAKING MOMENTUM

The automotive industry is one of the world's largest industries in terms of yearly market turnover (i.e., many hundreds of billions of dollars), and it either directly or indirectly employs tens of millions of workers globally. Another important factor is the capital intensity needed to manufacture the tens of thousands of components per vehicle. The cycle of disruption was not fast-moving, in contrast to what we've observed in other industries, from mobile phones to music publishing. As the normal scenario, either the industry's OEMs or first tier suppliers were undermining the anticipated change. Back in 2013, the traditional industry leaders propagated the message that neither a search engine company nor an entrepreneur experienced in developing digital payment methods were qualified enough to create an effect as strong and complex as theirs. That was the industry's state of mind until a few game-changing events unfolded, including:

- In 2017, Tesla introduced the Model 3 and received more than three hundred thousand pre-orders — all together worth over fourteen billion dollars in future sales. This electric sedan's performance shocked the whole automotive industry.

- Tesla's introduction of an over-the-air (OTA) update, and its successful installation of the semi-autonomous feature, were successfully deployed overnight for all of its customers. The industry felt another shock as the traditional automotive players at that time were completely against the concept of OTA. Most of the leaders in the game were convinced that the vehicle is a mission-critical machine for which such a technique is neither safe nor robust as it does not follow established industry standards and norms. In sum, the vehicle architecture is not designed to support OTA functionality and will therefore be dismissed by the majority of the customer base.

- Google's LiDAR, or Light Detection and Ranging system, was perceived in the market at that time as an expensive and unrealistic technology owing to the cost of tens of thousands of dollars per vehicle. What the traditional automotive players did not realize was that Google was going through the standard technology maturation and commercialization lifecycle. Just refer to Waymo (formerly the Google self-driving car project) and its Honeycomb LiDAR to see how the price dropped from $75,000 to $7,500 in few years.

THE INNOVATIVE DINOSAUR

ENTERPRISE LEADERSHIP MENTAL PERCEPTION JOURNEY TOWARD INDUSTRY DISRUPTION

Denial Phase

The Industry leaders at this phase are at a mental state of not perceiving the change and are convinced that the industry is protected by its special nature.

Exploration phase

During the exploration phase, the traditional industry leaders start to realize that two worlds of completely different frames of reference are existing. The output is shocking & they started to realize, that a new era is coming.

Collaboration phase

During this phase traditional players start to interact, propose & collaborate. A series of internal processes and cultural adjustments start to be able to adapt to the new dynamics.

Confrontation phase

This phase result is completely dependent on the output of the other three phases.
The actions taken in this phase determine the future competitive positioning of the organization.

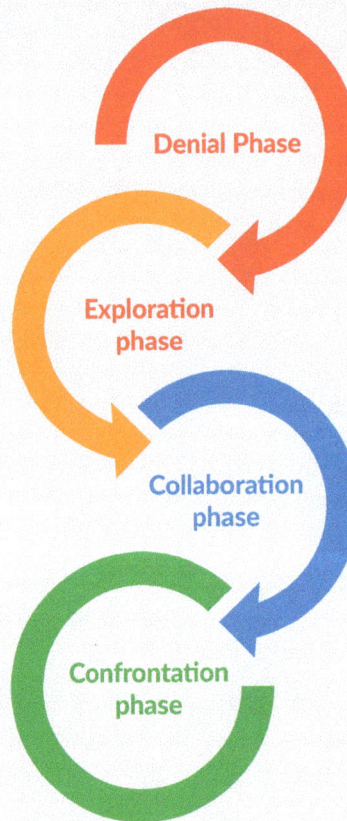

THE INNOVATIVE DINOSAUR

INDUSTRY LEADERS DISRUPTION PERCEPTION JOURNEY

Against that backdrop of disruption, the traditional automotive industry players have gone through various phases of realization. First came the denial phase in which industry leaders stood tall as change advanced, convinced that their sector's strong and complex nature and history were the ultimate form of protection against any and all disruptive forces. A phase of exploration followed, and so the traditional industry leaders turned a critical eye to Silicon Valley's leading disruptors to determine their competitors, be they future partners or eventual replacements. The traditional industry leaders, in turn, realized that there are two worlds with two distinct frames of reference at play:

- The emergence of the Silicon Valley leading disruptors in the game did not set the start of production (SOP) date — which are the magic words in the automotive industry. "When do you plan to have your SOP," the industry hypothetically asked. "When we feel that our products meet our expected UX and are ready for commercialization," the valley hypothetically responded. This answer perplexed the traditional automotive professional.

- The new entrants are not committed to specific quantities of components Rather, they request a feature that needs an R&D effort without calculating the target selling quantities. Automotive leaders are used to cost-plus pricing models, and they perceive the quantity commitment as a must for securing their investment. The emerging players, on the other hand, believe that a specific feature, which brings a specific benefit, must be strived for and achieved, thus R&D costs will be paid regardless of the potential risks and final outcome. They are used to prices based on the perceived-value pricing model.

- When the traditional automotive leaders started to explore the world of their counterparts, they found themselves sitting with founders and CEOs in the valley. Decisions are made at such meetings — without the need for an approval cycle or returning back to top management and the board of directors. This model was foreign to traditional automotive professionals who are accustomed to a structured chain of command and seniority with respect to approval cycles and decision-making.

- The discussion begins to cover the project lifecycle and forecasted delivery dates. It is normal in the automotive industry to have a R&D cycle of three to five years, from order intake to the start of production. A medium-scale R&D project is usually in the range of tens of thousands of hours of efforts with hundreds of engineers, all accompanied by many quality standards, processes, and checks that may reach forty to fifty percent of the overall R&D effort. The new entrants development model is strikingly different: it's agile and lean complete with a shortened sprint or release cycle.

THE INNOVATIVE DINCSAUR

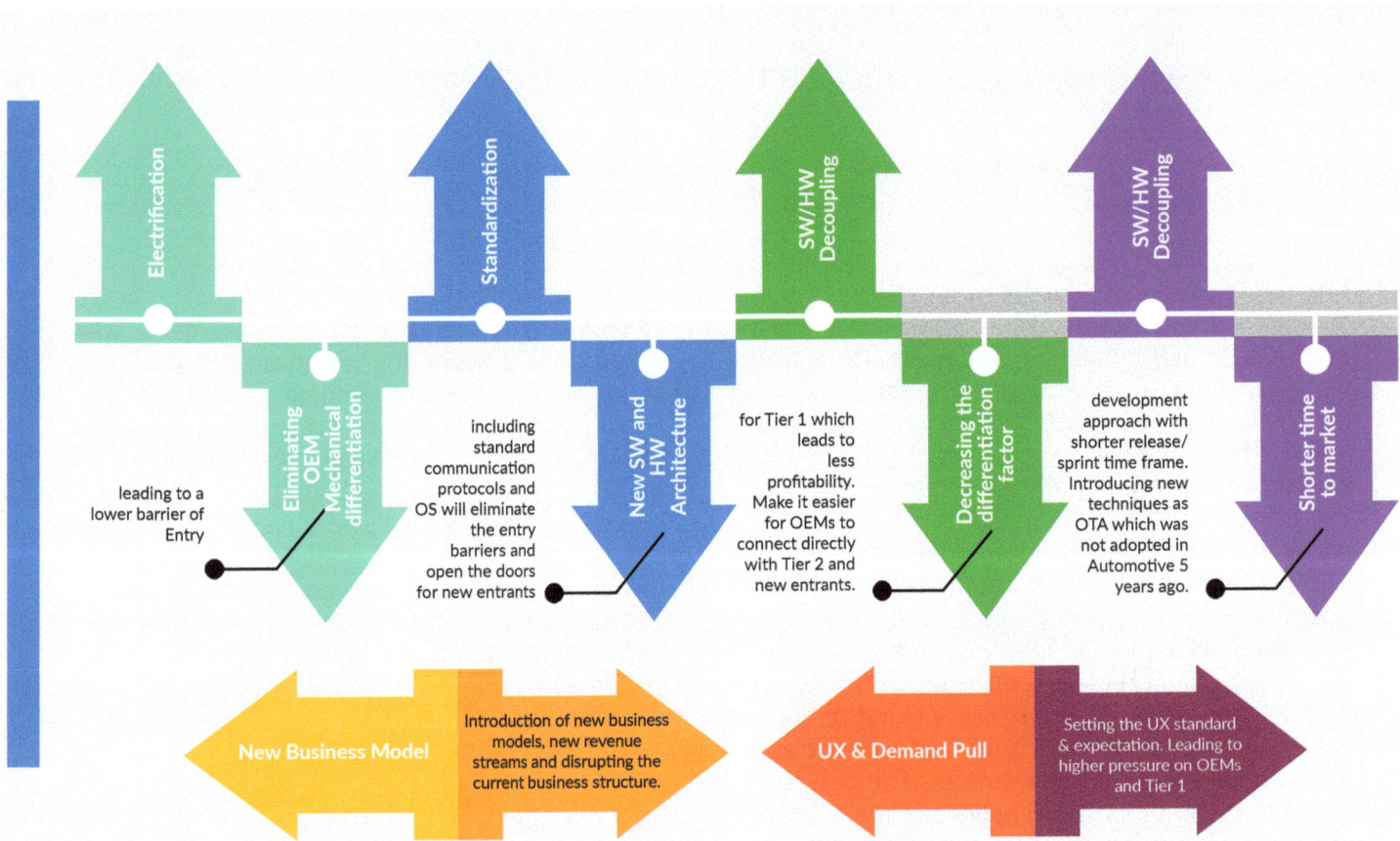

Electrification

Eliminating OEM Mechanical differentiation

leading to a lower barrier of Entry

Standardization

New SW and HW Architecture

including standard communication protocols and OS will eliminate the entry barriers and open the doors for new entrants

SW/HW Decoupling

Decreasing the differentiation factor

for Tier 1 which leads to less profitability. Make it easier for OEMs to connect directly with Tier 2 and new entrants.

SW/HW Decoupling

Shorter time to market

development approach with shorter release/ sprint time frame. Introducing new techniques as OTA which was not adopted in Automotive 5 years ago.

New Business Model

Introduction of new business models, new revenue streams and disrupting the current business structure.

UX & Demand Pull

Setting the UX standard & expectation. Leading to higher pressure on OEMs and Tier 1

Designed by: Motaz Agamawi
www.theinnovativedinosaur.com

THE INNOVATIVE DINOSAUR

THE COLLISION OF TRADITIONAL AND NEW ENTRANTS

When the traditional and new worlds collided in the midst of the exploration phase, the output was so shocking that the veteran automotive players admitted in turn that revolution was nigh and thus their futures uncertain. Another phase, one of conservative collaboration, emerged between these two pushed and pulled worlds, beginning with the traditional automotive players move to interact, propose, collaborate, and launch a series of internal processes and cultural adjustments in their organizations.

They knew that they could never adapt to the new dynamics of the near future without understanding the forces of change now circulating throughout their industry. Many trials have succeeded, while many others have failed. At this phase, we may posit a major shift in the thought processes and outlooks of the traditional players. Many of them have understood the change correctly, while many others are still struggling because they're going in the wrong direction, off target. At the time of writing, the industry seems to be locked in a phase of confrontation as it faces the new norm. The outcome of this phase will remain unclear and uncertain for the next few years. Some of the key elements of the automotive disruption include:

- Electrification is eliminating the mechanical barrier, which was fortifying the position of the OEMs and first tier suppliers. The architecture of the future car will be completely different, and the OEMs are currently searching for another differentiation factor than the engine and mechanical design.
- The vehicle electronic and SW architecture is undergoing a major change right now. Both SW and HW decoupling is moving faster than the established players had anticipated. Communication stake and special automotive communication protocols will vanish in the next couple of years, as automotive grade
- Ethernet is already regarded as the dominant communication protocol of today and future, even though it has not yet reached the diffusion phase.
- The architecture of distributed electronic control units (ECU) will be replaced by domain control units (DCU). We are moving toward data centers on wheels, and the Tesla computation architecture will be the closest to what the near future has in store for us.
  Software and electronic interfacing standardization are eliminating the barriers to entry, leaving space for new players to explore. More open and standard ecosystems will be in place, thus allowing ecosystem partners to participate and build different use cases, just like the mobile application stores of today.
- The advancement of AI, coupled with increased innovative and intuitive features for vehicles and the forward-facing direction of DCU and data-center-on-wheels architecture, demands more standard computational platforms. Accordingly, new entrants from the digital domain, like NVIDIA and others, are expected to gain considerable ground in the area of in-vehicle computation.

DOMAIN CONTROLLERS DISRUPTIVE

The standardization of the communication protocols, along with the anticipated demand increase for connectivity, are leading to a new demand for in-vehicle connectivity, which was traditionally served through telematics solutions. The forecasted entrance of traditional communication technology providers, including Cisco, Huawei, and Avaya, is expected to dominate in the game. Even future competition from both Google and Amazon may be on the horizon. The human-machine interface and intuitive technology are ascending, while traditional in-vehicle electronic switches face disruption. As digital display devices gain more ground, competition from Samsung and other players gains momentum.

The disruption coming from new and anticipated business models in vehicle revenue streams is tremendous. Car sharing, new mobility solutions, and in-vehicle data are disrupting the current state and nature of business. In-vehicle, advertisement, and content consumption are setting the scene for previously uncharted revenue streams that are expected to reach trillions of dollars over the next ten to fifteen years.

The Value Chain is in the process of restructuring

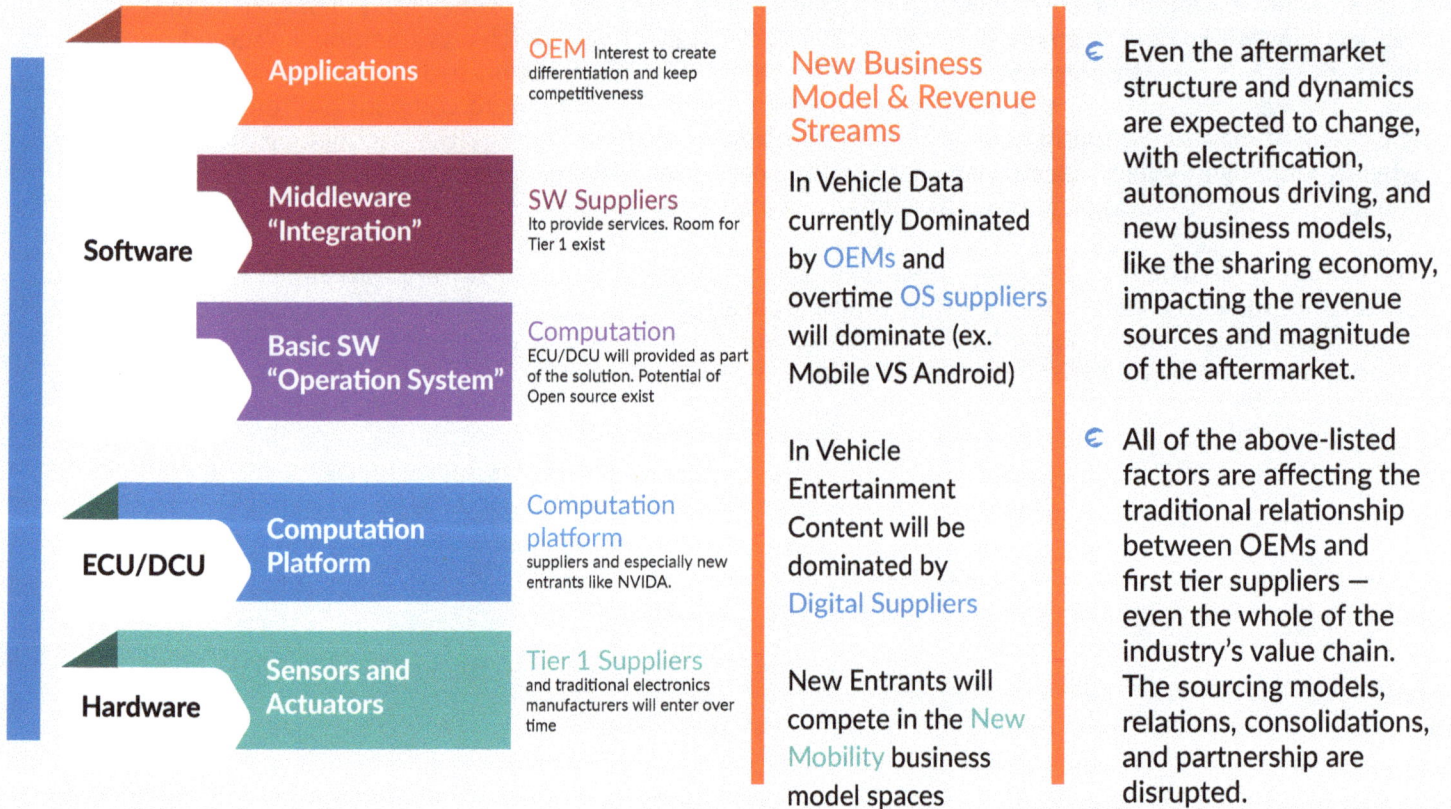

Software

Applications
OEM Interest to create differentiation and keep competitiveness

Middleware "Integration"
SW Suppliers Ito provide services. Room for Tier 1 exist

Basic SW "Operation System"
Computation ECU/DCU will provided as part of the solution. Potential of Open source exist

ECU/DCU

Computation Platform
Computation platform suppliers and especially new entrants like NVIDA.

Hardware

Sensors and Actuators
Tier 1 Suppliers and traditional electronics manufacturers will enter over time

New Business Model & Revenue Streams

In Vehicle Data currently Dominated by OEMs and overtime OS suppliers will dominate (ex. Mobile VS Android)

In Vehicle Entertainment Content will be dominated by Digital Suppliers

New Entrants will compete in the New Mobility business model spaces

€ Even the aftermarket structure and dynamics are expected to change, with electrification, autonomous driving, and new business models, like the sharing economy, impacting the revenue sources and magnitude of the aftermarket.

€ All of the above-listed factors are affecting the traditional relationship between OEMs and first tier suppliers — even the whole of the industry's value chain. The sourcing models, relations, consolidations, and partnership are disrupted.

THE INNOVATIVE DINOSAUR

DISRUPTION FORECASTED VALUE CHAIN IMPACT

After more than a century of stability and structure, the automotive industry of today first veered toward mobility and then e-mobility. The industry dynamics are transforming, supply and value chain leaders are disrupted, and business and revenue models are going through an unexampled build-up phase. New digital players are not aiming to wipe out the traditional players since they need the existing manufacturing capabilities and capacities. Digital disruptors are going to knock the value chain down a level, though, upholding the perceived value profitability through new business models and revenue streams while pushing the heavy lifting onto the shoulders of existing traditional players alone. The challenge for these weight-bearing players is not simply existential — rather, it is more about profitability and preserving their preferred place in the value chain. In response, the traditional automotive players will either surrender or fight back in this game of positioning, perception, and value creation. The coming days, weeks, months, or a couple of years at the most, will reveal the winner of this changed and changing game.

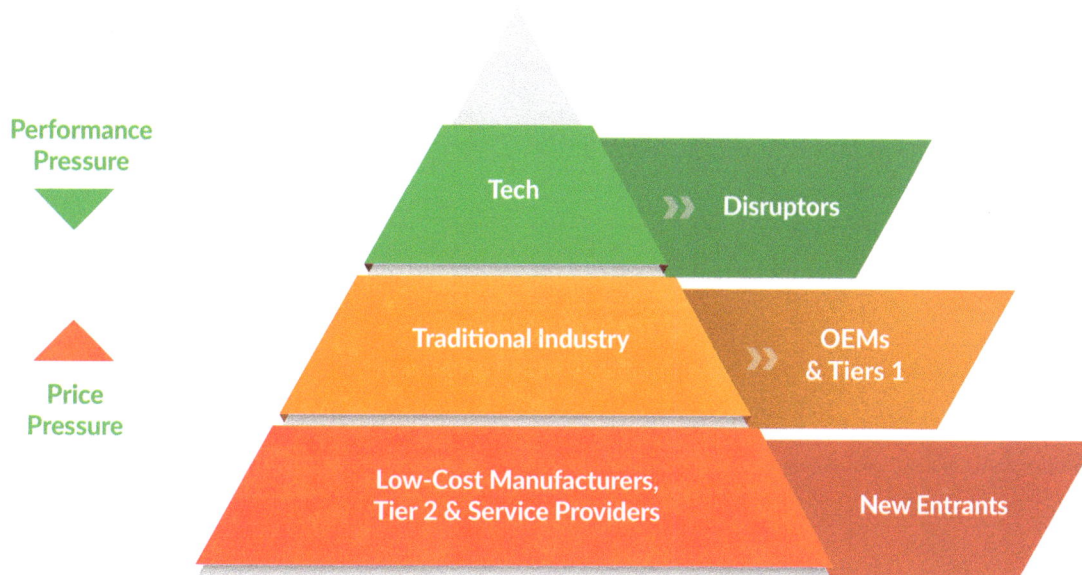

THE
INNOVATIVE
DINOSAUR

AUTOMOTIVE 10 YEARS VALUE CHAIN STRUCTURE FORECAST

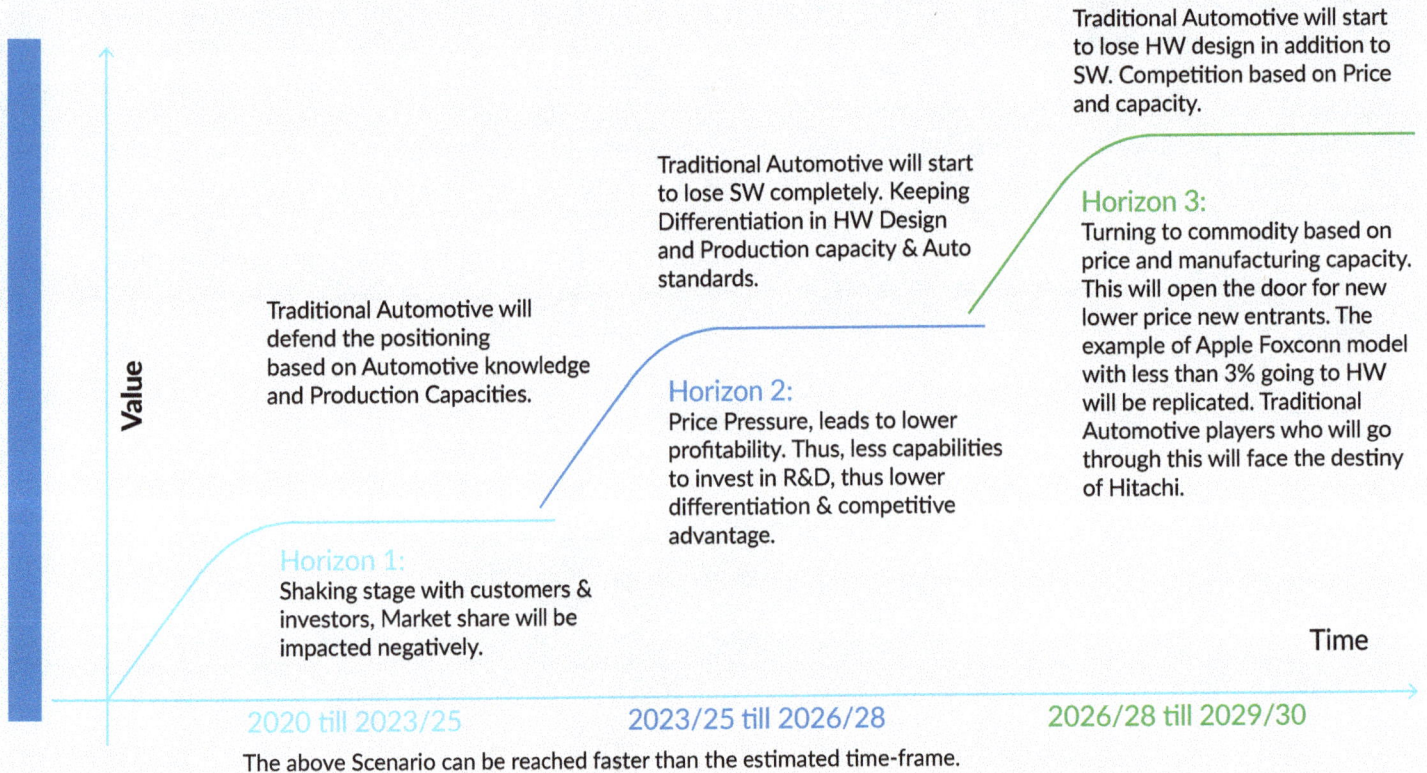

Traditional Automotive will start to lose HW design in addition to SW. Competition based on Price and capacity.

Traditional Automotive will start to lose SW completely. Keeping Differentiation in HW Design and Production capacity & Auto standards.

Horizon 3:
Turning to commodity based on price and manufacturing capacity. This will open the door for new lower price new entrants. The example of Apple Foxconn model with less than 3% going to HW will be replicated. Traditional Automotive players who will go through this will face the destiny of Hitachi.

Traditional Automotive will defend the positioning based on Automotive knowledge and Production Capacities.

Horizon 2:
Price Pressure, leads to lower profitability. Thus, less capabilities to invest in R&D, thus lower differentiation & competitive advantage.

Value

Horizon 1:
Shaking stage with customers & investors, Market share will be impacted negatively.

Time

2020 till 2023/25   2023/25 till 2026/28   2026/28 till 2029/30

The above Scenario can be reached faster than the estimated time-frame.

THE INNOVATIVE DINOSAUR

CHAPTER 4:
SOFTWARE AS
THE PRIMARY SOURCE
OF DISRUPTION

Today's products and solutions are composed of a combination of mechanical components, electronics, sensors, actuators, and software. Together, they are designed and assembled to deliver a specific use case, and to achieve a desired business model objective. We can find them in a range of systems and components with various levels of complexity. This complex architecture of diversified domains has been integrated into many everyday devices.

Although of the recent introduction of software components compared to other elements, its contribution in today® products and solutions is increasing dramatically. Software, communication, and internet connectivity are major building blocks in this era of digital disruption. Additionally, software platforms and technologies are the key contributors to the desired business and revenue models of today. In many cases, the advancement of a specific industry business model is contingent on the maturity and capabilities of the software element.

In this chapter, we will dive into the nature and elements of software, with an aim to compare and/or contrast it with the other heavyweight disciplines: the electronical and the mechanical, including hardware. Such contextualization and descriptive insights will guide us toward a deeper understanding of the core differences and needs that a traditional manufacturing enterprise must consider while being immersed — perhaps by force of circumstance — in the digitalization journey.

CHAPTER FOUR LIST OF TOOLS, DIAGRAMS, AND ILLUSTRATIONS

1. TID Illustration: Modern Systems Components
2. TID Illustration: Modern Systems Components Critical Path
3. TID Illustration: Modern Systems Components SW as a Driver
4. TID Illustration: Software Nature
5. TID Illustration: Summary of SW Nature
6. TID Illustration: Embedded SW Main Disruption Elements

CHAPTER FOUR SECTIONS:

- є Understanding the Nature of Software
- є Complexity of Embedded Software
- є Embedded SW Disruption Elements

**THE
INNOVATIVE
DINꞒSAUR**

CHAPTER FOUR LIST OF REFERENCES & EXTRA READINGS

1. Systems Engineering Body of Knowledge (SEBoK)
2. The Nature of Software: What's So Special About Software Engineering, IBM
3. Software Engineering for Automotive Systems: A Roadmap, Future of Software Engineering
4. A Survey on the State and Future of Automotive Software Release and Configuration Management
5. Software Engineering for Automotive Systems: A Roadmap
6. 4 Common Software Challenges in Automotive Manufacturing
7. New matrix to boost R&D efficiency, BCG
8. Productivity drivers in Automotive SW development, McKinsey
9. Kauppi, Dave. 2008. Sell A Software Company - The Valuation Dilemma. articles base
10. KOHERS, N. KOHERS and T. 2004. Information sensitivity of high-tech industries: evidence from merger announcements. Applied Financial Economics. 2004.
11. MERGERS & ACQUISITIONS AND TECHNOLOGICAL PERFORMANCE. VALENTINI, GIOVANNI. 2005. s.l.: Academy of Management, 2005.
12. Mergers & Acquisitions: A Strategy for High Technology Companies. Daunt, Jacqueline A. 2003. s.l.: Fenwick & West LLP, 2003.

COMPONENTS AND SUBCOMPONENTS OF TODAY'S SOLUTION & PRODUCTS

Electrical
System

Software
Platform

STEP
01

STEP
02

STEP
03

STEP
04

STEP
05

Mechanical
Platform

Sensors and
Actuators

Business
Model

Today's products and solutions are composed of a combination of mechanical, electronics, sensors, actuators, and SW. Together, they are designed and assembled to deliver a specific use case and achieve a desired business model objective. We can find them in a range of systems and components with various complexity levels. This complex architecture of diversified domains integrated can be found in many everyday devices, with the most complex in industrial machines, robots (both industrial and home use), as well as in aviation, military vehicles, weapons, and medical devices. We can turn to mobile phones, IoT devices, and game consoles for mid-range complexity, and to smart gadgets, like smart watches and electronic cigarettes, for the low-range.

Designed by: Motaz Agamawi
www.theinnovativedinosaur.com

THE INNOVATIVE DINOSAUR

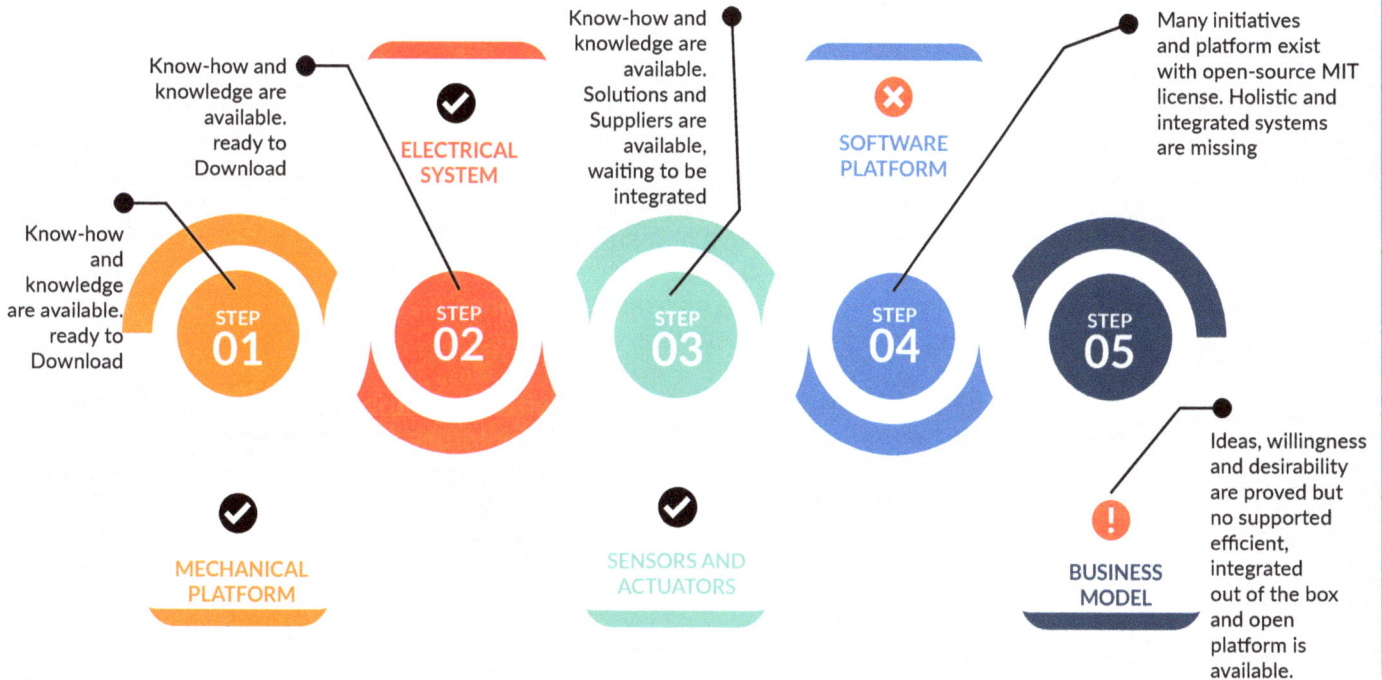

Know-how and knowledge are available. ready to Download

ELECTRICAL SYSTEM

Know-how and knowledge are available. Solutions and Suppliers are available, waiting to be integrated

SOFTWARE PLATFORM

Many initiatives and platform exist with open-source MIT license. Holistic and integrated systems are missing

Know-how and knowledge are available. ready to Download

STEP 01

STEP 02

STEP 03

STEP 04

STEP 05

MECHANICAL PLATFORM

SENSORS AND ACTUATORS

BUSINESS MODEL

Ideas, willingness and desirability are proved but no supported efficient, integrated out of the box and open platform is available.

Designed by: Motaz Agamawi
www.theinnovativedinosaur.com

THE INNOVATIVE DINOSAUR

Maturity varies from domain to domain. Mechanical systems and components are the most mature as the oldest discipline in the game; cutting-edge electronics systems architecture and standards then follow from a maturity perspective.

Thus, the sensors and actuators, although such a category is always linked to and dependent on advancements in basic research, be it the discovery or invention of new smart material, or the proof of new physical capabilities. Although the sensors and actuators R&D are always linked to the advancement of the basic scientific research and discovery of new materials, their general development and industrialization are considered far more mature compared to the SW discipline. Until 1980 and the rise of PC, the software industry was not as popular as of today. Advancements in computer science, and its related disciplines' maturity and complexity, are recent given that the discipline has been in existence for less than forty years.

Although of its recent introduction compared to other elements, software contribution into days products and solutions is increasing dramatically. Software, communication, and internet connectivity are major building blocks in this era of digital disruption. Additionally, SW platforms and technologies are the key contributors to the desired business and revenue models of today. In many cases, the advancement of a specific industry business model is contingent on the maturity and capabilities of the SW element.

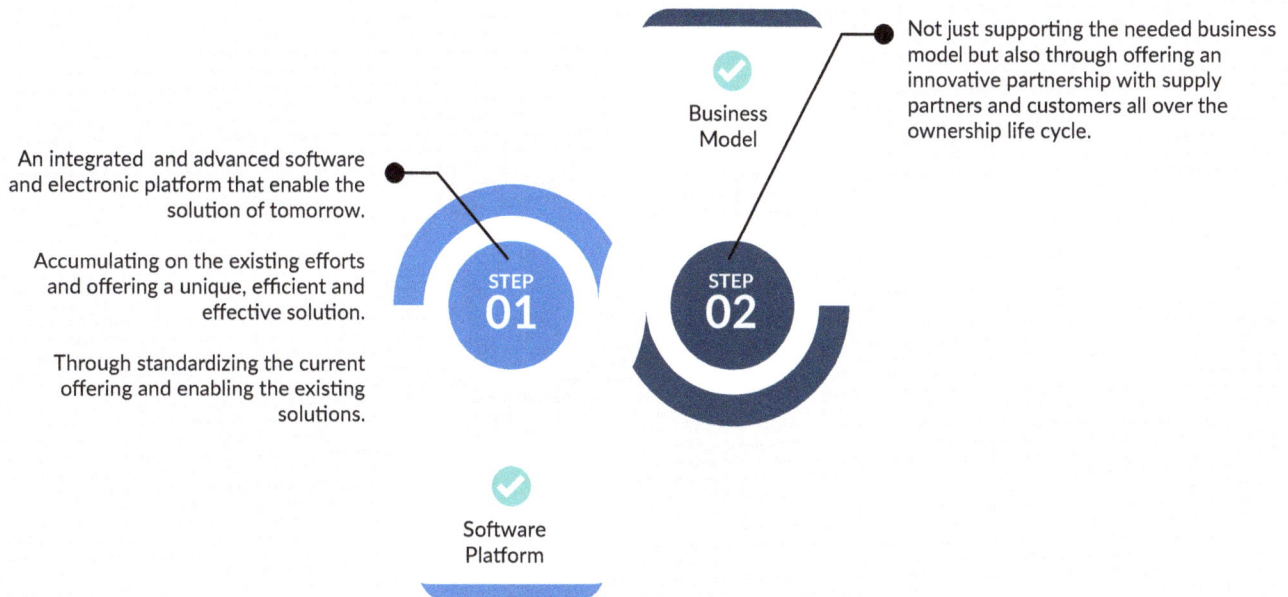

An integrated and advanced software and electronic platform that enable the solution of tomorrow.

Accumulating on the existing efforts and offering a unique, efficient and effective solution.

Through standardizing the current offering and enabling the existing solutions.

Business Model

Not just supporting the needed business model but also through offering an innovative partnership with supply partners and customers all over the ownership life cycle.

STEP 01

STEP 02

Software Platform

Designed by: Motaz Agamawi
www.theinnovativedinosaur.com

THE INNOVATIVE DINOSAUR

Business models that support advanced modularity based on open architecture often encourage pay-as-you-go and upgrade - as - you - go frameworks that are designed to turn devices into a revenue generation source. This transformation supports the shared resources economy, suits the desired customer trends lifestyles, and empowers target users through ease of collaboration, often leading to the lowest total cost of ownership. This is what of the industry, what it's looking to achieve. It's what customers are calling for and suppliers are struggling to provide. The critical path forward for many industries is the introduction of SW as a component that's fully integrated with their products, solutions, and platforms design.

Based on the above, the ability to understand the nature of SW in general and of embedded SW in particular is crucial for enterprise leaders, project managers, product designers, industrial teams, support frontliners, commercial teams, and even different enterprise support functions, including human resources, finance, administration. In the next section, we will delve into the nature and elements of SW, with an aim to compare and/or contrast it with the other heavyweight disciplines: the electronical and the mechanical. Such contextualization and descriptive insights will guide us toward a deeper understanding of the differences and needs that a traditional manufacturing organization must consider while being immersed — perhaps by force of circumstance — in the digitalization journey.

UNDERSTANDING
THE NATURE OF SOFTWARE

"Software entities are more complex for their size than perhaps any other human construct because no two parts are alike," the American computer scientist Fred Brooks famously wrote in 1987. "If they are, we make the two similar parts into a subroutine — open or closed. In this respect, software systems differ profoundly from computers, buildings, or automobiles, where repeated elements abound."

As established in Brooks' essay, "No Silver Bullet: Essence and Accidents of Software Engineering," the profoundly unique nature of SW is manifest in following four chief characteristics: complexity, conformity, changeability, and invisibility.

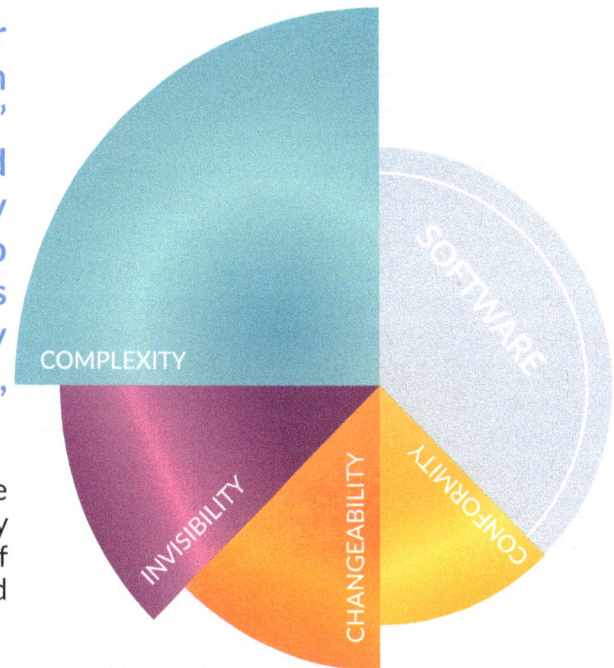

COMPLEXITY

SOFTWARE

INVISIBILITY

CHANGEABILITY

CONFORMITY

THE
INNOVATIVE
DINOSAUR
WHAT IF DINOSAURS WERE INNOVATIVE!

Designed by: Motaz Agamawi
www.theinnovativedinosaur.com

THE
INNOVATIVE
DINOSAUR

COMPLEXITY

Software systems are composed of many unique interacting parts that are encapsulated in different logical representations, including routines, functions, classes, and objects that are invoked when needed and not replicated. They have either a dynamic or static nature of invocations, interactions, couplings, and transition from a state to another. Having interfaces that are designed to interact with data sources and other external systems or service components. Software provides functionalities for components that are embedded, distributed, and/or data-centric. This complex nature leads to the need for complex methodological testing techniques, methods, and tools to help discover hidden defects that in most cases pop up during operations, before resulting in undesired additional work.

CONFORMITY

Physical products have inherited natural rules that it must adhere to. Software, on the other hand, must   comply with requirements that are represented in a set of developed components and interfaces to other internal parts and connecting to a defined set of external world elements related to its operation scope. During SW component execution, it is extremely difficult to detect logical, functional, and timing-related bugs. Physical products are not the same as tolerance between the interfaces of the system is the cornerstone of manufacturing and assembly. In SW, interfaces must have the exact match on the number, type, and couplings of parameters. The inability to identify conformity issues in the beginning of the project may lead to problems as the target SW feature will not meet the needs of the product under development. In the case that a lack of conformity is identified late in the project execution, an effort will need to be exerted to replace the inappropriate component with one that matches the requirement and design specified.

CHANGEABILITY

In the late stage of the project and maintenance, the SW is the most frequently updated and modified element. This does not mean that the SW code can be easily modified or changed. The nature of conformity can lead to changing a piece of SW code that's too complex to achieve. Changing a single part of a SW component can yield undesired results in the same component or other parts of the integrated system, thus further work and modifications may be needed before reaching optimum performance.

INVISIBILITY

Software is an intangible element with no physical properties, but its effect on the execution of a digital device can be observed. Software is represented in the use of a set of standard forms of illustration, including software requirements specification (SRS), design documents, entity-relationship diagrams, workflow diagrams, flow charts, and source code. These elements are used to describe, illustrate, model, and abstract the requirements and designs, but they are not the SW itself. They help us visualize the invisible.

Software has no physical properties

Software is the most frequently changed element of intensive systems.

Software alone is useless, as it's always a part of a larger system.

Risk management for software projects is predominantly process oriented.

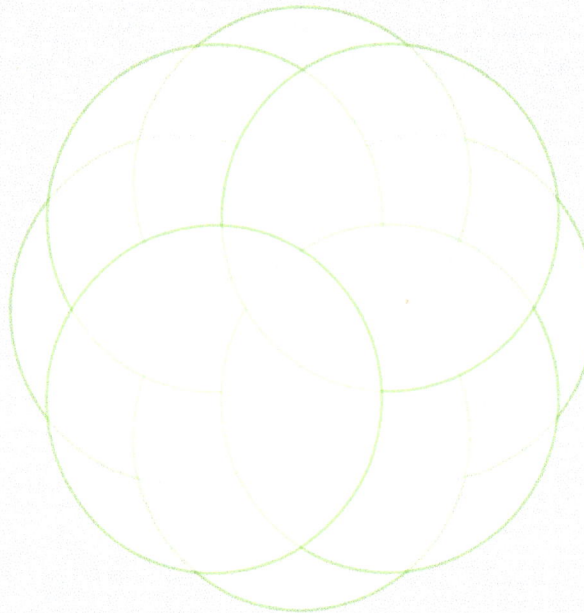

Software is the product of intellect - intensive teamwork.

Productivity of software developers varies widely than the productivity of other engineering disciplines.

Estimation and planning for software projects is characterized by a high degree of uncertainty, which can be at best partially mitigated by best practices.

Designed by: Motaz Agamawi
www.theinnovativedinosaur.com

THE INNOVATIVE DINOSAUR

COMPLEXITY OF
EMBEDDED SOFTWARE

Embedded SW is a SW code that is written to control a device or machine. It is usually developed to operate over a specific target HW platform composed of an ECU- Electronics Control Unite and operating system referred to as target. And it's commonly partnered with time, memory, and processing capabilities constraints.

Today, many traditional products include functionality that is managed by SW components. Countless precedents exist in our day-to-day life, from home appliances, personal gadgets, and industrial machinery to mobility machines (vehicles, buses, trains, boats, drones, airplanes, and military transportation). Medical devices, surgical robots, and electronic cigarettes can also be added to that list. Since SW and electronics are penetrating all industries, it's vital for us to dig deep into the special nature of embedded SW, which can be summarized as follows:

- Heterogeneity of SW
- Multidisciplinary domain of knowledge
- Distribution of SW
- Variants and configurations
- Unit-based cost model

Each of the above-listed elements will be illuminated by an automotive industry-related example, as it's facing a major disruption coming from the increased use of SW in the vehicles of today.

HETEROGENEITY OF SW

Embedded SW is diverse, ranging from entertainment and office-related ones to safety-critical real-time control ones. Historically, the methods and models of control theory were poles apart from those of the computer science domain. Tools such as MATLAB and Simulink are used to model differential equations supporting the control theory applied implementations. On the other hand, engineers in business information processing are increasingly keen to employ standard modeling methods and techniques to express data and behavior as the Unified Modeling Language (UML), plus other kinds of discrete data flow and state machine models. In embedded development, these separate engineering cultures have to be united to reflect all relevant aspects of the different engineering domains. The absence of widely accepted standards for modeling and development approaches explains part of the complexity that faces embedded SW development projects. Embedded full production systems and platforms have not yet been achieved due to the absence of commonly adopted standards and the diverse offering of tools from different vendors that are not yet ready to be integrated.

MULTIDISCIPLINARY DOMAIN OF KNOWLEDGE

Integrated embedded systems generally involve various skills from a wide range of disciplines. The different SW components and systems are constructed based on separate functions and routines that exchange data over a communication medium. In many cases, the topology of the included SW systems is as complex as the distributed computer networks, thus computer science and computer engineering skills are required. Such software systems and components are connected to various HW components, like sensors and actuators, that generate, consume, and process physical values in real time. The SW must respond to these inputs and outputs based on classical control theory constraints. In another type of system, like as the powertrain, the understanding of mechanical engineering and as of today for electric motors the electrical and power management engineering is mandatory. All of this is leading to the challenge of forming teams of diverse knowledge and experience backgrounds and, in many cases, with different logical paradigms and structured thinking approaches.

DISTRIBUTION OF SOFTWARE

The architecture of single traditional embedded systems includes tens, or in some cases hundreds, of processors that implement hundreds of features that users interact with. Such features are composed of many other atomic SW functions that address different issues, tasks, and routines covering various use cases and customer interactions. Functions do not stand alone, but rather they have high mutual dependency. The SW and communication distribution architecture is dependent on the physical product component and subsystems breakdown. In the communication domain, such a feature interaction creates high complex dependencies between the individual features; in time, this emerged as a pressing issue. Combine this complex nature with the intricacy of an inhomogeneous and nonstandard technical infrastructure as real time operating systems, middleware and diverse special communication protocols communicated over several bus systems acting as the communication backbone between the different processing units.

VARIANTS AND CONFIGURATIONS

In order to grasp the complexities of variants and configurations, we will carefully observe the automotive domain, as it is stunningly complex in this regard.

A premium car typically has about eighty electronic fittings that can be ordered depending on the country. Simple yes or no decisions for each function yield a possible maximum of 2^{80} variants. Each model is usually produced for up to eight years. OEMs are responsible for providing support for at least fifteen years after the purchase of a vehicle. The lifecycle of HW components, like CPUs- Central Processing Units or DSPs- Digital Processing Units, is much less, say, up to five years. After the first three years of production, a quarter of the original ECUs-Electronic Control Units in the car have to be replaced by newer ones due to discontinuation. Software may be modified at much shorter intervals, though, typically several times a year. In particular, the comparatively short CPU lifecycles enforce changes in a vehicle's SW or HW system during the production period and maybe also in the development phase. This means that over time, various versions of each piece of SW in a car may emerge. When defective ECUs are replaced, or when a SW update is performed as part of vehicle maintenance, configurations containing hybrids of old and new SW can be created. New SW versions are introduced when exchanging entire ECUs, or during maintenance by way of 'flashing' techniques for replacing the SW of an ECU. When exchanging entire ECUs, or updating the respective SW, we must be sure that the new SW correctly interoperates with the rest of the vehicle SW. If not, compatibility issues will turn up. With its ever-expanding use of integrated SW, today's vehicle increasingly inherits the characteristics of a complex IT system.

UNIT-BASED COST

For industries that operate in a highly competitive mass market with strong cost pressure, competition over price requires permanent optimization. As a consequence of these combined forces, engineers concentrate on reducing the amount of necessary memory and computation power. Following that, code is written and directly optimized for specific individual processors. The SW must be closely attuned to the processors' characteristics for optimization to occur, plus any attempt to squeeze the code into as little memory as possible requires a further set of code optimizations. As a result, it becomes a grueling task to port the code to another processor, perhaps creating an infinite loop-like nuisance. Later on, it will be difficult to add any functionality to the system, change parts of the code, and fix defects. The code is more complex than necessary — for instance, in terms of strong coupling between modules — so changing it becomes an arduous task. Moreover, reusing this code in future models or on other processors is next to impossible. This optimization technique leads to a high probability of bugs, therefore finding them may become even more difficult — especially since application logic issues are now obscured by optimization. Thinking exclusively in terms of unit-based costs in conjunction with the associated need for optimizations will render the SW complex and difficult to handle. Eventually, time to market (TTM), maintenance costs, and the risk of not finishing a development project are substantially increased.

THE DISRUPTION OF EMBEDDED SW

When SW players enter a new frontier, they often push toward standardization or the adaptation of the target market practice to existing SW industry norms and convert what exists into more complex IT architecture. This phenomenon became manifest when Apple entered the music and mobile industries, and when Google and Tesla entered the automotive industry.

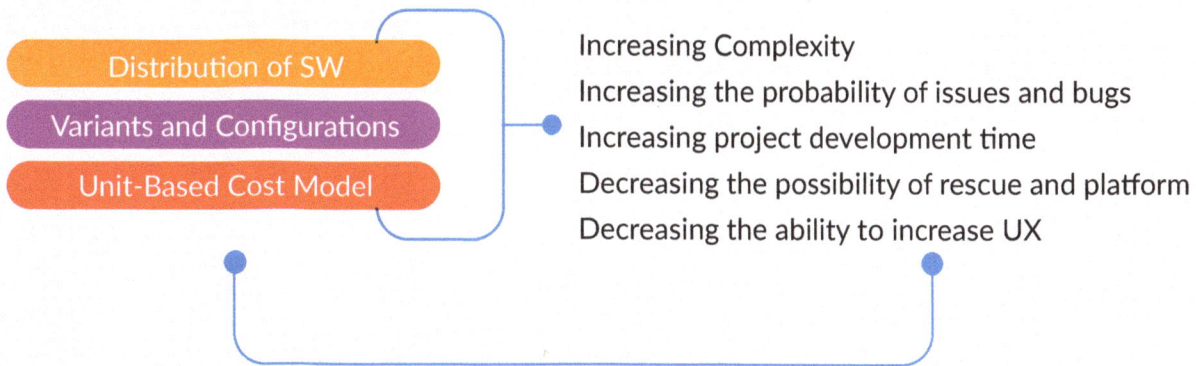

Distribution of SW

Variants and Configurations

Unit-Based Cost Model

Increasing Complexity
Increasing the probability of issues and bugs
Increasing project development time
Decreasing the possibility of rescue and platform
Decreasing the ability to increase UX

Disruption Elements

Architectural Innovation to decrease the complexity
Standard complex IT architecture which is leading to open standard
Ability to invest in platforms and reuse to reduce cost and speed time to market
Better abilities to increase UX efficiently

Designed by: Motaz Agamawi
www.theinnovativedinosaur.com

THE INNOVATIVE DINOSAUR

CHAPTER 5:
THE DIGITAL VERSUS TRADITIONAL INDUSTRIAL ENTERPRISE

A business organization can be defined as a structured body of people that is guided by leaders whose methods of evaluating different team members and decisions are translated into processes. Organization values are revealed in those processes, and organizational culture is shaped by these values; what an organization can and cannot achieve is perhaps defined by its culture.

In this chapter, we will establish the elements that constitute the output or result of the leaders' daily actions and decisions, which are ultimately based on their vision for how the work should be completed, be it better or best. The objective is not to determine the winning or superior type of organization, but rather to ascertain that producing cutting-edge technologies does not make a manufacturer a digital- or technology-based organization. Furthermore, the implementation of such technologies, like the Cloud, data science, and Chatbot, does not mean that the organization is digitally transformed. To be deemed a digital enterprise, many organizational aspects — including processes, methods, tools, and governance mechanisms — must be addressed and thoroughly explored.

CHAPTER FIVE SECTIONS:

- ℰ Process and Methods
- ℰ Software Development Toolchain
- ℰ Software Development Teams
- ℰ Project Management
- ℰ Supporting Functions
- ℰ Commercial Teams
- ℰ Business Model
- ℰ Product Design
- ℰ Organization Leadership

**THE
INNOVATIVE
DINⅭSAUR**

CHAPTER FIVE LIST OF REFERENCES & EXTRA READINGS

1. The role of manufacturing versus services in economic development, by Jostein Hauge and Ha-Joon Chang

2. Manufacturing Economy vs. Service Economy: Implications for Service Leadership, by Daniel T. L. Shek, Po P.Y. Chung and Hildie Leung

3. Seizing the Future: The Dawn of the Macro industrial Era. Book Review by GOSLIN, LEWIS N.

4. Leadership, change and responsibility, by Joop Remme, Stephanie Jones and others

5. Designing and managing the supply chain, by Simchi-Levi, and Kaminsky

6. Strategic Management, a dynamic perspective, by Mason A Carpenter and Gerard Sanders

7. Winning, by Jack Welch with Suzy Welch

8. Influence without Authority, by Allan R. Cohen and David L. Bradford

9. Our Iceberg is melting, by Holger Rathgeber, John Kotter, and Kazuhiro Fujihara

10. Thinking Wrong, by John Bielenbergm Mike Burn and others

11. On Competition, by Michael E. Porter

12. The fifth discipline, by Peter Senge

Now that we have reached a common definition and understanding of SW nature in general and of embedded SW in specific, let us go through the various organizational elements that differentiate traditional manufacturing or industrial enterprises from digital enterprises.

The objective is not to determine the winning or superior type of organization, but rather to ascertain that just because an organization is producing cutting-edge technologies, it does not necessarily make them a digital or technology-based organization. Furthermore, the implementation of such technologies, like the cloud, data science, and Chatbot, does not mean that the organization is digitally transformed. To be deemed a digital enterprise, many organizational aspects — including processes, methods, tools, and governance mechanisms — must be addressed.

But first, let us agree on a nuanced definition of an organization:

It is a structured body of people that is guided by leaders whose methods of appraising different team members and decisions are translated into processes. Organization values are revealed in those processes, and organizational culture is shaped by these values. What an organization can and cannot achieve is perhaps defined by its culture.

The elements below constitute the output or result of the leaders' daily actions and decisions, which are ultimately based on their vision for how work can be done, be it better or best.

**THE
INNOVATIVE
DINESAUR**

Stewardship VS
Technology Management

Process VS Team
Knowledge & Competencies

Single Purpose
VS UC & UX

SW as Component
VS as Product

Cost Plus VS
Perceived Value

Implementation VS
Development Teams

4Ps & 7Ps VS
Technology Adoption

Tangible VS
Ambiguate Intangible

Process & control
VS agile and lean

ORGANIZATION
LEADERSHIP

PROCESS AND
METHODS

PRODUCT
DESIGN

SOFTWARE
DEVELOPMENT
TOOLCHAIN

BUSINESS
MODEL

SOFTWARE
DEVELOPMENT
TEAMS

COMMERCIAL
TEAMS

PROJECT
MANAGEMENT

SUPPORTING
FUNCTIONS

Designed by: Motaz Agamawi
www.theinnovativedinosaur.com

THE
INNOVATIVE
DINƆSAUR

PROCESS AND METHODS

Industrial and manufacturing-based organizations have robust processes and methods that are governed by audits and different control systems. The brainware industry, (like the SW which is the leading part in Digital industry) has its own processes and methods, but they are embedded — by default — in their day-to-day toolchain and operational conduct manifesto.

Another important factor in the brainware industry is the technical competency of its teams and management levels. In a manufacturing company, the quality of the final product can be dramatically increased by adjusting and enforcing a specific process and then providing the essential training to the target team. Conversely, in the brainware industry, the same result cannot be achieved by simply revisiting and enforcing a given process, instead the target team's technical competency and toolchain must be positioned with precision.

Processes are the translation of organization leadership, vision, conduct, and daily decisions. They are reflections and projections of beliefs and values as well as the best practices formulated by management. Methods are the representation of how such processes are implemented. The organization is shaped around a series of processes and corresponding methods, and its limits are thus bound by them.

SOFTWARE DEVELOPMENT TOOLCHAIN

Two perspectives must be considered when tackling the toolchain topic. The first is related to an industrial organization that provides a software component as part of its total solution offering. In this case, the toolchain requirements and its sophisticated level of integration represent the needs and desired objectives to be met. In short, this outlook leans more toward integration and validation testing. The second perspective is related to a SW development organization, which provides SW as a product. In this case, the SW is the main business line. The toolchain, here, represents the organizational culture and encompasses the varied parts of the SW development lifecycle.

The trials to manage and control software development process in the same way as other disciplines are not successful. Software has a special nature that distinguishes it from HW or mechanical design and development. The recommended path for success is by way of our understanding of this nature and adherence to the SW industry's standards and norms.

As an example, continuous integration (CI) and continuous delivery (CD) represent the difference between digital and traditional organizations. What is confirmed is that the CI/CD robustness and usage were fully implemented in SW-based organizations a few years ago, while industrial-based organizations continue to struggle with such implementation. Traditional industry leaders tend to believe that their domain has a special nature, thus they cannot follow the best standard SW practices — and that is one of the main reasons why such entities are struggling in the digital domain. A couple of years ago, many traditional entities were convinced that agile development methodology was only suitable for pure SW houses, and so many of them developed their own agility-based methodologies. The result was unsatisfactory, though, as they walked the line between traditional and modern development methodologies.

THE
INNOVATIVE
DINESAUR

The design of the organization toolchain is a critical element for shaping and defining the final SW product output. The toolchain itself encapsulates the philosophy of the organization in the management and delivery of SW. It will either limit or extend the team's capabilities and agility in addition to the final quality of delivery. Organizations must design and deploy the toolchain with utmost awareness so that it matches the desired objective. For traditional enterprises, it is recommended to assign the responsibility of benchmarking, selecting, and implementing the SW development toolchain to a seasoned internal or external SW specialist— or else the results will likely mirror those that we see today in many struggling enterprises today.

SOFTWARE DEVELOPMENT TEAMS

Building the technical team competency of any organization is based on the organization's identification of its core competency, which is a result of defining the entity's central competitive edge and value proposition. By nature, industrial organizations define their core value proposition differently than digital or SW-based organizations. Talent and technical competency development differ with respect to both hard and soft skills as well as in the process of talent acquisition and the talent development paradigm, even from an early stage.

A simple yet highly significant example is the organization's labeling of the team as either the human resources or talent management department. This difference in terminology indicates a philosophy that is reflected in the result of execution.

Another key differentiation is the technical team organization structure and reporting lines, which will be covered in the organization-focused part of this section. It is worth mentioning now, though, that in SW-based organizations there is a clear distinction between the SW development team (those who develop software) and the implementation team (those who configure software). But, in many manufacturing-based organizations, such skill and process differentiations are not in place.

PROJECT MANAGEMENT

Project management (PM) for a tangible product or project is completely different from intangible ones. Digital products and SW solutions are intangible by nature, with a high dynamic change and major ambiguity.

The skills needed to manage digital, SW, and brainware products or projects are at variance with both hard and soft skills perspectives. Managing such types of ambiguous and dynamic projects require a professional who has a dee understanding of the related nature and skills — one that is not usually found in the normal PM process. In manufacturing-based organizations, PMs often come from manufacturing backgrounds, and, in many cases, they are supported by one or more colleagues who lead the SW component of the project. Since the role of the PM chiefly entails decision-making and customer interfacing, and due to either the ignorance or the less perceived importance of the SW part from the PM leads to the mismanagement of the SW-related projects.

In digital or SW-based organizations, PMs often come from SW technical backgrounds, thus their knowledge of the issues and nature of the project is suitable for achieving tasks at hand and future goals from both decision-making and customer interfacing perspectives. The difference is clear and can be summarized who is leading the PM either SW or other and the result will be based on the answer.

THE INNOVATIVE DINESAUR

SUPPORTING FUNCTIONS

The charter and code of conduct of any supporting team, including finance, procurement, facility, logistics, and others, are a result of the organization's overall culture and desired objectives. In manufacturing-based organizations, the supporting functions are more geared toward process and control; as the supporting functions evolve, so too do the complexities. On the other hand, the supporting functions of digital or SW-based organizations are more agile and lean: they are not preoccupied with that which is better, but rather with that which is worth the wait regarding any given decision.

By way of simple illustration, the majority of manufacturing enterprises' costs are allocated for purchasing material, components, and building factories, which can reach up to seventy percent of the yearly incurred costs. Accordingly, it's common to have a robust and, in some cases, complex purchasing process. On the contrary, for digital or SW-based enterprises, the highest costs are the personal ones, which can reach up to seventy percent of the total yearly incurred cost. An hour of an individual's time is the most expensive item in the profit and loss statement — meaning, any process must be designed in the favor of increasing the output of each single team member, and so leaner and more agile supporting team processes will be in place.

Another example is the IT or IS team structure, process, and policies. The charter of an IT or IS department in an industrial organization is not the same as the digital or SW-based one. Further afield, the policies and process to manage an IT infrastructure that serves information workers are not the same as the ones used for the management of the majority of SW developers. The level of restrictions and complexities is different: we will never find a digital or SW-based organization that restricts its team members to installing a piece of SW or changing a machine IP until IS approval or permissions have been granted. The opposite case will be in place in an industrial-based organization. In sum, the rationale behind each case is based on the nature of the business and industry in addition to the majority of users' sophistication level.

THE
INNOVATIVE
DINOSAUR

COMMERCIAL TEAMS

The commercialization process and lifecycle of tangible versus intangible products or projects are worlds apart from the process and team skills perspectives of both marketing and sales lifecycle. Selling ambiguous and unrealized ideas, along with the ability to identify and tackle needs that are not clearly expressed by customers, and then going through a process of matching all of this with the appropriate portfolio offerings and/or solution needs, require skill sets that are less relevant to tangible traditional sales.

Even high-tech and digital or SW marketing strategies and skills are different. The latter variety of marketing, for instance, is neither about the 4Ps nor 7Ps, and even the techniques and approach followed in the various stages of the technology adoption lifecycle for the different types of target customers is completely different. The demand generation and its capturing are shaped and executed with a different approach, just as with the evaluation of new product development selection criteria and decisions. New product development validation lifecycle, minimum viable product (MVP) definition, pivoting, and early-adaptor acquisition strategies are different.

BUSINESS MODEL

The business and revenue models are completely different between traditional and digital-based organizations. Pricing strategies are different, too, with cost-plus versus perceived-value strategies, which in return impact the revenue model either in terms of asset sales or subscription based, pay-as-you use, and even 'freemium' (free and premium) strategies.

The game console is an example of a manufacturing-based product business model Sony's PlayStation and Microsoft's Xbox series follow a model that revolves around selling the console HW at almost the cost of production, with the main revenue streams coming from the sales percentage taken from the game publishers, which is based on game sales. Also, the pricing of the gadgets, which compromises a considerable part of the revenue model. Multiple factors influence the strategy formulation paradigm and approach. One of the most important factors is the depth of the organization's pockets, as they affect the ability to invest and design a higher risk revenue strategy. The pockets' depth is a result of the organization's overall profit structure and ability to attract either internal or external investments for new ventures.

THE INNOVATIVE DINOSAUR

Another central difference is the R&D cost management strategy. For many of the manufacturing-based organizations' R&D arms, cost is handled in the manner of the cost of goods sold (COGS) philosophy. Therefore, either a target customer will pay in full or part for the cost of R&D, and the final product is sold at cost-plus or markup prices. Although this strategy is useful for minimizing the cost of R&D, it impacts the end profitability, which, in return, yields less of an economic impact for the new product development and innovation. In contrast, digital or SW-based organizations are handling the cost of R&D, innovation, and even innovation failure in a completely different approach. Indeed, this leads to higher risk but in return bestows the ability to price the final product based on the anticipated customer perceived value, which is, in most cases, far greater than the real cost of the product and thus results in greater profit margins.

PRODUCT DESIGN

Product design is another key divergence between traditional manufacturing and digital or SW-based organizations — in particular, whether the HW (mechanical/electronics) or the SW team will take the lead. Traditional manufacturing-based organizations will appoint the HW team. We have a sensor, an actuator, or even machinery that will be produced or manufactured, so the HW team starts to define the specs and compile the product and/or system design. At a later stage, the SW team is brought on to add the related SW it designed based on the HW capabilities or limitations and functionalities.

In digital or SW-based organizations, the opposite process is applied. The product requirements, architecture, and design are set in place, and then begins the acquisition process of the best-in-class HW to meet such product specification and functional requirements. It is a different approach for the system level design, which implies many future consequences. No one can claim which approach is better, but rather it is a result of organization structure, culture, and desired objectives.

Another clear split between the two organization types — worlds — is the customer centricity and UX- user experience approach while building a new product. The mental paradigm of digital or SW-based organizations in this domain is distinct, which implies that the difference is the means and tools used in such processes. Google's newly introduced internet router (extender), for instance, pays attention to details and the UX in ways unseen before in the market.

THE INNOVATIVE DINOSAUR

ORGANIZATION LEADERSHIP

Leaders structure, influence, and design organizations. Their actions and code of conduct are translated into the organization processes, which formulates its values. The organizational culture is shaped by these values and defines what can and cannot be achieved.

Leaders are paid to establish a vision and mission as well as to strategize and make decisions on a daily basis. They hire and assign diverse managerial levels of decision-makers on behalf of the organization, and they shape and approve the product development strategies while setting the tone for customer relationship management. In essence, leaders are often made along a lengthy or long-lasting path of experience that informs and inspires their frame of reference. This is reflected in the execution of the leader's duties and responsibilities, thus a cascade effect reaches all levels of leaders and decision-makers in a given organization.

In the management academic literature, two contradictory types of top leaders are unpacked: the steward and the entrepreneur or innovator and what in between. Perhaps the most famous example of the steward is John Sculley, the former CEO of Apple from 1983 to 1993. And for the entrepreneurial or innovative leader, the most famous example is, without a doubt, Steve Jobs, who founded Apple Inc. in 1976. In going through these two leadership examples, the difference will be clear between traditional manufacturing leaders and digital or SW leaders. It is not a comparison drawn to determine which leadership style is better, but rather it provides us with a clear distinction between the characteristics and frame of references associated with each of the two types of leaders.

If an organization is facing a digital disruption wave and its leadership is coming from a different domain with a different frame of reference, then the situation will be exceptionally challenging as the leaders' perception of the change — namely, what is needed for the future — is based on their previous work experience Naturally, the top management team comes from the core of the organization domain — but, with limited digital experience in most cases. As a result, the team will likely fall into a deep chasm of their best efforts, one that's based on what experience they gained and what they have extracted from the best practices over years. Many of those cases include organizations that have great chief technology officers (CTO) and a brilliant VP for digitalization

**THE
INNOVATIVE
DINƎSAUR**

or an experienced leader as the head of global software delivery. We will find that such professionals come from electronic, mechanical, and industrial backgrounds with limited or no real practical experience in SW development. These unexpected players can be good professionals, but they are working based on their best efforts, perceiving, and making decisions from their own frame of reference — which is oftentimes irrelevant or unsuited to a digital or SW decision. They offer their honest advice to the organization's leaders based on what they know and what they think will work better. In time, though, a problem surfaces: the leaders and the organization neglect the fact that these unexpected players or professionals are not digital or SW experts, thus in many cases their best efforts are the main reason behind failure. Humans tend to make decisions within the bounds of our acquired knowledge and experience as well as the information at hand. We are guided by a mental map of ideas, thoughts, and information perception toward what we (think we) know best.

During a period of disruption, bringing professionals with digital and SW experience into the fold as part of the organization leadership and top management is vitally important. At the same time, the number of digitally aware and experienced team members must be increased. These professionals must be empowered, given the needed room to lead the needed change, and encouraged to play the role of advocacy. Bringing in an insider without a track record of practical digital or SW experience is generally a route to disaster, signaling the beginning of the end for many enterprises. To avert disaster, leaders must take heed of the magnitude of change vis-à-vis the organization's true capabilities and competencies. The true, deep and effective digital transformation will never be achieved without the full belief and sponsorship of the most senior leaders, as if they are the maestro and the rest of the organization is the orchestra. Together, they perform a desired musical piece with expertise and mutual support.

CHAPTER 6:
ASSESSING THE ENTERPRISE'S DIGITAL AND CREATIVE READINESS

The objective of this chapter is to propose a set of techniques, methods, and tools that will help us in identifying an organization's digital and innovation capability readiness. We propose such an assessment through the application of three types of deep analysis and audits:

PRE-AUDIT BUSINESS DEFINITION QUESTIONS

A predefined set of questions are listed. Answering these questions will help to define the business, understand its nature, and guide the audit accordingly. Moreover, answering these questions guarantees a common understanding of the business among stakeholders, either eliminating or mitigating ambiguity.

ENTERPRISE'S DIGITAL READINESS

A quick audit for digital readiness is provided. With this set of enterprise aspects, we will be better equipped to understand where traditional organizations stand in comparison to digitally-driven ones. This is an essential step for understanding the organization's status quo.

ENTERPRISE'S INNOVATION AUDIT

This audit offers organizations an overview of their strengths and weaknesses with respect to technical innovation management, thus enabling them to highlight the areas that they should examine in greater depth. The model defines the scope of what organizational aspects should be audited.

The combination of these three audit types provides us with a 360-degree view of an enterprise's digital and innovation readiness. Based on the audit results enterprise strategy teams and top management will be able to identify gaps, set desired improvements and objectives, and ultimately design the appropriate transformation strategies. Such strategies will be translated into actionable initiatives and product portfolio management approaches, all of which are covered across the chapters of this book.

**THE
INNOVATIVE
DINESAUR**

CHAPTER SIX SECTIONS:

- ∈ Pre-Audit Business Definition Questions
- ∈ Enterprise Digital Readiness
- ∈ Enterprise Innovation Audit

CHAPTER SIX LIST OF TOOLS, DIAGRAMS, AND ILLUSTRATIONS

1. TID Canvas: Enterprise Innovation Audit Main Elements
2. TID Canvas: Enterprise Innovation Audit Main Questions
3. TID Canvas: Pre-Business Definition Audit Canvas
4. TID Canvas: Enterprise Innovation Maturity Canvas Detailed Guide
5. TID Canvas: Enterprise Innovation Maturity Evaluation Grid
6. TID Canvas: Enterprise Innovation Maturity Roadmap Canvas
7. TID Canvas: Enterprise Digital Maturity Ladder
8. TID Canvas: Enterprise Digital Readiness Canvas
9. TID Table 1: Enterprise Digital Readiness Score Card

THE INNOVATIVE DINESAUR

CHAPTER SIX LIST OF REFERENCES & EXTRA READINGS

1. Designing a Better Business, by Patrick van der Pijl, Justin Lokitz and Lisa Kay Solomon
2. The Service Innovation Handbook, by Lucy Kimbell
3. Value Proposition Design, by Alex Osterwalder, Yves Pingeur and others
4. Business Model Generation, by Alex Osterwalder and Yves Pingneur
5. McKinsey 7S Framework
6. Development of a Technical Innovation Audit, by Vittorio Chiesa
7. ISO 56002:2019, Innovation management, Innovation management system, Guidance
8. Innovation360.com
9. Boardofinnovation.com
10. Certified Change Management Professional
11. Association for Strategic Planning
12. KPI Institute

THE
INNOVATIVE
DINOSAUR

ENTERPRISE PRE-BUSINESS DEFINITION AUDIT CANVAS

Scope

What is the industry we are operating in?
What are we offering?
Which business field are we operating in?
What is our industry type (service, manufacturing, research, other)?
What is the type of our entity (customer interfacing, R&D center, offshore center, manufacturing center, distribution platform, or other)?
Where are we positioned in the value chain?

Customer

Who is our customer, the one who pays directly to us?
Who is our user, the one who uses our product, does it differ from the customer?
How do our customers perceive us (leaders, followers, laggards)?
How do we reach our customers?
Are we "a good to have" or "a must have" for our customers?
What are our customers needs, wants and demands?

Competition

Who are we competing with?
What is our competitive advantage?
What is our differentiation factor?
Who is our substitute?
What is our core competency?

Offering

What do we offer to our customers
What is our value proposition?
What is the product or service that we are selling?
What is our business model?
What is our sale/revenue volume?
What is our order intake volume for the years to come?
What is our operating margin and net profit?
How are our revenues distributed over products or business units?
How are our revenues distributed geographically?
Which product or service is generating the highest margins and which is generating the lowest?

Organization

What is our organization core functions?
What is our organization support functions?
How many team members do we have in our organization (full time, & outsourced)?
How many countries do we operate in?
How many sites do we have (production, distribution, operations,...)?
How many team members are included in each entity type?
Does each entity type has different nature than the others?
What is our cost structure and what is the main cost elements?

Research & Development

How do we define innovation, invention and creativity?
How do we distinguish and innovate?
How do we measure innovation impact?
How do we support innovation?
What is the percentage of sales revenue coming from innovative new products/services?
How much do we spend on R&D and innovation?
What is the percentage of engineers and scientists compared to others within our team members?
What is our innovation strategy?
What processes, policies, methods and tools do we have to support research and innovation?
What is the level of sponsorship from the top management for the research and innovation?
What is our innovation management team structure?
How many team members do we have dedicated for innovation activities?
Do we have the proper innovation competencies within our team?

Designed by: Motaz Agamawi
www.theinnovativedinosaur.com

THE INNOVATIVE DINOSAUR

PRE-AUDIT BUSINESS DEFINITION QUESTIONS

Before starting the Enterprise Innovation Capability Audit, we need to define our business. A predefined set of questions are listed. Answering those questions helps in defining the business, understanding its nature and directing the audit into the proper directions. Also, we use these questions to guarantee the common understanding of the business between different stakeholders and eliminate the ambiguity as much as possible.

GOAL

- The main objective of this set of questions is to provide a common and agreed upon understanding of the various aspects of the business between the interested stakeholders.
- It also helps the auditor and innovation strategists to better understand the business — think, a holistic 360-degree view.
- In many cases, the resulting answers may be used with the target groups attending the audits to ensure that all participants have the same degree of knowledge and understanding of the business.

HOW TO USE

- First, we must identify the main stakeholders.
- A sample representing the different groups of the enterprise is then decided upon, including top management, and middle management. It must also incorporate many functions, from technical R&D, production, operations, and sales to marketing, in addition to support functions like HR and finance.
- Design workshops with each group of no more than twelve members. The workshops should not exceed two hours.
- The output of each workshop will be a set of answers commonly agreed upon between the attendees. The auditor must consolidate the output of the different workshops with an objective of achieving single answer for each of the audit questions. The common answers are considered as a definition for the different aspects of the business addressed in the audit.
- This definition is to be used as the chief guideline for the full strategize process.
- It is recommended that the auditor share the final definition and results with all of the stakeholders.

THE
INNOVATIVE
DINESAUR

DETAILS

1. Scope Definition

- What is the industry that we are operating in?
- What are we offering?
- Which business field are we operating in?
- What is our industry type (e.g., services, manufacturing, or research)?
- What type of our entity (e.g., customer interfacing, R&D center, offshore center, manufacturing center, and distribution platform)?
- Where are we positioned in the industry value chain?

2. Customer Definition

- Who is our customer (i.e., the one who pays us directly)?
- Who is our user (i.e., the one who uses our product, even if they differ from the customer)?
- How do our customers perceive us (e.g., as leaders, followers, or laggards)?
- How do we reach our customers?
- Are we a "good to have" or "must to have" in the eyes of our customers?
- What are our customers' needs, wants, and demands?

3. Competition Definition

- Who are we competing with?
- What is our competitive advantage?
- What is our differentiation factor?
- Who is our substitute?
- What is our core competency?

4. Offering Definition

- What do we offer to our customers?
- What is our value proposition?
- What is the product or service that we are selling?
- What is our business model?
- What is our revenue model?
- What is our sales or revenue volume?
- What is our order intake volume in the coming years?
- What is our operating margin and net profit?
- How are our revenues distributed over our products or business units?
- How are our revenues geographically distributed?
- Which product or service is generating the highest margins, and which one is generating the lowest?

5. Organization Definition

- What are our organization's core functions?
- What are our organization's support functions?
- How many team members do we have in our organization (e.g., full-time, part-time, and outsourced)?
- How many countries do we operate in?
- How many sites do we have (e.g., production, distribution, and operation)?
- How many types of entities do we have (e.g.,
- R&D, manufacturing, and distribution)?
- How many team members are included in each entity type?
- Does each entity type have a different nature than the others? If yes, we need to specify the differing nature.
- What is our cost structure, and what are the main cost elements?

6. Research and Innovation Definition

- How do we define innovation, invention, and creativity?
- How do we distinguish between research and innovation?
- How do we measure innovation impact?
- How do we support innovation?
- What is the percentage of sales or revenue coming from new innovative products or services?

- How much do we invest on R&D and innovation?
- What percentage of our team is engineers and scientists, and where do they rank among the other members?
- What is our innovation strategy?
- What processes, policies, methods, and tools must we possess to support both research and innovation?
- What level of sponsorship is there from the top management for   research and innovation?
- What is the structure of our innovation management team?
- How many of the team members are dedicated to innovation activities?
- Does our team hold the required innovation competencies?

THE INNOVATIVE DINOSAUR

ENTERPRISE DIGITAL MATURITY LADDER

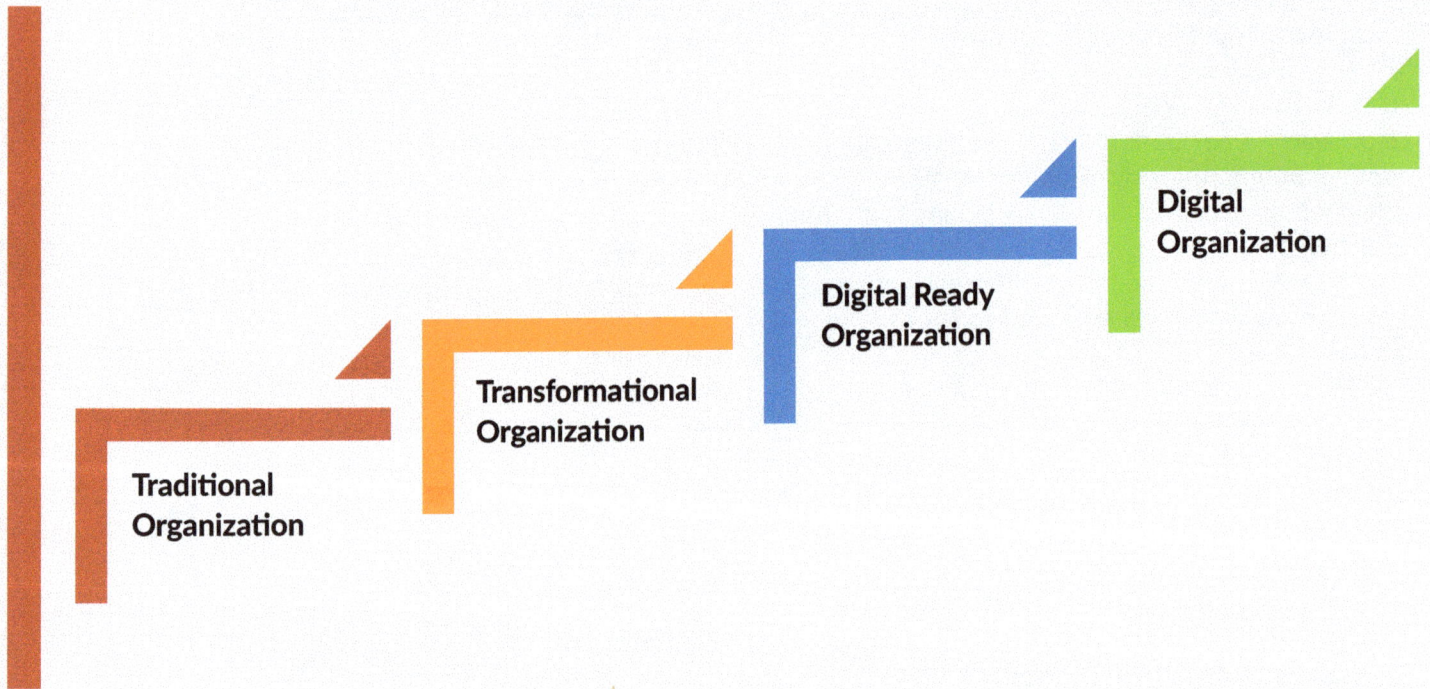

Traditional Organization

Transformational Organization

Digital Ready Organization

Digital Organization

Designed by: Motaz Agamawi
www.theinnovativedinosaur.com

THE INNOVATIVE DINOSAUR

ENTERPRISE DIGITAL READINESS CANVAS

Process & Methods	Traditional	1	2	3	4	Digital
SW Development Tool Chain	Traditional	1	2	3	4	Digital
SW Development Teams	Traditional	1	2	3	4	Digital
Project Management	Traditional	1	2	3	4	Digital
Support Functions	Traditional	1	2	3	4	Digital
Commercial Teams	Traditional	1	2	3	4	Digital
Business Model	Traditional	1	2	3	4	Digital
Product Design & Customer Centricity	Traditional	1	2	3	4	Digital
Organization Leadership	Traditional	1	2	3	4	Digital
User Experience Design	Traditional	1	2	3	4	Digital
Ecosystem Approach	Traditional	1	2	3	4	Digital
Profitability Structure	Traditional	1	2	3	4	Digital
Lean & Agility	Traditional	1	2	3	4	Digital
Time to Market	Traditional	1	2	3	4	Digital

Designed by: Motaz Agamawi
www.theinnovativedinosaur.com

THE
INNOVATIVE
DINOSAUR

GOAL

The goal of this step is to examine the fourteen elements that define a digital organization. After a prompt survey, the results will help us in determining the stage of readiness for any given enterprise. Following that, this result will guide the strategy formulation to be implemented for the needed transformational initiatives and program — which will be ultimately designed to achieve the desired digital transformation and enterprise innovation strategies.

HOW TO USE

- Identify the key stakeholders.
- Decide a sample representing the different groups from within the enterprise. Including top management, middle management, teams. Also the sample must include different functions including R&D, production, operations, sales, marketing and preferred to include support functions as HR, Finance and others.
- Set workshops with each group separately, group size to be not more than 12 members. Also workshop not to exceed 2 hours.
- It is recommended to share the output of the Pre-Audit Business Definition Questions with the target participants.
- This will help in guaranteeing a common understanding and alignment between all of the parties.
- The audit is to be conducted with the scoring grid mentioned in the next section. Definitions of each audit element mentioned in the grid may be modified or adjusted based on the nature and needs of a given enterprise.
- Each participant is to answer the questions mentioned in the evaluation grid.

THE INNOVATIVE DINOSAUR

ᴄ At the end of the audit and during the analysis phase, each element will have a score between one and four. This represents the average of all answers. We can apply this by summing the complete results of the fourteen elements, before dividing it by fourteen. It is the decision of the analyst to apply the average rounding technique following the desired on. One of the techniques can be as follows:

- ᴄ We have fourteen different audit element.
- ᴄ Each element has a score from one to four.
- ᴄ Lets consider that, we have 10 participant answering our audit
- ᴄ For each pillar you will conduct the summation of the result of each individual and divide by the number of participant. So in our example if we assumed that for a specific element each of the participants gave a score of four. Then this element summation will be 40. If we divided the forty by ten then this pillar score is four. In case of fractions please apply the rounding technique.
- ᴄ Then to be able to identify the overall readiness score which must be between one to four. Conduct a summation for the fourteen elements and then divide by fourteen. In our example if we assumed that all the participants are giving a score of two for each element. Then the summation will be twenty eight. Divide twenty eight by fourteen the result will be two. Please do not forget to round to the nearest.
- ᴄ Different techniques can be applied, the objective is to achieve a consolidated average score per element and a single average value representing the organization overall stage of digital readiness.

ᴄ The above process must be applied to all of the participants' feedback and then a global average is to be calculated.

ᴄ The global average will lead to the organization's overall place within the enterprise digital maturity ladder and, in turn, the identification of its stage of digital readiness.

ENTERPRISE DIGITAL READINESS SCORE CARD

In the following chart, 1 is purely traditional and 4 is purely digital. Your choice is based on your own point of view. This grid is designed to provide guidance while conducting the organization digital readiness through fourteen different organizational elements that defines the boundaries between traditional and digital organization.

After answering the digital readiness score card, the enterprise will be able to spot its position within the digital maturity ladder. Gaps will be identified and strategies for the needed transformation will be ready to be compiled.

THE INNOVATIVE DINᴄSAUR

PROCESS & METHODS

Traditional	Transformational	Digital Ready	Digital
• Processes are rigid and complex, not lean.	• Exceptions exist for some teams of a special nature in which more lean and agile processes are applied.	• Initiatives for implementing more lean and agile processes are in place.	• Processes and methods are lean, agile, and governed with a clear service level agreement.
• They are oriented toward process robustness, enforcement, and control.	• A special approval for such exceptions is needed.	• Partial implementations for decreasing the complexity of the process exist with a clear service- level agreement (SLA).	• Team competencies and skills take the highest priority in terms of development — higher than the processs monitoring and control aspects.
• The process and methods are perceived as more important elements than the team's competencies and skills.	• The existence of different SW systems to manage some of the process without integrated interfaces to allow the different system to exchange the needed data and information between each other.	• Balancing the robustness of the process and the increases in team competencies and skills is supported by the organization's top management.	• Complete automation for the process and methods is implemented through fully integrated SW management information systems.
		• Existence of SW systems that manage all the processes with partial integration for the different systems, allowing a semi-automated data and information exchange between the different systems.	• Self-service features are supported by the SW systems accessible to different team members.

SW DEVELOPMENT TOOLCHAIN

Traditional

- Software toolchains are separated with no integration for the different systems together.
- Manual or nonstandard transfer of source code and artifacts from a stage of development to another.
- Software development processes, standards, and methods are either included in templates or do not yet exist.
- Toolchain elements are not up to date, fragmented, or coming from different providers with a nonhomogeneous UX.

Transfor-mational

- SW development life cycle is managed through a well-defined toolchain with minimal integration.
- All processes and standards are documented, and the teams are trained.
- Manual reviews by experts and senior team members are regularly followed.
- The existence of manual transfer of code and artifacts from a stage of development to another.
- Toolchain elements are fragmented — coming from different providers with nonhomogeneous UX.

Digital Ready

- Full integration occurs between the various toolchain elements with no manual transfers for source code and artifacts.
- Automated implementation occurs, too, for different quality gates between the different stages of development.
- Product quality is in focus.

Digital

- The complete implementation of CI- Continuous integration and CD- Continuous Delivery/Development are in place.
- Fully homogenous and up-to-date toolchain is implemented.
- Product quality is guaranteed through the proper quality gates between the different development stages through automated workflows.
- All processes, standards, and best practices are forced, monitored, and controlled through the development toolchain.

THE
INNOVATIVE
DINOSAUR

Traditional

- ∈ Software quality measures concern process quality measure more than final product quality.
- ∈ Toolchain concerns SW integration needs more than SW development needs.

Transfor-mational

- ∈ The mix between process quality adherence and product quality measures exist.
- ∈ Toolchain is more oriented toward SW integration needs than SW development needs.

Digital Ready

Digital

SW DEVELOPMENT TEAMS

Traditional

- R&D organization structure is complex, with more of a focus on mechanical and/or electronics.
- Software teams represent the minority within the R&D organization.
- Thus, SW R&D is following the systems, mechanical and electronics directions, requirements, and processes.
- Software teams are perceived as followers, and they do not participate in the product or system requirement definition.
- Moreover, SW is perceived as the easiest part to be

Transfor- mational

- The only difference between transformational and traditional organization is the increase of importance of SW.
- Increased importance leads to increases in the number of SW team members within the overall R&D teams.

Digital Ready

- As the importance of SW rises, it represents a more strategic differentiation factor.
- Organizations shift their focus to SW R&D teams, SW itself begins to have a clear role within the overall product or system requirement definition, although it does not lead the product development process.
- Organizations then start to realize the complexity of the SW changes in addition to the implications associated with such complex systems.
- Software R&D is led by a management team with SW experience that reports to an R&D management with no SW experience.

Digital

- The seniority of the SW teams has shifted from a hierarchy depicted as a pyramid to a diamond shape: the majority of the team is mid-career members, and there is a small number of top experts and junior members.
- Investment in team competency and skills is in place.
- Software skills, including development, testing, and implementation, are properly defined and the needs of each group are properly addressed.
- Software-based productivity measures, which are collected, analyzed, and reported on by the SW toolchain automatically and transparently, are properly implemented.

THE
INNOVATIVE
DINOSAUR

Traditional	Transformational	Digital Ready	Digital
modified or changed. SW R&D is led by non-SW experienced management. ϵ The hierarchy of seniority in SW teams is not balanced with more junior members. ϵ Team skills and experience do not match the desired organization's technical roadmap. ϵ There is no clear differentiation between SW development teams and SW integration or configuration with no clear differentiation in career progression and competency building. ϵ The management approach to increase	SW experience. The SW team's hierarchy of seniority starts to move toward maturity with a balanced number of junior members compared to mid-career ones. ϵ Investment in team competency and skills are in place. ϵ Differentiation between SW development and SW implementation or configuration is defined and considered. ϵ Software productivity measures considering quality of work delivered and KPIs related to rework and the cost of defects are also in place.		

Traditional	Transfor-mational	Digital Ready	Digital

Traditional

productivity through increasing the number of SW development team members, which usually leads to a more complex status.

€ SW team's productivity is measured by exerted efforts in combination with the number of lines of code productivity more than the quality of work delivered.

€ There is no clear measure for the quality of work delivered per team and per individual.

€ Rework and cost of defects are not measured.

PROJECT MANAGEMENT

Traditional

- Project management organization is built around the industrial and manufacturing aspects.
- Project managers come from industrial and manufacturing backgrounds and without digital or SW experience.
- Their knowledge, skills and experiences are born of or based on more tangible products.
- With only limited experience when it comes to managing ambiguous customer requirements, they are incompetent at effectively estimating the needed time, associated cost and design the

Transfor-mational

- The major difference between transformational and traditional organization project management is that the SW complexity and importance has increased from an operational perspective.
- Based on the increased importance of SW the project management organization starts to inject SW assistant project manager roles into projects with high software components contribution.
- The introduction of a mechanism to support project managers with the SW projects follows.

Digital Ready

- A separation between traditional project management and digital or SW management is established.
- The leading project players are still the traditional project managers, but Software project managers are more empowered.
- A governing Project Management Office (PMO) is also established to supervise and resolve conflicts between the two project managers types, though the non-SW project managers have the final say.

Digital

- Software project managers are leading the projects while also receiving support when needed from industrial or manufacturing project managers.

Traditional	Transfor-mational	Digital Ready	Digital
appropriate pricing schema for the customer change requests.	Still, the responsibility of customer interfacing falls on the project managers. c The newly introduced role is not having the proper empowerment and thus the problems are not resolved as desired.		

SUPPORT FUNCTIONS

Traditional	Transformational	Digital Ready	Digital
∈ Support functions are strictly following processes. ∈ They are more aligned with control than providing support and execution. ∈ In short, they have less agility and are less lean.	∈ Same dynamics as traditional enterprise. ∈ Except that support teams are forced through the management to provide support in a more efficient manner to some special teams or exceptional situations or projects.	∈ Support functions are transforming more toward agile and lean teams for most of the processes. ∈ Service-level agreements (SLA) related to the provided services are in place and followed. ∈ Support functions prioritize effective execution over monitoring and control.	∈ Effective support teams are in place with a clear mandate of participating in the overall organization objectives. ∈ The efficiency and effectiveness of the provided services are the main objectives to be achieved. ∈ Support functions provide end-to-end services with a mindset that the internal teams are their target customers. ∈ The internal customer satisfaction of the delivered services is measured and then corrective actions or improvements are implemented by the support functions.

THE
INNOVATIVE
DINOSAUR

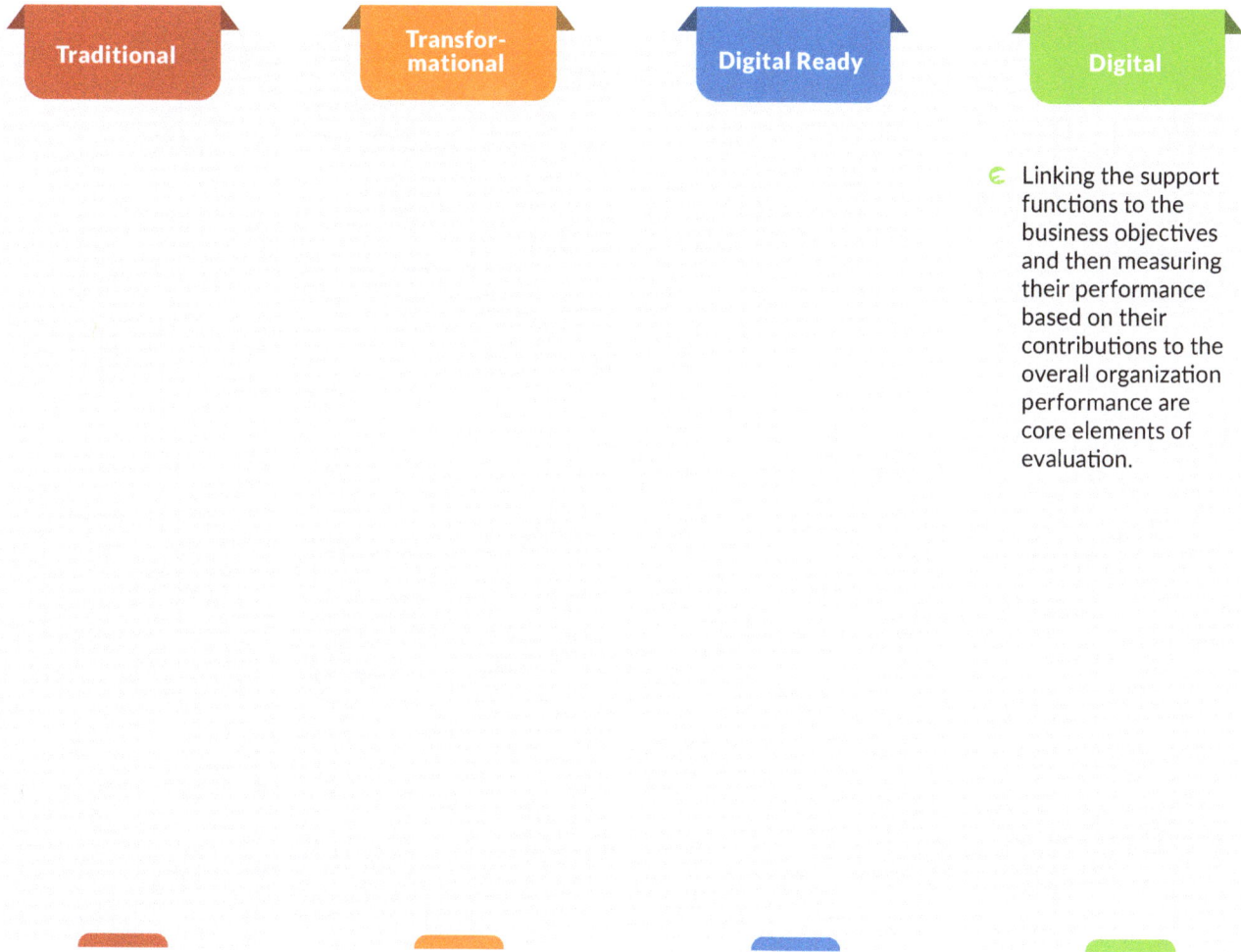

Traditional	Transfor-mational	Digital Ready	Digital

Linking the support functions to the business objectives and then measuring their performance based on their contributions to the overall organization performance are core elements of evaluation.

COMMERCIAL TEAMS

Traditional

- Commercial organizations are built around the traditional business model for tangible products.
- As product life cycle and product marketing depend on the traditional techniques, channels, and means for customer demand generation and demand capturing.
- The organization's approach toward the different stages of the technology adoption life cycle is not considered.
- New product development selection criteria are more conservative and toward market pull with limited customer validation techniques implementation.

Transfor-mational

- Closer to the traditional organization behavior but with conservative exploration for the digital models.

Digital Ready

- Mixing between the traditional and digital commercial models.
- The majority of the offerings and techniques that are implemented lay emphasis on traditional models.

Digital

- The digital commercial model is completely followed, and the stages of the technology adoption lifecycle are fully considered and tailored to the different target customer segments.
- New product development selection criteria are not conservative; rather, it's toward technology push with fully- implemented customer validation techniques that are supported by an agile pivoting capability.

THE INNOVATIVE DINOSAUR

BUSINESS MODEL

Traditional

- Both business and revenue models are centered around asset sales.
- Pricing strategies, for instance, are built on cost-plus techniques.
- The R&D and innovation efforts are mainly paid by enterprises business- to-business (B2B) customers, leading to low impact on the innovation investments.

Transfor-mational

- Same as the traditional enterprise.
- The exploration and testing of new business or revenue models are conducted but with no actions executed.

Digital Ready

- The majority of the products and services follow traditional business and revenue models.
- There is a shift toward digital and SW pricing strategies.
- Most of the new product development R&D investments are carried by the organization, and its trials of applying perceived value pricing strategies are in order.

Digital

- The full digital and SW business and revenue models are applied.
- A fusion of revenue models exist within the portfolio, including asset sales as well as subscription-based, pay-as-you-use, and even freemium strategies.
- Perceived- value pricing strategies are followed.

THE
INNOVATIVE
DINOSAUR

PRODUCT DESIGN & CUSTOMER CENTRICITY

Traditional	Transfor-mational	Digital Ready	Digital
℮ The experts on the HW (mechanical or electronics) domain lead the product design phase. ℮ User-centric and design-thinking approaches are not followed as product functionality is emphasized over UX through the product usage journey.	℮ Close to the traditional enterprise. ℮ The exploration and testing of user-centric, design-thinking, and UX-driven approaches are conducted through the implementation of training and workshops for a select number of team members.	℮ Product design leadership is often a hybrid of HW and SW experts. ℮ Investments in cultural transformation initiatives related to design-thinking, user-centric, and UX are made.	℮ Software experts lead the product design phase. ℮ Thus, product design follows the user-centric, design-thinking, and UX paradigm.

THE INNOVATIVE DINOSAUR

ORGANIZATION LEADERSHIP

Traditional	Transfor-mational	Digital Ready	Digital
⊂ The backgrounds and experiences of organization leaders are completely formulated within the traditional domain. ⊂ Digital and SW experience may be found at the lower-middle management layers within the organization's different departments. Who are not empowered.	⊂ The backgrounds and experiences of the organization's leaders are completely formulated in the traditional domain. ⊂ A limited number of second-tier executives have digital and SW domain experience, thus they are not empowered.	⊂ The backgrounds and experiences of the organization's leaders represent a mixture of the traditional and the digital, but with much more of the former than the later.	⊂ The leaders of the organization come from a SW and digital background and experience.

THE INNOVATIVE DINOSAUR

UX DESIGN

Traditional	Transformational	Digital Ready	Digital
℮ Product functional and nonfunctional requirements as performance are taking the focus ℮ The UX is not considered and customer validation techniques are not followed.	℮ Concepts of UX are explored but not integrated as part of the new product development and product design.	℮ With continuous trials to help increase the product portfolio, UX is taking center stage. ℮ Investments in the domain of UX are applied by adding experienced members to the team and integrating the proper processes within the wider scope of the new product development. ℮ Customer validation is integrated into the new product development life cycle.	℮ The UX is considered part of the corporate DNA, values, and culture. ℮ Meanwhile, team members attempt to build products and services that are functional, efficient, and beautiful.

ECOSYSTEM APPROACH

Traditional	Transfor-mational	Digital Ready	Digital
€ Products are closed and standard interfaces for integration are unavailable. **€** External partners and ecosystem stakeholders have no means to integrate or build any extended functionalities or use cases.	**€** The ecosystem approach is explored as some interactions with external stakeholders unfold. **€** Product interfaces are not available for the ecosystem partners, and the cooperation business model to encourage external ecosystem stakeholders to engage into a business relation does not exist. **€** Based on rigid internal processes, the absence of standard product interfaces coupled with the unavailability of a clear business model for ecosystem partners leads that most of the ecosystem partnership trials are facing failure.	**€** Product standard interfaces are designed with the objective to be available for external ecosystem stakeholders, who have limited access to those interfaces. **€** Focus on achieving a clear ecosystem business model emerges but within a trial scope. **€** Partnership deals with ecosystem stakeholders are evaluated and executed on a case-by-case basis without any standard process that gives the external ecosystem stakeholders the ability to go through such a process on a self-served basis.	**€** Standard product and services interfaces are designed, implemented, and launched to be available for all of the external ecosystem stakeholders, along with supported self-service features and capabilities. **€** The necessary partnership information, technical documentation, and partnership business model information are available and accessible to the ecosystem partners, who are, in turn, building new functionalities and use cases.

THE INNOVATIVE DINOSAUR

PROFITABILITY STRUCTURE

Traditional	Transformational	Digital Ready	Digital
- Profitability structure is based on the fixed cost-pricing strategy, which leads to minimum net profits. - This hinders the company's overall corporate ability to invest in the future.	- Similar to traditional organization but explorations and trials to diversify the product portfolio pricing strategy and revenue sources are taking place. - Such explorations may build on added-value services while extending the current offering to diversify the revenue sources, and thus, increasing the product or services portfolio profitability structure.	- A mix of cost-plus and perceived-value pricing strategies are leading to greater profitability, but the full potential has yet to be achieved.	- A high profitability structure is achieved through a diversified portfolio of products, services, and a multi-tier business and revenue models.

LEAN AND AGILITY

Traditional	Transfor-mational	Digital Ready	Digital
∈ Processes are not lean, and agility does not exist.	∈ Same as the traditional organization.	∈ Lean and agile processes are in progress, with an observable increase in enhanced efficiency and effectiveness. ∈ A fast time to market is achieved for a specific set of products and services in the product portfolio.	∈ Organization processes are lean and agile with continuous improvement plans.

TIME TO MARKET

Traditional	Transfor-mational	Digital Ready	Digital
∈ The commercialization life cycle to convert ideas into realized products is slow. ∈ Time to market takes longer compared to the overall market dynamic structure and needs.	∈ Same as the traditional organization but some trials are taking place to adopt the product development processes by adding some special exceptions for projects of a special nature to be developed and introduced in a more efficient manner.	∈ A fast time to market is achieved for a specific set of products and services in the product portfolio.	∈ A fast time to market is achieved through the acceptance of the fail fast-win fast approach.

THE
INNOVATIVE
DINOSAUR

DIGITAL READINESS AUDIT FINDING DETAILS

Audit Finding details is a setup that is recommended to be completed at least by the audit to clearly state the findings related to each of the above-described fourteen elements. This step to be completed by each of the audit participants, including each participant's justifications for their choices, is optional. It is better to include this step, though, as it will give insights into each of the participants — still, it is not mandatory and should be left to the discretion of the auditor.

Digital Enterprise Element	Audit Finding
Process & Methods	
SW Development Toolchain	
SW Development Teams	
Project Management	
Support Functions	
Commercial Teams	
Business Model	
Product Design & Customer Centricity	
Organization Leadership	
UX Design	
Ecosystem Approach	
Profitability Structure	
Lean & Agility	
Time to Market	

**THE
INNOVATIVE
DINESAUR**

ENTERPRISE INNOVATION AUDIT MAIN ELEMENT

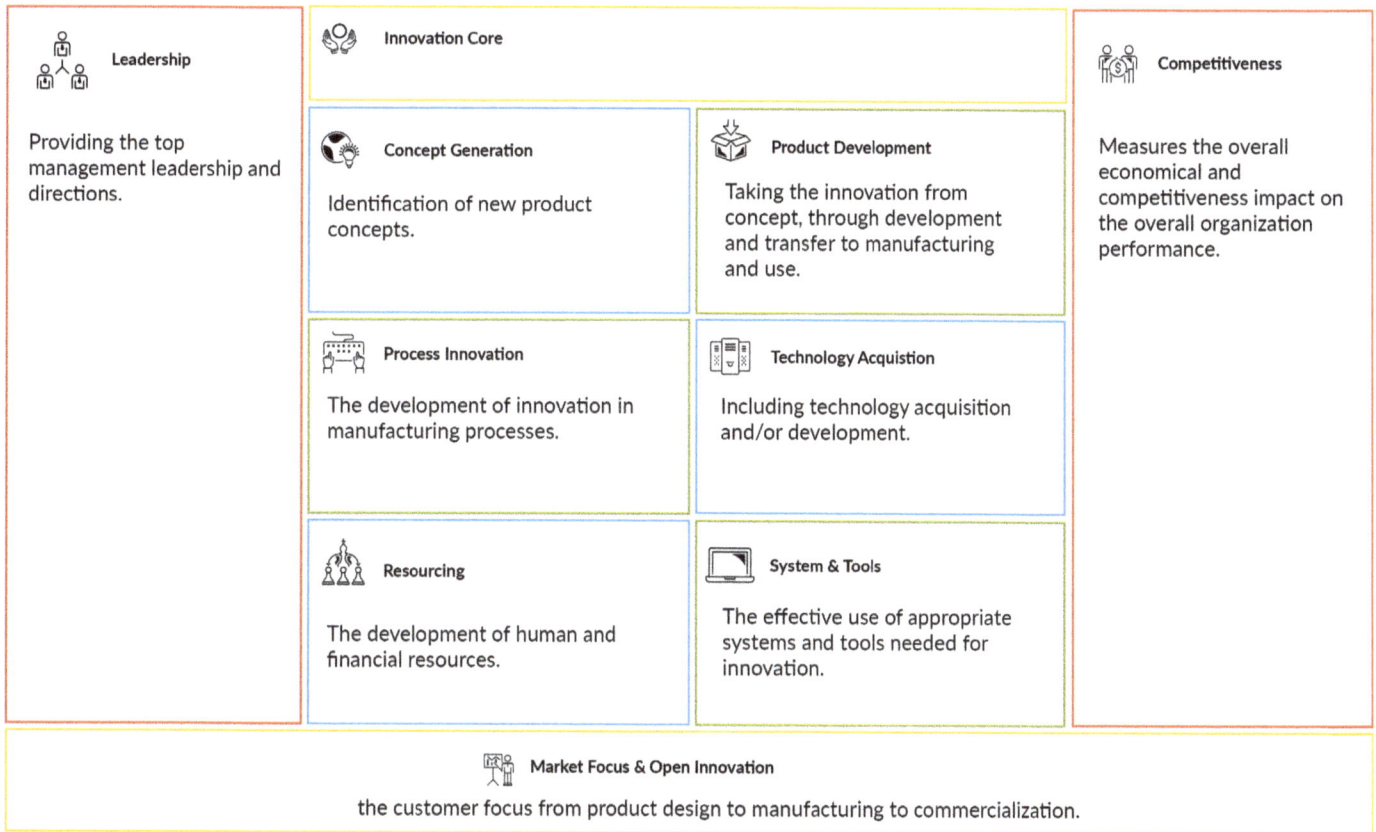

Leadership

Providing the top management leadership and directions.

Innovation Core

Concept Generation

Identification of new product concepts.

Product Development

Taking the innovation from concept, through development and transfer to manufacturing and use.

Process Innovation

The development of innovation in manufacturing processes.

Technology Acquistion

Including technology acquisition and/or development.

Resourcing

The development of human and financial resources.

System & Tools

The effective use of appropriate systems and tools needed for innovation.

Competitiveness

Measures the overall economical and competitiveness impact on the overall organization performance.

Market Focus & Open Innovation

the customer focus from product design to manufacturing to commercialization.

Designed by: Motaz Agamawi
www.theinnovativedinosaur.com

THE INNOVATIVE DINOSAUR

"Innovation audit is an essential first step for any organization that wants to adopt innovation as part of its strategy."

Innovation audits are an examination of current innovation practices. With such insight, the management team gains alternative and additional measures and techniques that may help them increase —even maximize their innovation capabilities.

In this section, we will provide a quick overview on Italian researcher Vittorio Chiesa's technical innovation audit, which focuses on the individual processes necessary for innovation and the degree to which the best practices are being used and implemented effectively. Chiesa's framework implies either an internal or external assessment of the practices used through comparison with the best known practices.

Understanding the Pillars of the Technical Capability Innovation Audit:

- **Concept Generation:** identifying new product concepts.
- **Product Development:** moving innovation from concept to development and then transferring it to manufacturing and use.
- **Process Innovation:** developing innovation in the manufacturing processes.
- **Development and Management:** including technology acquisition and /or development.
- **Resources:** developing human and financial resources.
- **Systems and Tools:** effectively utilizing the appropriate systems and tools needed for innovation.
- **Leadership:** leading and directing the top management. In reviewing the practices that are adopted to manage the innovation, we can assess: The degree to which there is an appropriate business process in place.
- The deployment of good practice, and the breadth of its use.
- The degree to which each practice meets the best-known standards.

The Chiesa's model covers four main processes: the identification of new product concept generation; taking innovation from concept to product launch; the development of innovation in the production process; and the development and management of the needed technology for each technology acquisition and development. The process and performance audits are to be done in tandem.

THE INNOVATIVE DINOSAUR

The objective of the complete audit is to offer companies an overview of their strengths and weaknesses with respect to technical innovation management, thus enabling them to highlight the areas that they should closely (re)examine. The model sets the scope of what is to be audited.

The model should view innovation as a business process, and it should directly address the managerial processes and organization mechanisms through which innovation is performed.

ENTERPRISE INNOVATION AUDIT
MAIN ELEMENT

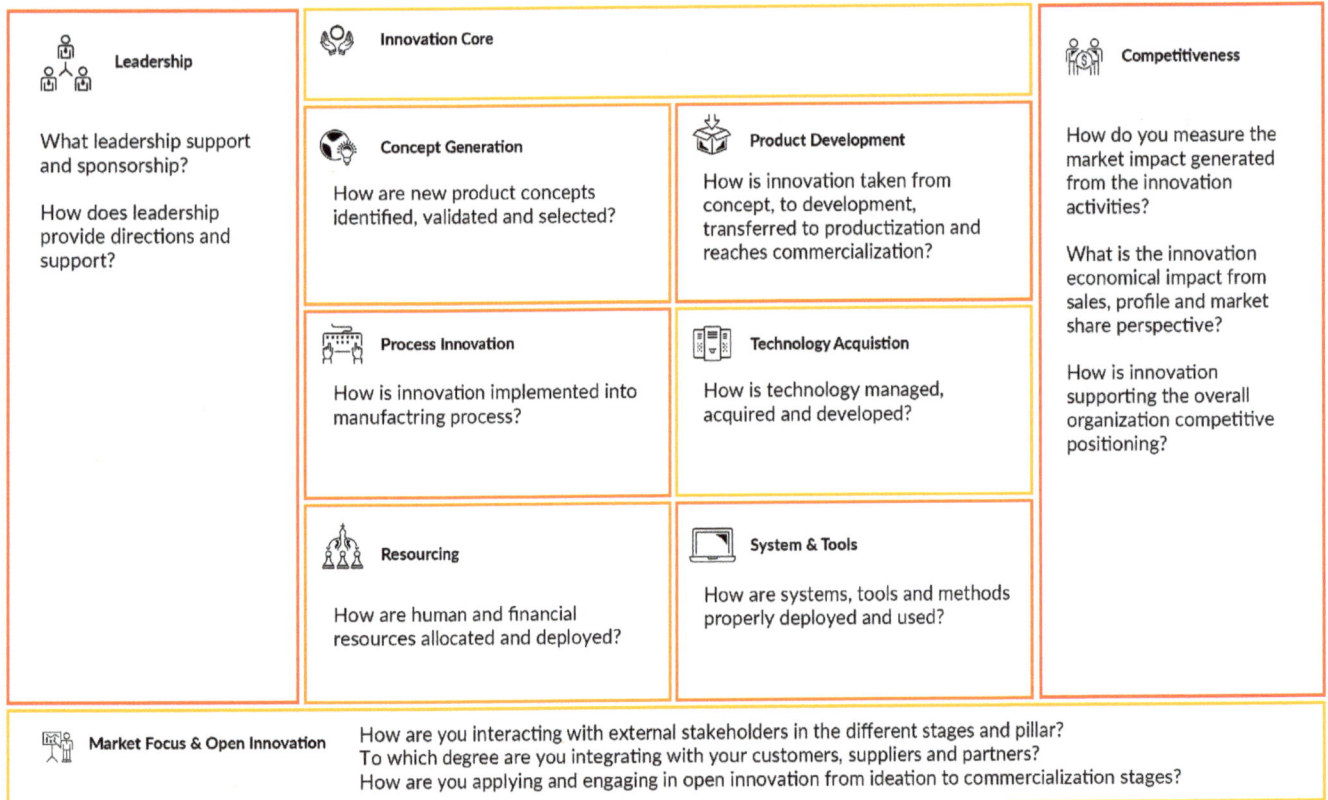

Leadership

What leadership support and sponsorship?

How does leadership provide directions and support?

Innovation Core

Concept Generation

How are new product concepts identified, validated and selected?

Product Development

How is innovation taken from concept, to development, transferred to productization and reaches commercialization?

Process Innovation

How is innovation implemented into manufactring process?

Technology Acquistion

How is technology managed, acquired and developed?

Resourcing

How are human and financial resources allocated and deployed?

System & Tools

How are systems, tools and methods properly deployed and used?

Competitiveness

How do you measure the market impact generated from the innovation activities?

What is the innovation economical impact from sales, profile and market share perspective?

How is innovation supporting the overall organization competitive positioning?

Market Focus & Open Innovation

How are you interacting with external stakeholders in the different stages and pillar?
To which degree are you integrating with your customers, suppliers and partners?
How are you applying and engaging in open innovation from ideation to commercialization stages?

THE INNOVATIVE DINOSAUR
WHAT IF DINOSAURS WERE INNOVATIVE

Designed by: Motaz Agamawi
www.theinnovativedinosaur.com

THE
INNOVATIVE
DINOSAUR

WE HAVE CREATED A CHECKLIST OF PROCESSES AND CONCEPTS FOR EACH PILLAR

Concept Generation
- How are new product concepts identified, validated, and selected?

Product Development
- How is the innovation moved from concept to development and then transferred to productization before reaching commercialization?

Process Innovation
- How is the innovation implemented into the manufacturing process?

Technology Acquisition
- How is technology managed, acquired, and developed?

Resources
- How are the human and financial resources allocated and deployed?

Systems & Tools
- How are the systems, tools, and methods deployed and used?

Leadership
- What is the leadership support and sponsorship?
- In what ways do the leaders provide directions and support?

Market Focus & Open Innovation
- How are external stakeholders interacted with in the different stages and pillars?

- To what degree the enterprise is integrating customers, suppliers and partners
- How the enterprise is applying and engaging in open innovation, from ideation to commercialization stages.

Competitiveness
- How is the market impact generated from the innovation activities measured?
- What is the innovation's economic impact from sales, profile, and market share perspectives?
- How is the innovation supporting the organization's overall competitive positioning?

There are many debates about the effectiveness and accuracy of enterprise technical innovation capability audits. Based on personal practical experience, I can confirm that such audits are quite useful for enterprises of different maturity stages in understanding the status quo related to the enterprise innovation capability and readiness. Once the status quo is understood through a structured framework and methods, innovation professionals are capable of formulating and implementing suitable strategies and initiatives that better manage and foster the enterprise's innovation capabilities.

ENTERPRISE INNOVATION AUDIT

		New Concept Generation	Inventiveness & Creativity	Innovation Planning	Exploiting Innovation
Core	**Concept Generation**	What is the sources of Innovation?	How is the org. structured to support & encourage Innovation?	How are you planning for innovation and TDP?	How do you asses, evaluate, select and fund innovation?
		Team Work & Organization	Idea to Manufacturing	Manufacturing to market	Industrial Design & Process
	Product Development	How NPD is managed & cross functional teams are integrated?	How are Engineering and Manufacturing linked, & changed are handled?	How are Manufacturing &Product design integrated and linked?	How are customer, experience and needs considered the process?
		Manufacturing Strategy	New Processes Imp.	Continuous Improvement	
	Process Innovation	How is existing capability assesed, & matched to market demand?	How are suppliers integrated & the ability to adapt based on capability VS needs?	Process, method & tools to identify gaps and benchmarking?	
		Technology Monitoring	Technology Strategy	Management of IP	
	Technology Acquisition	How are systematic monitoring of trends, technologies, competitors in place?	How is technology selection applied and Technology Development Plan compiled?	How is IP protected and exploited in a systematic manner?	
Support		Systems	Tools & Methods	Quality Assurance	
	Systems & Tools	How are systems in place to support NPD?	How are they placed to promote creativity, capture customer feedback & measure performance?	How is quality integrated in the life cycle?	
		Goals for Innovation	Funding	Talent Management	Organization Structure
	Resourcing	How are support functions and resources integrated & allocated?	How are funds allocated, flexible and managed?	How is talent sourced, engaged, involved and trained?	How are R&D, Manufacturing, support functions & resources integrated & allocated?
Input		Customer Involvement	Continuous Monitoring	Open Innovation	
	Market Focus	How is customer validation and feedback integrated?	How are needs, demands & competition monitored & considered ?	Degree of open innovation involvement and openness to external stakeholders	
		Strategy & Structure	Human Capital Allocation	Climate for Innovation	
	Leadership	How much is innovation strategy integrated in corporate strategy?	How much is org structure in favor of supporting innovation?	How does org. encourage ideation, risk taking and intrapreneurship?	

Designed by: Motaz Agamawi
www.theinnovativedinosaur.com

THE INNOVATIVE DINOSAUR

After understanding the basic concepts and pillars of the enterprise innovation capability audit, we can start discussing a simple method for conducting, executing, evaluating, and planning based on the audit findings. To be able to evaluate and audit each pillar of the enterprise innovation capability audit framework, we have designed major questions to be answered for each sub-pillar.

Goals

- ⊂ Assess the main pillars that define the enterprise innovation and inventiveness capabilities.
- ⊂ Identify the status quo of the enterprise innovation processes, methods and tools capability, maturity. and readiness.
- ⊂ Understand the current capabilities to better plan how to achieve the desired maturity.
- ⊂ Identify the gaps, weaknesses, and strengths compared to the desired state to be achieved.
- ⊂ The audit analysis result is the major input for all the steps to be followed, from planning to execution.

How to Use

The enterprise innovation capability audit pillars, excluding the competitiveness pillar, can be categorized into three main groups. The first group includes the core pillars, the second includes the support pillars, and the third includes the input pillars, which have a direct impact on the overall enterprise innovation capability.

- ⊂ The enterprise technical innovation capability audit is recommended to be conducted by a professional innovation audit assessor.
- ⊂ The assessor needs to conduct interviews with different stakeholders in order to fill the audit questions.
- ⊂ The target groups to be interviewed are recommended to represent the various populations of the organization, including different seniority levels, genders, ages, and, most importantly, the number of years served within the organization.
- ⊂ Interviewing the top management is essential, including the CEO of the enterprise, with an objective to understanding their perspective and perception of innovation.
- ⊂ It is recommended to formulate an internal innovation committee with wide supporter and influencer participation — in case the enterprise does not yet have an established innovation management function.
- ⊂ If it is acceptable from the perspective of top management, it will be optionally preferred to include a limited number of external stakeholders, like suppliers, partners, and maybe even customers, to understand their perceptions and expectations from the enterprise innovation position.
- ⊂ The audit needs to be conducted on an annual basis by following the PDCA methodology.

**THE
INNOVATIVE
DINESAUR**

DETAILS

To be able to evaluate and audit each pillar of the enterprise innovation capability audit framework, we have designed major questions to be answered for each sub-pillar. The detailed guide includes each question in a consolidated view.

Core Pillars	Concept Generation	Main Pillar Question: How are new product concepts identified, validated, and selected?	
		New Concept Generation	What are the sources of innovation? **Audit implications:** • Systematic monitor for market needs • Use feedback from customer • Building long-term relationships with customers
		Inventiveness & Creativity	How is the organization structured to support and encourage innovation? **Audit implications:** • Supporting new product ideas and initiative from employees • Rewarding entrepreneurial behavior • Circulating new product ideas • Structuring organization for favoring creativity and inventiveness
		Inventiveness & Creativity	How is the organization planning for innovation and the Technology Development Plan (TDP)? **Audit implications:** • Cross-functional screening of new product concept • Matching technological capabilities to market needs • Market-led planning process • Prioritizing product development projects • Integrating processes for generating new product concept, planning product innovation, and releasing new product

THE INNOVATIVE DINOSAUR

Product Development

Exploiting Innovation

How does the organization assess, evaluate, select, and fund innovation?

Audit implications:
- Evaluating alternatives for developing new business opportunities
- Selecting venture alternatives for entering new businesses
- Using governmental funding mechanisms

Main Pillar Question: How are new product concepts identified, validated, and selected?

Teamwork & Organization

How are new product development (NPD) managed and cross-functional teams integrated?

Audit implications:
- Managing the product development process
- Integrating all relevant functions in the product development process
- Facilitating communication among the different groups
- Managing process/task parallelism
- Rapid feedback, from manufacturing to design and engineering
- Defining the roles of project managers in the organization
- Use of cross-functional teams

Idea to Manufacturing

How are engineering and manufacturing linked and changes handled?

Audit implications:
- Linking manufacturing and engineering
- Handling engineering changes

THE INNOVATIVE DINOSAUR

Manufacturing to Market   How are manufacturing and product design integrated and linked?

Audit implications:
- Incorporating industrial design into product development
- Use of internal and external design experts

Industrial Design & Process   How are customers, experiences, and needs considered in the process?

Audit implications:
- Creating mechanisms for customer requirements information to be integrated into product design

Manufacturing Strategy   How are customers, experiences, and needs considered in the process?

Audit implications:
- Evaluating the capabilities of existing production processes
- Establishing a formal procedure for generating a manufacturing strategy
- Matching the process capabilities to the requirements of the marketplace
- Linking process innovation to product innovation
- Allocating resources to develop new process technologies
- Monitoring sources of new process innovation

New Process Improvement   How are suppliers integrated, in particular, their ability to adapt based on capability versus needs?

Audit implications:
- Matching technology complexity to adaptive capacity
- Managing the links with suppliers in the development and implementation
- Accompanying production process innovation with the appropriate
- changes in the organization
- Modifying performance measure to reflect the capability of the new process

THE INNOVATIVE DINOSAUR

Continuous Improvement How are processes, methods and tools implemented to identify gaps and conduct benchmarking?

Audit implications:
- Identifying opportunities for improvement in the process
- Integrating process improvement with quality control
- Benchmarking production process performance
- Involving manufacturing process developers in improvement after installation

Technology Acquisition

Main Pillar Question: How is technology managed, acquired, and developed?

Technology Monitoring Is there a systematic monitoring of trends, technologies, and competitors in place?

Audit implications:
- Systematically monitoring trends in existing and future technologies
- Assessing competitors' technology capabilities
- Identifying emerging technologies
- Understanding the organization's core technologies and competencies
- Building the required core competencies based on technology capabilities
- Relating technology to the business objectives and strategies

THE INNOVATIVE DINOSAUR

Support Pillars

System & Tools

Technology Strategy

How is the technology selection applied and the technology development plan compiled?

Audit implications:
- Choosing sources of technologies either in-house development, licensing, partnering, and/or external alliances
- Use of both qualitative and quantitative methods to evaluate R&D projects
- Corporate procedure for selecting R&D projects
- Identifying key issues in R&D organization, to support the firm's technology policy
- Favoring communication, and creating structural interface of R&D with other functions to optimize resources corporate-wide

Management of Intellectual Property

How is intellectual property (IP) both protected and exploited in a systematic manner?

Audit implications:
- Protecting IP, from patents to trademarks and copyrights
- Exploiting IP

Main Pillar Question: How are new product concepts identified, validated, and selected?

Systems

What systems are in place to support NPD?

Audit implications:
- Information and products used to support the process for product development
- Systems enhancing communication in the innovation process

THE INNOVATIVE DINOSAUR

Tools & Methods

How are the tools and methods are placed to promote creativity, capture customer feedback, and measure performance?

Audit implications:
- Using tools to capture customer feedback, needs, and demands
- Using tools for design of new products
- Using tools for promoting creativity
- Using tools to capture new product development ideas
- Using tools to capture the organization's best practices and knowledge sharing
- Using tools to capture customer complaints, incidents, and proposals for improvement
- Using all organization data sources together to generate correlations, insights, and accessibility for different team members within the organization

Quality Assurance

How is quality integrated in the life cycle?

Audit implications:
- Managing quality in the design
- Managing quality in the development
- Managing quality in the aftermarket
- Integrating process improvement and product innovation with quality management

Resources	Main Pillar Question: How are human and financial resources allocated and deployed?

Goals for Innovation

How are support functions and resources integrated and allocated?

Audit implications:
- Identify the key roles needed for managing innovation processes
- Recruiting, developing, evaluating, and rewarding human resources
- Establishing career development paths for technical people

Funding

How are R&D and innovation related funds allocated, and managed?

Audit implications:
- Stability of funding of R&D activities and technology acquisition
- Sharing risks and reducing costs of innovation through alliance networks
- Flexibility of funding with respect to product and process development

Talent Management

How is talent sourced, engaged, involved, and trained?

Audit implications:
- Identifying the talent's core distinctive competencies
- Capitalizing on the core competencies by building the proper soft and hard skill sets through continuous talent development programs
- Designing and implementing the proper performance evaluation mechanisms
- Implementing effective talent acquisition strategies for current and future competency needs
- Building and enforcing suitable technology-based organizational culture and mode of operations with processes, policies, and methods that reflect the business agility paradigm

Leadership	**Organization Structure**	How are R&D, manufacturing, support functions, and resources integrated and allocated? **Audit implications:**

Organization Structure

How are R&D, manufacturing, support functions, and resources integrated and allocated?

Audit implications:

- Defining the organization's mission in terms of technology and innovation
- Integrating innovation strategies with corporate strategies and plans
- Identifying the organization's core competencies
- Defining the perspectives of innovation and technical functions
- Designing the role of the organization's support functions in the innovation process, and how they support enforcing and leveraging the corporate innovation culture, from process, policies, methods to tools

Main Pillar Question: What is the leadership role in supporting and sponsoring innovation activities, initiatives and how do they provide guidance and strategic directions?

Strategy & Structure

To what degree is the innovation strategy integrated with the corporate strategy?

Audit implications:

- Determining the overall innovation management strategy, either in-house or external
- Defining the innovation competitive measure and Key Performance Indicator (KPI), including the corporate innovation impact definition
- Guaranteeing the innovation objectives reach all levels of the organization
- Defining the organization's priorities and balancing between normal operation and innovation resource allocation, including conflict resolution mechanisms

Leadership

THE
INNOVATIVE
DINOSAUR

Leadership

Organization Structure

How are R&D, manufacturing, support functions, and resources integrated and allocated?

Audit implications:

- Defining the organization's mission in terms of technology and innovation
- Integrating innovation strategies with corporate strategies and plans
- Identifying the organization's core competencies
- Defining the perspectives of innovation and technical functions
- Designing the role of the organization's support functions in the innovation process, and how they support enforcing and leveraging the corporate innovation culture, from process, policies, methods to tools

Main Pillar Question: What is the leadership role in supporting and sponsoring innovation activities, initiatives and how do they provide guidance and strategic directions?

Strategy & Structure

To what degree is the innovation strategy integrated with the corporate strategy?

Audit implications:

- Determining the overall innovation management strategy, either in-house or external
- Defining the innovation competitive measure and Key Performance Indicator (KPI), including the corporate innovation impact definition
- Guaranteeing the innovation objectives reach into all levels of the organization
- Defining the organization's priorities and balancing of normal operation and innovation resource allocation, including conflict resolution mechanisms

THE INNOVATIVE DINOSAUR

Human Capital Allocation To what degree does the organizational structure favor and/or support innovation?

Audit implications:
- Defining the enterprise innovation management function roles, responsibilities, and structure
- Allocating the proper caliber from competency and capacity perspectives
- Allocating the needed resource capacity for innovation and new product development activities
- Defining the relationship between innovation organization and other internal organizations and functions

Climate for Innovation How does the organization encourage ideation, risk-taking, and intrapreneurship?

Audit implications:
- Encouragement of new idea development, risk-taking, and intrapreneurship
- Defining a performance measurement system for encouraging innovation
- Identifying the degree to which innovation processes and policies are shared and understood across the organization

Market Focus	Main Pillar Questions: How does the organization interact with external stakeholders in the different stages and pillars? To which degree are they integrating with their customers, suppliers, and partners? And how are they applying and engaging in open innovation, from the ideation to commercialization stages?
Customer Involvement	How are customer validation and feedback integrated? **Audit implications:** • Implementation of idea validation strategies and the degree of involvement of current and anticipated customers • Integrating customer feedback and opinions in idea selection processes • Weight of customer desirability in the idea selection • Availing the channels and processes for validating ideas, proof of concepts and prototypes with target customers • Integrating the insights of customer relations management (CRM) into the innovation process • Integrating incident and management systems with the innovation process • Implementing mechanisms for capturing customer feedback and improvement proposals within the new product development lifecycle

Continuous Monitoring

How are needs, demands, and competition monitored and considered?

Audit implications:
- Continuous monitoring of industry trends and new technologies
- Continuous monitoring of consumer needs and expectations
- Continuous monitoring of megatrends, demographics, and social changes or disruptions
- Continuous analysis of consumer buying habits and purchasing criteria
- Continuous analysis of competing products
- Continuous analysis of competitors' offerings
- Continuous monitoring and analysis of changes in industry dynamics
- Continuous monitoring of direct and indirect competition offerings substitutes and major disruptions coming from other industries
- Monitoring of emerging startups and new business models

THE
INNOVATIVE
DINOSAUR

Open Innovation

To which degree are the open innovation initiatives and activities involving external stakeholders?

Audit implications:
- Involvement with universities and research centers
- Implementation of industry academia collaboration processes and strategies
- Allocation of external funds and research support programs participation level
- Engagement in activities that provide sponsorship of research and postgraduate activities
- Engagement in activities that support undergraduate activities and involvement
- Active participation with standard bodies and business representative organizations
- Implementing strategies, policies, and processes for scientific publications and conferences and other types of engagement with the scientific community
- Level of involvement with startup communities and existence of processes and policies supporting such partnerships
- Establishing a startup funding mechanism
- Existence of merger and acquisition strategies with needed allocated funds

ENTERPRISE INNOVATION MATURITY EVALUATION GRID

Core

Concept Generation

New Concept Generation	Inventiveness & Creativity	Innovation Planning	Exploiting Innovation

1 2 3 4 — 1 2 3 4 — 1 2 3 4 — 1 2 3 4 — 1 2 3 4

4

Product Development

Team Work & Organization	Idea to Manufacturing	Manufacturing to market	Industial Design & Process

3 1 2 3 4 — 1 2 3 4 — 1 2 3 4 — 1 2 3 4 — 1 2 3 4

2

Process Innovation

Manufacturing Strategy	New Process Implementation	Continuous Improvement

1 1 2 3 4 — 1 2 3 4 — 1 2 3 4 — 1 2 3 4

Technology Acquisition

Technology Monitoring	Technology Strategy	Management of IP

1 2 3 4 — 1 2 3 4 — 1 2 3 4 — 1 2 3 4

Support

4
3   **Systems & Tools**

Systems	Tools & Methods	Quality Assurance

1 2 3 4 — 1 2 3 4 — 1 2 3 4 — 1 2 3 4

2
1   **Resourcing**

Goals for Innovation	Funding	Talent Management	Organization Structure

1 2 3 4 — 1 2 3 4 — 1 2 3 4 — 1 2 3 4 — 1 2 3 4

Input

4
3   **Market Focus**

Customer Involvement	Continuous Monitoring	Open Innovation

1 2 3 4 — 1 2 3 4 — 1 2 3 4 — 1 2 3 4

2
1   **Leadership**

Strategy & Structure	Human Capital Allocation	Climate for Innovation

1 2 3 4 — 1 2 3 4 — 1 2 3 4 — 1 2 3 4

THE INNOVATIVE DINOSAUR
WHAT IF DINOSAURS WERE INNOVATIVE!

Designed by: Motaz Agamawi
www.theinnovativedinosaur.com

THE INNOVATIVE DINOSAUR

The enterprise internal maturity canvas is a scoring grid that provides a consolidated visual representation for the overall enterprise innovation capability audit pillars. The results will indicate the overall or average status of the enterprise innovation capability audit in a single view — one that helps guide the organization to the proper and suitable internal innovation strategy design.

Goals

- ∈ Represent audit result in a visual consolidated view
- ∈ Consolidate understandings of enterprise innovation readiness and capabilities
- ∈ Identify current gaps and areas of improvement Summarize enterprise innovation audit finding

How to Use

Based on your designed detailed questionnaire answers, mark each sub-pillar result, on a scale of one to four. Next, calculate the average of each sub pillars and mark the scale; the score of each main pillar is the result of the average of the related sub-pillars scales. Following that, calculate the average of each category's related main pillars and then mark the scale accordingly. The scale of each sub-pillar will encompass a clear definition to be used throughout the audit process, or the predefined questionnaire to be used by the auditor. The evaluation grid scoring card is customizable and can thus be tailored or adapted to specific requirements, needs, enterprise natures, and target contexts.

The context and objectives of the audit may differ from one organization to another. For instance, a service-based organization requires a certain customization that is irrelevant or nonessential to a manufacturing-based enterprise. Also, within the same organization, different business entities may require their own distinct version of the evaluation score card. Offshore and global delivery centers may have different natures —even different definitions. Based on these assumptions, and in many cases, the evaluation grid score card design may need customization, even in the same organization's entities. While designing the evaluation grid score card, the audit implications under each pillar and sub-pillar mentioned in the Enterprise Innovation Maturity Canvas must be considered and followed, particularly when applying the needed customization.

Details

For each sub-pillar below, the score card will be arranged on a scale of 1 (unsatisfactory) to 4 (excellent).

ENTERPRISE MATURITY EVALUATION GRID SCORE CARD

	1	**2**	**3**	**4**
New Concept Generation	Ad-hoc development of new product concept	Limited customer contact Product concept developed internally within single function Idea is internally generated, evaluated and developed without any validation from an external stakeholder.	New product concept sought out in the marketplace and research conducted into customer needs Involvement of marketing and technical functions in developing and screening new product concepts	Direct long-term relations with customers to access feedback and identify needs Continuous screening of opportunities and new trends Clear communication strategy for acquiring different team feedback, in particular, those working with customers
Innovation Planning	No planning	Planning for the next generation	Planning for up to two generations	Long-term planning for three generations Market-driven innovation planning

THE INNOVATIVE DINOSAUR

Inventiveness & Creativity

- The business environment discourages creativity
- New ideas are encouraged, but risk-taking is avoided
- Risk-taking to implement new ideas is encouraged
- Innovative and entrepreneurial behavior is rewarded
- Resources are available to fund unplanned activities

Teamwork & Organization

- No teamwork and little communication exist between the areas of functional expertise
- Some use of functional expertise or functionally based teams, but no project discipline or involvement of other functions
- Limited use of multi-functional teams; these project teams are disciplined and review progress
- Widespread use of multi-functional teams, with the early involvement of all
- Strong team leadership, with teams empowered to make decisions

Process of Innovation

- Not actively seeking new technology to support business processes
- No manufacturing, service, or business process strategy
- Process technology bought off-the-shelf and installed
- Without customization the technology often drives the process.
- Business strategies ensure that process capabilities support market or customer needs
- Investment(s) made in improving and developing systems and technologies
- Strong links between product, service, and process development
- Technology remains current with new processes

THE INNOVATIVE DINOSAUR

Market Focus

- Absence of market and competitors analysis
  No market channels

- Ad-hoc consumer interaction and consideration
- Ad-hoc competitor information
- Weak distribution channels
- No marketing activities

- Knowledge on consumer needs and competitors
- Existence of distribution channels
- Ad-hoc marketing activities

- Detailed market analysis and clear view on consumer needs
- Detailed competitive analysis and product competitive edge
- Well-established market channels and distribution
- Professional marketing plan and communication

Climate for Innovation

- Short-term financial viability and the avoidance of risk are encouraged at the expense of innovation

- General encouragement for innovation, but little or no measurement or reward for it

- Innovation is customer-driven
- Performance measures for innovation are reviewed regularly at the most senior business level

- Management encourages and rewards risk-taking and new ideas
- Each and every employee understands how technology and service development drive innovation

Goals for Innovation

- Little or no management involvement in innovation

- No innovation goals
  The value of innovation is not represented at the most senior business level

- Innovation and technology capability seen as a means of gaining a competitive edge and/or improving services

- Explicit and challenging goals are set for innovation with an understanding of how it can shape strategy in the long term

THE INNOVATIVE DINOSAUR

Human Capital Allocation

€ No human resource planning (HRP) for innovation; key innovation skills are missing from the business

€ The human resources needed for innovation are generally known and available, but slow to be accessed and applied

€ The skills required for innovation are identified and then fully resourced through recruitment and training

€ The business grows innovation competency through ongoing skill and career development in all functional areas

Funding

€ Status quo budget process, that is, no new thinking or fundamental changes from the previous year

€ Industry average levels are the baseline, with product or service development and training budgets being subjected to sharp fluctuations year after year

€ Policies are in place on how product or service development and training should be funded

€ Efforts to ensure that capacity for this is available from suppliers and external support functions

€ Financial resources are related to the potential contributions of products and services

€ Development and training can make to the business over the short- and long-term, with minimal fluctuations despite cash flow variations

Systems

€ Limited use of information or communication systems

€ The primary use of information and communication systems are within specific functional areas

€ There is widespread use of information and communication systems, but primarily for internal one-way information flow

€ Few systems link with suppliers and customers.

€ Systems are geared to improve business processes, service development, and delivery, in addition to shortening delivery times

€ Systems for both internal and external collaboration are in place

Tools

- No significant usage of business or process management tools
- Ad-hoc tool usage, with no clear objectives
- Some use of tools to improve products, service and process effectiveness and innovation.
- Widespread use of appropriate tools to capture customer needs and to ensure the effectiveness of products, services and process design.

Quality Assurance

- Status quo budget process, that is, no new thinking or fundamental changes from the previous year
- Industry average levels are the baseline, with product or service development and training budgets being subjected to sharp fluctuations year after year
- Policies are in place on how product or service development and training should be funded
- Efforts to ensure that capacity for this is available from suppliers and external support functions
- Financial resources are related to the potential contributions of that product or service
- Development and training can make to the business over the short- and long-term, with minimal fluctuations despite cash flow variations

Technology Monitoring

- No systematic means for internal and external environment competitive analysis and monitoring
- Narrative identification of core competencies Absence of core competency continuous improvement plans Absence of formal systematic monitoring for external and internal environments
- Systematic analysis for both external and internal environments in place
- Formal identification of core competency
- Absence of core competency improvement plans
- Technology acquisition and core competency strategies are not integrated with corporate business strategy
- Continuous systematic monitoring for both internal and external environments
- Core competency continuous improvement plans
- Technology roadmaps are in place, with consideration for future disruptive technologies
- Technology and business strategies are integrated, serving one other

Technology Strategy

- Absence of technology acquisition strategy
- No process for R&D projects identification in place
- No evaluation mechanism in place

- Technology acquisition sources are identified
- Quantitative evaluation for R&D projects are in place
- Favoring communication with other teams, without formal channels, is in place

- R&D issues are identified using formal procedure
- R&D project's selection procedure is in place
- Technology strategy is not formally designed
- Communication channels are in place

- Distinctive technologies are identified, and acquisition strategy is in place
- Technology acquisition is linked to business strategy
- Continuous qualitative and quantitative measures are in place
- Communication is encouraged, and formal channels are defined

Management of IP

- Absence of IP Strategy and process

- IP is encouraged but without a formal process

- IP is encouraged
- Formal IP process is in place
- Required funds are available
- Absence of IP strategy IP generation is not linked to organization strategy

- IP strategy is in place, serving organization objectives
- IP process and funds are in place

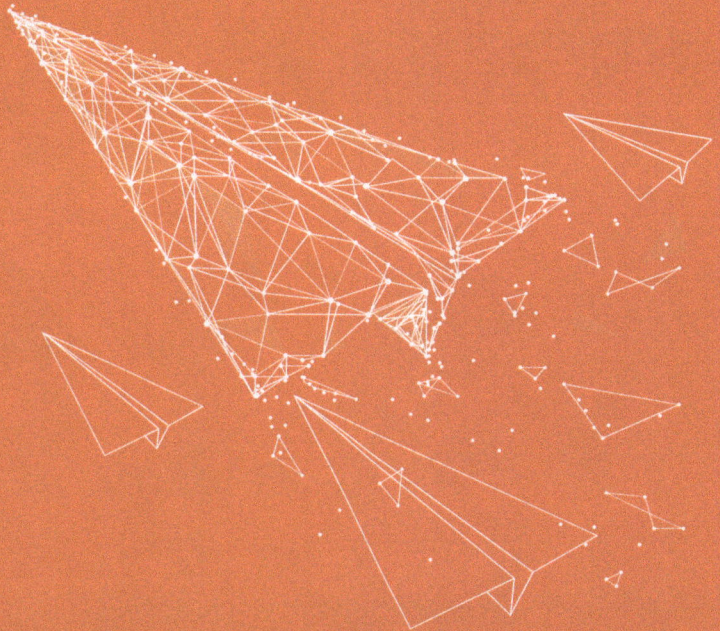

CHAPTER 7:
ENTERPRISE MANAGEMENT OF TECHNOLOGY, EXPLORED

We can define technology management as the integrated planning, designing, optimization, operation, and control of technological products, processes, and services. Or, for a more succinct definition, it is an organizational framework made for the use of technology and thus the human advantage. The central function of the technology management role is to gain insight into the value of certain technologies linked to the organization, fortifying the enterprise against its marketplace competitors by applying and/or producing the best innovative solutions in the game.

It is only when a technological advancement finds its market that research-and-development efforts are rewarded in terms of economic and social impact. Technological breakthroughs present new frontiers and vistas for industrial development and economic growth. When we talk about technology, we must mention technology innovation. Since scientific discoveries and basic research generally emerge without instantaneous commercial value, they fall into the hands of universities and research centers. Inventions are described as the applied science through which scientific discoveries are shaped into physical structures and processes; they may or may not be developed into marketable products. Innovation, on the other hand, is the adoption of invention(s) and the process(es) through which invention is introduced to markets, i.e., the commercialization process. Even though markets (buyers) may ignore the innovation, by diffusing it, the wealth creation process is initiated.

In this chapter, we will

- Define the main characteristics of differentiation between the management of technology and the management of business administration paradigms and
- Reach a common understanding of the terms "technology" and "innovation."

THE
INNOVATIVE
DINOSAUR

CHAPTER SEVEN LIST OF TOOLS, DIAGRAMS, AND ILLUSTRATIONS

1. TID Illustration: Forms of Technology
2. TID Illustration: Innovation Wealth Creation
3. TID Illustration: Technology Generations S-Curve
4. TID Illustration: Distinction between Creativity, Invention and Innovation
5. TID Illustration: Sequence of Discovery, Invention and Innovation
6. TID Illustration: Types and Forms of Innovation
7. TID Illustration: Innovation Topology
8. TID Illustration: Key Stakeholders in Technology Innovation
9. TID Illustration: Product Technology Classification

CHAPTER SEVEN SECTIONS:

- ∈ What is meant by the term Technology?
- ∈ Management of Technology VS Management of Business Administration
- ∈ What is Innovation?
- ∈ Why is an Organization Innovative?

THE INNOVATIVE DINCSAUR

CHAPTER SEVEN LIST OF REFERENCES & EXTRA READINGS

1. Customized Management of Technology by Tarek Khalil
2. The Strategy of Management Innovation and Technology, Murray R. Millsom and David Wilemon
3. Entrepreneurship a contemporary approach
4. Futuring, the exploration of future, Edward Cornish
5. Entrepreneurship, starting and operating a small business, by Steve Mariotti
6. Innovation and Entrepreneurship by Peter F. Drucker
7. Exploring Innovation, by David Smith

WHAT IS MEANT BY THE TERM TECHNOLOGY?

To start, we need to agree on what is meant by 'technology,' both fundamentally and universally. Simply, technology is the way we do things. It is the knowledge applied in products, processes, tools, methods, and systems for achieving objectives and missions. In the context of development, it is the creation of goods and the delivery of services.

"In essence, technology is all of the knowledge, products, processes, tools, methods, and systems employed in the delivery of goods and services."

HARD WARE
The physical structure and logical layout of the equipment or machinery that is to be used to carry out the required tasks.

SOFT WARE
The knowledge of how to use the hardware in order to carry out the required tasks.

BRAIN WARE
The reason for using the technology in a particular way.

KNOW HOW
The practical knowledge of how to get Technology done.
As opposed to "know-what" (facts), "know-why" (science), Know-How is often a tacit knowledge

Designed by: Motaz Agamawi
www.theinnovativedinosaur.com

THE INNOVATIVE DINOSAUR

Growing out of this definition, technology assumes an array of forms, including hardware, software, brainware, and know-how. Hardware is the physical structure and logical layout of the equipment or machinery that may be used to carry out required tasks. Software is the collected knowledge on how to use the hardware in order to carry out those tasks. Brainware is the reason for using the technology in a particular way. And know-how is the practical knowledge of how to design, develop, and create a specific technology.

NATURAL RESOURCES ➤ PRODUCT TECHNOLOGY ➤ PRODUCTION TECHNOLOGY ➤ MARKET PLACE ➤ CUSTOMER SATISFACTION

By understanding the meaning of technology, we can then define 'technology management' as the integrated planning, design, optimization, operation, and control of technological products, processes, and services. Or, for a more precise definition, it is an organizational framework for the use of technology and the human advantage. The main function of the technology management role is to gain insight into the value of certain technologies for the organization, and to fortify the firm against its marketplace competitors by applying and/or producing the best innovative solutions in the game. As a set of robust and dynamic management disciplines, it helps organizations to oversee their technological fundamentals to create competitive advantages. The typical concepts of technology management include:

Technology strategy as the logic or role of technology in the organization

Technology forecasting as the identification of possible relevant technologies for the organization, possibly through technology scouting

Technology roadmap as the mapping of technologies to business and market needs

Technology project as a set of projects under development

Technology portfolio as a set of technologies in use

Innovation management as the integrated concepts of enterprise innovation management

High-tech marketing as the understanding of the special nature of technology marketing, like disruptive innovation concepts

THE
INNOVATIVE
DINOSAUR

MANAGEMENT OF TECHNOLOGY VS MANAGEMENT OF BUSINESS ADMINISTRATION

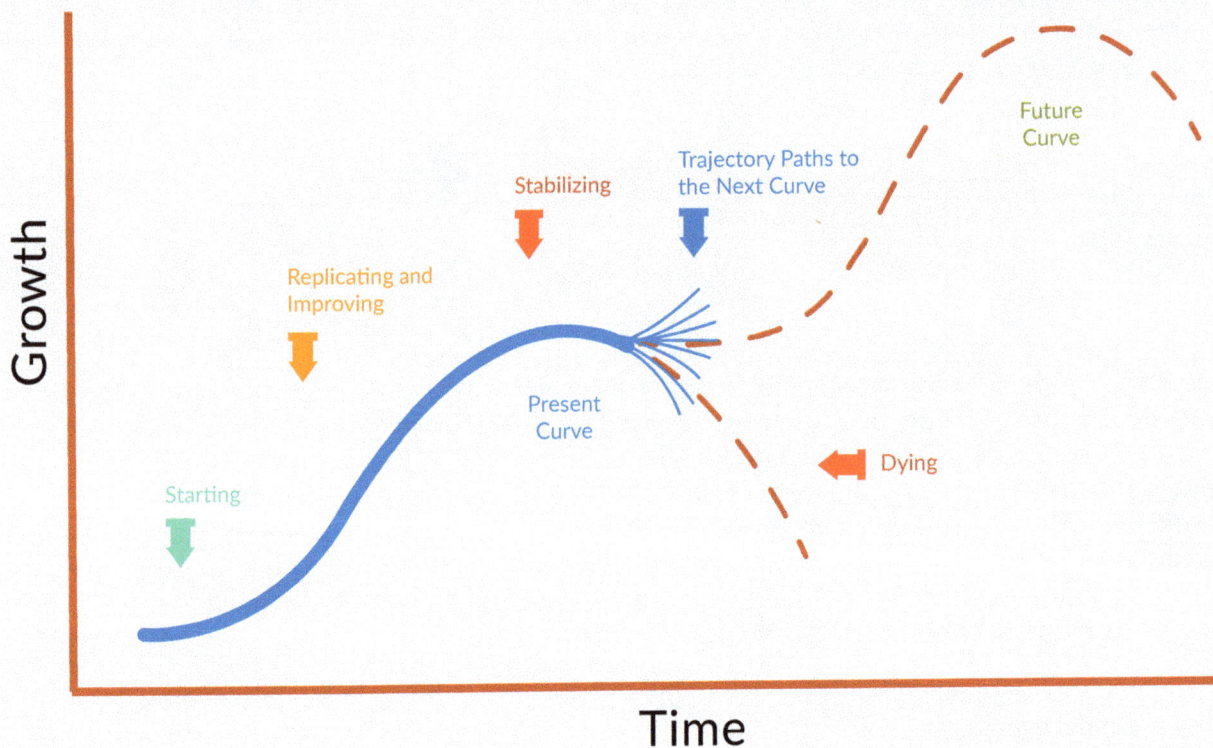

Designed by: Motaz Agamawi
www.theinnovativedinosaur.com

THE
INNOVATIVE
DINOSAUR

This decades-old social science theory suggests that all innovations follow a similar diffusion pattern, popularly known as the 's' curve, even though they are originally based upon the concept of a standard distribution of adopters. Such distribution follows a technology adoption lifecycle, which is a model that describes the acceptance of a new innovation according to the demographic and psychological characteristics of defined customer groups, named the 'adopters.' Clustered groups of adopters follow a normal distribution over a curve which is following a bell curve representation. In broad terms, the s-curve directs our attention to the four phases of a technology lifecycle: emergence, growth, maturity, and aging. Another major contribution to this area is Carnegie Mellon University's Capability Maturity Model Integration, which includes maturity-level testing for the determination of repeatability, definition, management, and optimization. This model indicates that any organization must master one level before being able to proceed to the next. And another comes from the Gartner Hype Cycle methodology, which presents a yearly 'hype cycle' that depicts technological trends and how, according to the firm, "they are potentially relevant to solving real business problems and exploiting new opportunities." Our modern technology marketing approach results in technologies being over hyped in the early stages of growth, although the proper understanding of this cycle helps technology managers to separate hypes from real drivers, compare technology business value with respect to the objectivity of analysts, and reduce the technology investment risk.

All together, these concepts form a formalized foundation for our approach to managing technology; meanwhile, they also lead to differentiations between traditional business management (MBA) and Management of Technology (MOT) disciplines.

THE INNOVATIVE DINOSAUR

WHAT IS INNOVATION?

Creativity	The ability to create something new	Perquisite of Invention and Innovation
Invention	The creation of something new	Results in new knowledge
Innovation	The Transformation of an idea or resource into useful application	Result in a new product, service or processes

Designed by: Motaz Agamawi
www.theinnovativedinosaur.com

THE
INNOVATIVE
DINOSAUR

Creativity is the ability to bring ideas, either new or renewed, to life. It is an ability, not an activity. People are either born or made creative, but we often train them out of their innovative impulses by imposing organizing principles and systems at every corner and in every mind. An invention may be a novel device, method, process, composition, or discovery. It may also signal improvement — a reimagining — or an alternate means for achieving an existing and desired outcome or function. While invention is the activity of bringing something new into the world, innovation is the process of doing new things and eventually introducing creative ideas, or inventions, to the market.

Creativity is an impetus of entrepreneurship, and innovation is the process of entrepreneurship. "Innovation," the late management consultant Peter Drucker once said, "is the means by which the entrepreneur either creates new wealth-producing resources or endows existing resources with enhanced potential for creating wealth." In other words, innovation implies multifaceted action, not simply thinking up a novel idea or method. After we pass through the illumination and verification stage of creativity, we may become inventors, but we are not yet innovators.

THE
INNOVATIVE
DINOSAUR

INVENTION

INNOVATION

MARKET PLACE

SCIENTIFIC DISCOVERY

It is only when a technological advancement finds its market that research-and-development efforts are rewarded in terms of economic and social impact.

Designed by: Motaz Agamawi
www.theinnovativedinosaur.com

THE INNOVATIVE DINOSAUR

Technological breakthroughs present new frontiers and vistas for industrial development and economic growth. Scientific knowledge focuses on natural phenomena, while staying neutral on the question of how such research and findings may be (mis)used. Historically, scientific knowledge and technology progressed slowly. By the mid-nineteenth century, though, science and technology started to interact with one another in immediate, unavoidable, and irreversible ways; the real explosion in knowledge and technology was triggered off. When we discuss science, we tend to highlight the disciples' endless discoveries — but when we talk about technology, we mention technology innovation. Since scientific discovery and basic research have no instantaneous commercial value, this is why they are the role of universities and research centers. Inventions are the applied science by which scientific discoveries are shaped into physical structures and processes. They may or may not be developed into marketable products. Innovation, on the other hand, is the adoption of invention and the process by which invention is introduced to markets through the commercialization process. Markets (buyers) may embrace or ignore the innovation. By diffusing the innovation, the wealth creation process is initiated.

Technology is an expression of human creativity. Managing technology requires continuous efforts in creating the technology itself or reimagining an existing one, developing novel products and services, and successfully marketing them.

It requires great creativity along with a system designed to exploit — maximize the benefit and usage of — them. Further afield, it requires an investment in research and development (R&D), which is often a costly endeavor, not to mention a potentially risky one, too. The management of technology is an investment in the future to be neither neglected nor its value underestimated. Technology creation and exploitation rely on a chain of events, starting with inventions and ending at the marketplace.

Innovation has many forms, with process or product innovation being among the most common and thus important.

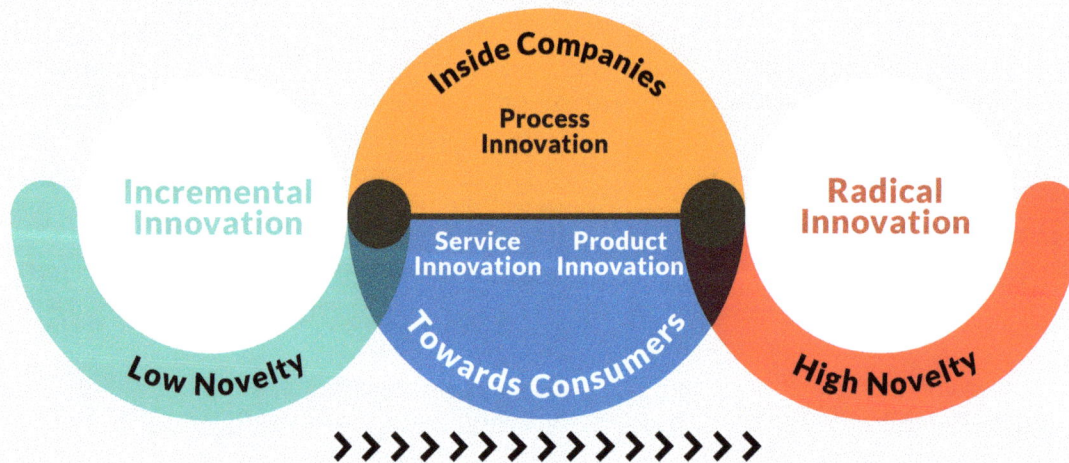

Inside Companies

Process Innovation

Incremental Innovation

Service Innovation   Product Innovation

Radical Innovation

Low Novelty

Towards Consumers

High Novelty

Designed by: Motaz Agamawi
www.theinnovativedinosaur.com

THE INNOVATIVE DINOSAUR

Process innovation is the implementation of a new or significantly-improved production or delivery method (e.g., major changes in techniques, equipment, and/or software). Product innovation is the creation and subsequent introduction of a new good or service, or an improved version of one already on the market. Companies may innovate either incrementally or radically, which are succinct ways of saying "little by little" or "full steam ahead." Incremental innovation is not about sweeping changes; rather, think of it as cost cutting or feature improvements in existing products or services. Radical innovation is about introducing something that does not yet exist. It involves circumventing, not fighting, competition: instead of fighting for market share, a company steps aside and simply creates its own market à la the Blue Ocean strategy — which is based on "an analogy to describe the wider, deeper potential to be found in unexplored market space.

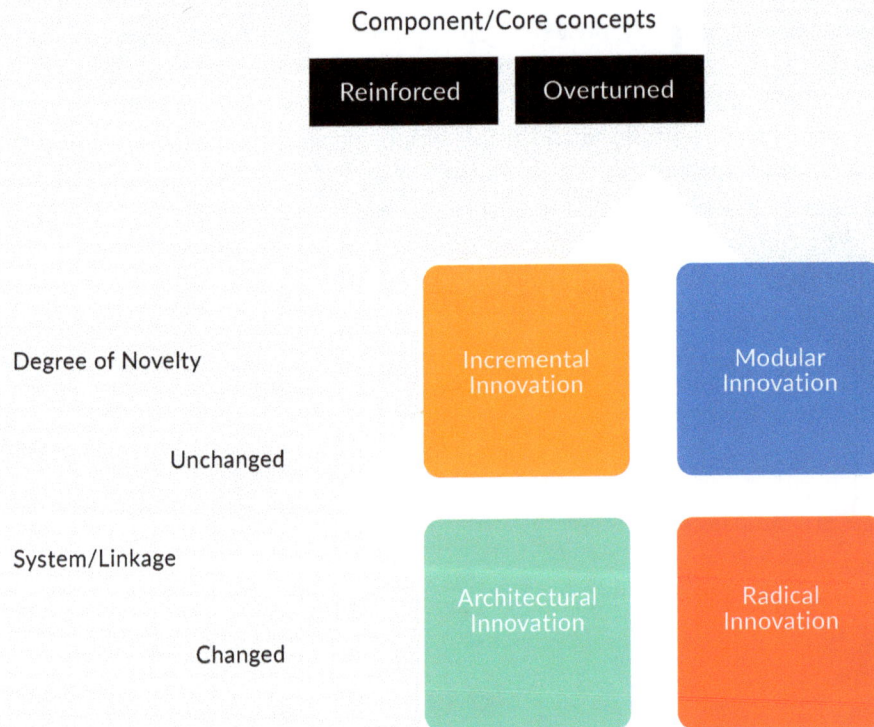

Designed by: Motaz Agamawi
www.theinnovativedinosaur.com

THE
INNOVATIVE
DINOSAUR

> ## TECHNOLOGY, AND ITS PROPER MANAGEMENT, CREATES WEALTH FOR NATIONS, ENTERPRISES, AND INDIVIDUALS ALIKE.

Business competitiveness is no longer a matter of choice: it's a matter of survival in a global marketplace. Technology is an indispensable aspect of most societies today, as though it's the engine of our modern lifestyles, signifying our society's standard of living. Enterprises are often built and organized to function around a core technology. The most successful ones utilize appropriate technology and manage technological change to gain an edge in the marketplace.

> ## WE CANNOT MANAGE INNOVATION: WE MUST MANAGE FOR INNOVATION.

To "manage for innovation" means that we design our processes, values, and culture to support fostering the needed creative environment. The main pillars of the innovative environment, based on Tarek Khalil's book *Customized Management of Technology*, include:

- Freedom
- Challenge
- Solid project management
- Sufficient time and resources
- Recognition
- Encouragement of pressure

THE INNOVATIVE DINOSAUR

Environment obstacles for creativity

- Constraints
- Evaluation and judgment
- Weak project management
- Insufficient time and resources
- Organization disinterest
- Overemphasis on statuesque
- Internal competition
- Unhealthy pressure

Characteristics of innovative organizations

- Motivated and motivational
- Fair evaluation of work (even failure)
- Mechanism for developing ideas
- Values creativity
- Sense of leadership
- Reward and recognition
- Sense of respect (others and self)
- Open, active Communication
- Orientation to risk
- Presence of sufficient time
- Presence of necessary expertise
- Allocation of effective funds
- Availability of material resources
- Mature systems and processes
- Availability of relevant information
- Quality of offered training
- Lack of so-called 'turf wars' (aka. office politics)
- Constructive, not destructive, criticism
- Wise management (absence of strict controls)
- No excess of formal structures

Fostering a culture of innovation is the cornerstone of any successful innovation initiative — and it's not just a top-down decision. Innovation is achieved through people, and people are not machines. They must be convinced by the innovation, and so the management challenge is to reach the seemingly unchangeable minds.

THE INNOVATIVE DINOSAUR

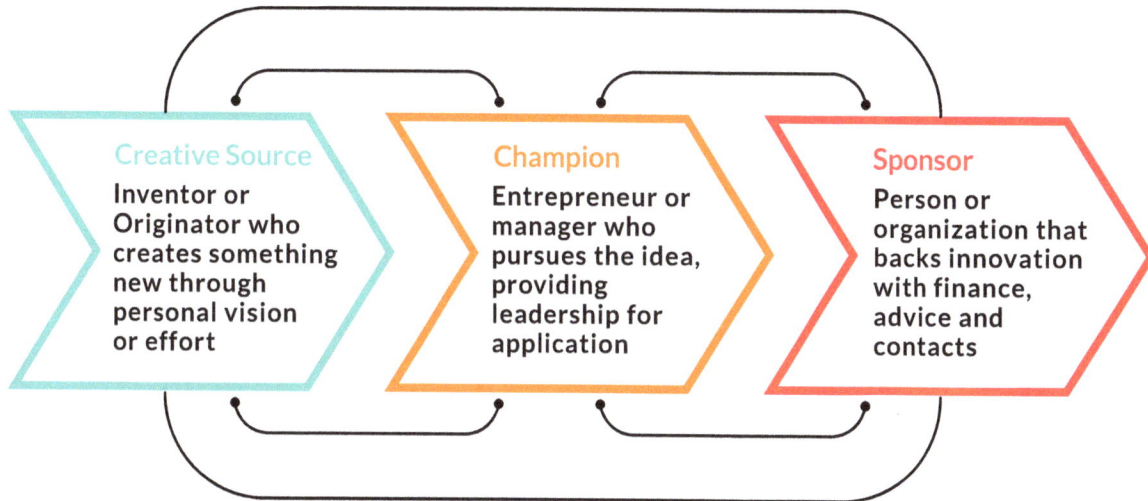

Creative Source
Inventor or Originator who creates something new through personal vision or effort

Champion
Entrepreneur or manager who pursues the idea, providing leadership for application

Sponsor
Person or organization that backs innovation with finance, advice and contacts

THE INNOVATIVE DINOSAUR
WHAT IF DINOSAURS WERE INNOVATIVE

Designed by: Motaz Agamawi
www.theinnovativedinosaur.com

THE INNOVATIVE DINOSAUR

For a technology innovation to succeed, there are essential players involved and key conditions to fulfill. All together, these professionals and organizational conditions satisfy the necessity for creativity and implementation. According to Customized Management of Technology, the following seven conditions are required for the success of technology innovation:

- ∈ An accomplished professional in an executive leadership position to reinforce strategic decisions that encourage the development of creativity and an innovation.
- ∈ An operational leader to conduct and oversee the fundamental duties related to adapting acquired knowledge into commercial goods and services.
- ∈ An evident demand for the commercial application by an adequate number of prospective consumers to offer grounds for a financial investment in an innovation.
- ∈ The product or service represents a worthwhile innovation that adds value to society.
- ∈ Solid cooperation between the essential players, from the top to the many diversified functions or teams in the organization; together, they must bring R&D to full fruition.
- ∈ Availability of resources and the supporting technology to succeed in the endeavor.
- ∈ Coordination with external players who may help steer the success of an innovation via their relationships with government agencies, investors, suppliers, and creditors.

The organization's ability to recognize its core competency relies upon its insight into what we know how to do best, or what we can do that no other organization can rival. A company that knows specific core competency must make sure that it has the capability to achieve it, at the very least in its immediate marketplace. In fact, a realized core competence may pave a pathway to a wide variety of markets. At the same time, it should also make a significant contribution to the perceived customer benefits of the product or service, especially one that's difficult for competitors to imitate. Core competency begets competitiveness, so companies need to select and target areas in which to build core competence in technology. Following that, they must move to possess state-of-the-art technology in those areas while tracking the impact on business and modifying their strategies accordingly.

In sum, to the companies that ask, "what do we do with our core competency?" — I suggest you develop your central capabilities, surround your competencies with barriers, deploy them as widely as possible, and realign all remaining activities.

Distinctive Technology

Technologies that give the company distinctive advantage

Basic Technology

Necessary for operation but does not distinguish the company from competitors

External Technology

Complimentary technologies required to fulfill the service, not related to the core business, do not distinguish the company from competitors and do not have a distinctive competitive advantage

Designed by: Motaz Agamawi
www.theinnovativedinosaur.com

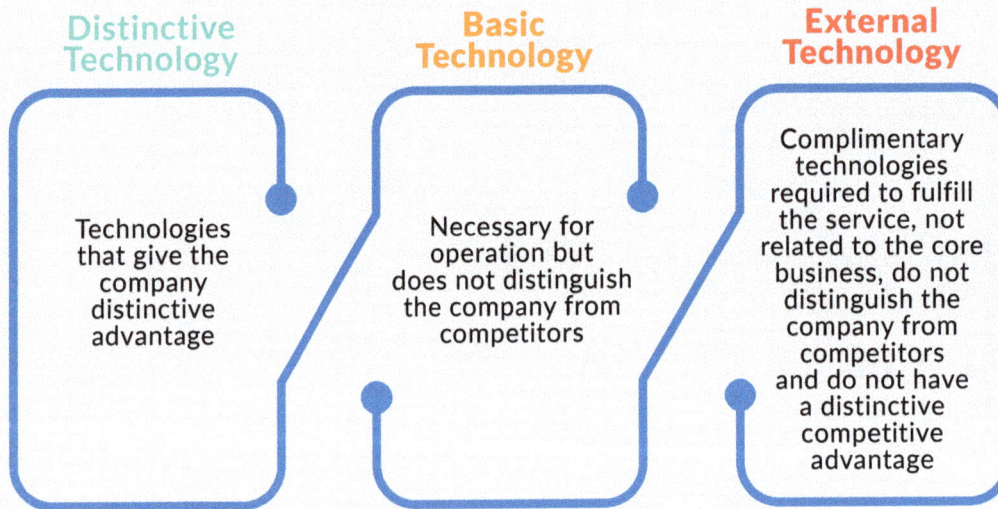

THE INNOVATIVE DINOSAUR

Next, the ability of the organization to conduct proper technology classification comesintofocus,ortheidentificationofitsdistinctive,basic,andexternaltechnologies. This classificatory process helps the organization properly and decisively build its own core competencies by understanding the technologies both at hand and within reach. Based on this classification, the organization prioritizes its investments and resources as follows.

- € Do not invest in basic technology development, but rather invest your time in understanding how to use and integrate it.
- € Acquire external technologies through partnership, alliances, or outsourcing, with a minimum investment of your own time.
- € Complete ownership of the distinctive technologies through in-house development.

CHAPTER 8:
BUILDING THE INNOVATION ORGANIZATION

The organization's true competencies are represented in the knowledge, know-how, and experiences of its own team. Accordingly, the enterprise innovation culture should empower, activate, motivate, educate, and engage team members in the enterprise innovation activities. Where do we begin — from the human desirability angle, or the technical feasibility angle, or the business viability angle? As if we are able to make sure that our team members possess the adequate desirability level to engage and participate in the innovation process, then we can manage to leverage both feasibility and viability. When the intersection between the three elements — human desirability, technical feasibility, business viability — occurs, this is the only time that the desired innovation impact can be reach.

The end goal of the enterprise's activities is to achieve a commercially successful and competitive offering. To do so, we must devise strategies that lead to different internal and external initiatives and programs. When integrated, these initiatives and programs accumulate new ideas for the idea funnel, introduce the most competitive concepts to the development stage, and then cultivate another set of the most developed ideas with impact and outreach in mind. But first, we must design innovation boosters while also collaborating externally with the various ecosystem stakeholders.

In this chapter, we will

- ⌁ Describe frameworks and methods that are to ensure that our strategies and initiatives are integrated to achieve our targets and objectives.
- ⌁ Assist enterprise innovation management teams in designing strategies, analyzing the taskforce personas to better understand their motives and achieve a high(er) level of engagement, and maintaining a unified view for all of the initiatives, programs, and activities that foster the impact of our innovation management investment.

**THE
INNOVATIVE
DINESAUR**

CHAPTER EIGHT SECTIONS:

€ Enterprise Innovation Strategy Starting Point: A User-centric Approach
€ Enterprise Innovation Fostering Strategy – Main Elements
€ Enterprise Innovation Maturity Roadmap Canvas
€ Enterprise Innovation Initiatives
€ Interactive Design Canvas
€ Enterprise Innovation 4I Approach
€ Enterprise Team Inventiveness Distribution

CHAPTER EIGHT LIST OF TOOLS, DIAGRAMS, AND ILLUSTRATIONS

1. TID Illustration: Enterprise Innovation Strategy Starting Point- A People Centric Approach
2. TID Illustration: Fostering Strategy - Main Elements
3. TID Illustration: Enterprise Innovation i4 Approach
4. TID Illustration: Enterprise Team Inventiveness Definitions
5. TID Illustration: Enterprise Innovation Initiative Interactive Canvas Details
6. TID Canvas: Enterprise Inventiveness Distribution
7. TID Canvas: Innovation Initiatives VS Inventiveness Persona Coverage
8. TID Canvas: Enterprise Innovation Initiatives Interactive Design Canvas
9. TID Canvas: Innovation Initiative Design Canvas
10. TID Canvas Example: Enterprise Innovation Maturity Roadmap - With Examples
11. TID Canvas Example: Innovation Initiative Interactive Design Canvas Examples

THE
INNOVATIVE
DINESAUR

CHAPTER EIGHT LIST OF REFERENCES & EXTRA READINGS

1. The Innovator's Dilemma, by Clayton M. Christensen
2. The Innovator's Solution, by Clayton M. Christensen
3. Game Storming, by Dave Gray, Sunni Brown and James Macanufo
4. Communicating the New, by Kim Erwin
5. Make space, by David Kelley
6. Gathering and Using Information for the Selection of Technology Partners. EDWIN J. NIJSSEN, RIK VAN REEKUM, and HENRIE¨TTE E. HULSHOFF.
7. Factors Required for Successful Implementation of Futures Research in Decision Making. Book Review by Glenn, T. J. Gordon and J. C. 2001
8. On the Future of Technological Forecasting. VARY COATES, MAHMUD FAROOQUE, RICHARD KLAVANS, KOTY LAPID, HAROLD A. LINSTONE, CARL PISTORIUS, and ALAN L. PORTER.
9. Kickbox foundation, by Adobe
10. Ideo tools
11. openideo
12. Innovation Academy
13. Certified Innovation Manager
14. IMP³ROVE
15. Global Innovation Institute
16. Infodev

THE
INNOVATIVE
DINOSAUR

ENTERPRISE INNOVATION STRATEGY STARTING POINT A PEOPLE CENTRIC APPROACH

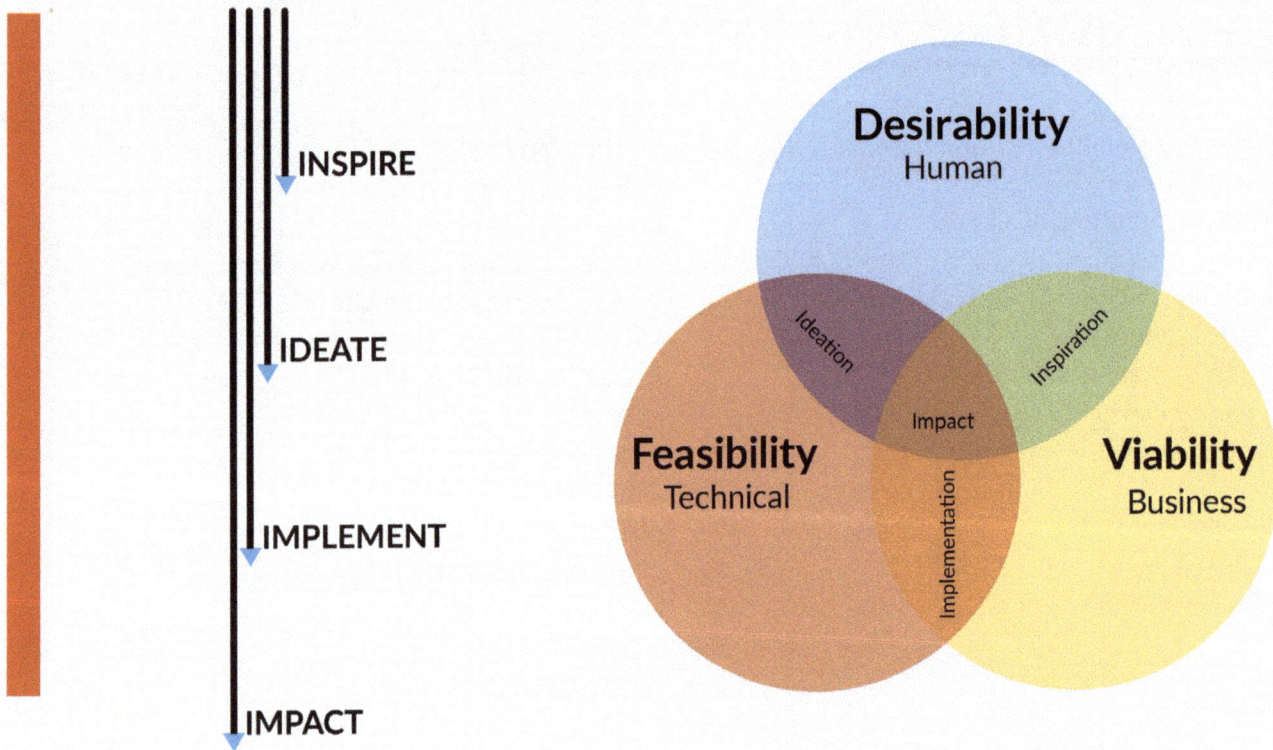

INSPIRE

IDEATE

IMPLEMENT

IMPACT

Desirability
Human

Ideation

Inspiration

Impact

Feasibility
Technical

Implementation

Viability
Business

THE INNOVATIVE DINOSAUR
WHAT IF DINOSAURS WERE INNOVATIVE?

Designed by: Motaz Agamawi
www.theinnovativedinosaur.com

THE INNOVATIVE DINOSAUR

> **It is all about people. We cannot manage innovation; we manage for innovation.**

DESCRIPTION

The most precious asset of any enterprise is its people. People, or team members, are the ones who develop and deliver products and then sell them to customers while offering their immediate and continued support. They develop experiences that lead to knowledge in the form of know-how, know-what, and know-when. From each late delivery and each product issue or bug, to each best practice, all the successes and all the failures are investments in the people employed and involved. In other words, the organization's true competencies are represented in the knowledge, know-how, and experiences of its own team.

GOALS

The enterprise innovation culture should empower, activate, motivate, educate and engage team members in the enterprise innovation activities.

THUS, THE QUESTION IS: WHERE DO WE BEGIN?

Is it from the human desirability factor, from the technical feasibility, or from the business viability aspects. As if we are able to achieve that our team members possess the adequate desirability level and will to engage and participate in the innovation process, then we can manage to leverage both feasibility and viability.

When the intersection between the three above-stated elements — human desirability, technical feasibility, business viability — occurs, this is the only time that the desired innovation impact can be reach.

THE INNOVATIVE DINOSAUR

- ∈ When human desirability and technical feasibility intersect, this is
- ∈ When ideation happens and great ideas start to evolve.
- ∈ When human desirability and business viability intersect, this is when inspiration strikes and a chain reaction of passion unfolds.
- ∈ When technical feasibility and business viability intersect, this is when ideas are implemented.
- ∈ When the three elements converge, in the form of intersecting ideation with inspiration and implementation, this is what leads to impact and innovation success.

> " "
> **INNOVATION SUCCESS AND IMPACT ONLY EMERGE WHEN HUMAN DESIRABILITY INTERSECTS WITH TECHNICAL FEASIBILITY AND BUSINESS VIABILITY.**
> " "

ENTERPRISE INNOVATION MATURROADMAP STRATEGY – MAIN ELEMENTS

Better Innovation Environment
by harnessing the collective power of our people, to be able to gather insights and ideas through a proven design thinking process.

Motivate

Educate

Fostering & transforming cultures

Connecting & engaging teams

People are the fuel of Innovation

Improve Innovation Culture
by valuing our people ideas and contribution across the entire organization. To increase company wide engagement and reduce silo mentality.

Facilitate

Recognize

Designed by: Motaz Agamawi
www.theinnovativedinosaur.com

THE INNOVATIVE DINOSAUR

HOW TO USE

THE ENTERPRISE INNOVATION FOSTERING STRATEGY NEEDS TO FOCUS ON:

- ϵ Creating a robust innovation environment, which can be achieved by harnessing the collective power of people (team members) to then gather their insights, ideas, and implementations, all through a proven design-thinking and
  enterprise innovation process, method, and/or platform.
- ϵ Improving innovation culture by valuing people, their ideas, and their contributions across the entire enterprise.
- ϵ Increasing enterprise-wide engagements and reducing or eliminating the insularity of the 'silo mentality' between different teams, departments, organizations, functions, and global sites.

ENTERPRISE INNOVATION MATURITY ROADMAP CANVAS

	Y-i Strategize & Inspire	Y-ii Standardize & Establish	Y-iii Implement & Foster	Y-iv Integrate & Grasp
Core				
Concept Generation				
Product Development				
Process Innovation				
Technology Acquisition				
Support				
Systems & Tools				
Resourcing				
Input				
Market Focus				
Leadership				

THE INNOVATIVE DINOSAUR
WHAT IF DINOSAURS WERE INNOVATIVE!

Designed by: Motaz Agamawi
www.theinnovativedinosaur.com

THE
INNOVATIVE
DINOSAUR

After completing the internal innovation capability audit and representing the resulted status quo (using the enterprise internal innovation audit maturity scoring grid), we can now begin designing the internal innovation maturity increase strategy, using the maturity roadmap canvas, to close the identified gaps.

GOALS

- The enterprise internal innovation maturity roadmap canvas helps us set our priorities and visualize our strategy by using a single canvas.
- For each of the twenty-seven sub-pillars, we will need to determine a start date and timeline for when the desired output is expected to be reached.
- For each sub-pillar, we need to design a measurable target and KPI, plus an estimated time frame and needed resources including budget

HOW TO USE

The enterprise's internal innovation maturity roadmap canvas assumes four main phases for increasing innovation capability and maturity.

The primary objective of this canvas is to prioritize the enterprises pillars, which will directly impact the decision of setting priority and sequence of launching your internal innovation initiatives which includes:

- Desired maturity state
- Planned time to achieve the desired state
- Availability of human and financial resources
- Support from the different internal stakeholders
- Readiness of internal teams
- State of the enterprise's overall internal innovation culture
- Degree of the internal processes' agility
- Commitment of top management and backers to go through the transformation strategy

- Clarity of the internal innovation strategy's objective and desired impact
- Technical competency readiness of the existing teams, especially in terms of technical industry and product portfolio knowledge
- Availability & competency of the internal innovation teams
- Customers and general industry stakeholders' perception of the enterprise's innovation capabilities and position

All of the above factors will impact the design of the transformation and internal innovation strategy. The enterprise's understanding of these factors will affect the speed of implementation.

THE INNOVATIVE DINOSAUR

ENTERPRISE INNOVATION MATURITY ROADMAP CANVAS - WITH EXAMPLES

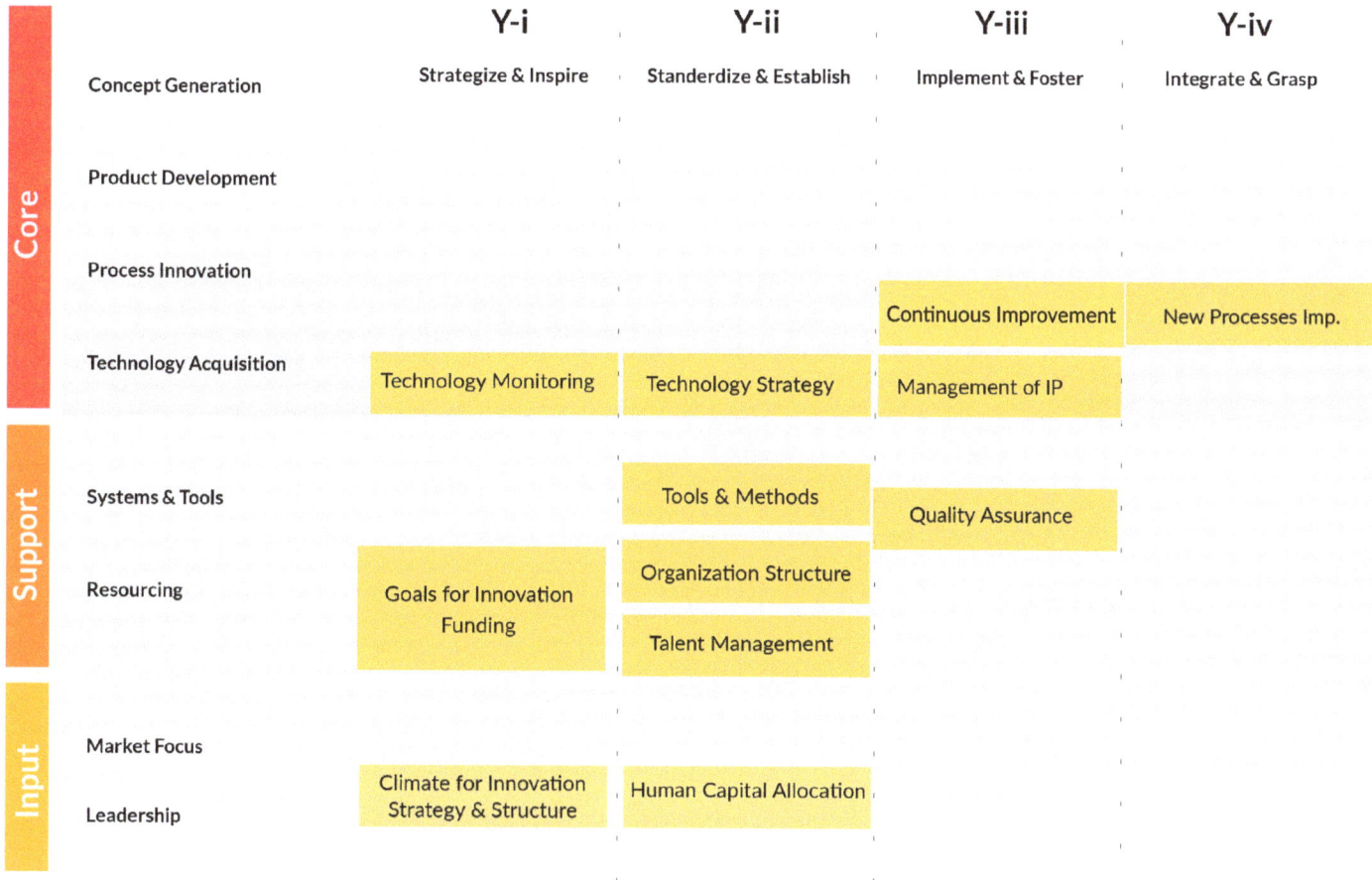

	Y-i	Y-ii	Y-iii	Y-iv
	Strategize & Inspire	Standerdize & Establish	Implement & Foster	Integrate & Grasp
Core — Concept Generation				
Product Development				
Process Innovation			Continuous Improvement	New Processes Imp.
Technology Acquisition	Technology Monitoring	Technology Strategy	Management of IP	
Support — Systems & Tools		Tools & Methods	Quality Assurance	
Resourcing	Goals for Innovation Funding	Organization Structure		
		Talent Management		
Input — Market Focus				
Leadership	Climate for Innovation Strategy & Structure	Human Capital Allocation		

Designed by: Motaz Agamawi
www.theinnovativedinosaur.com

THE INNOVATIVE DINOSAUR

ENTERPRISE INNOVATION INITIATIVES
INTERACTIVE DESIGN CANVAS

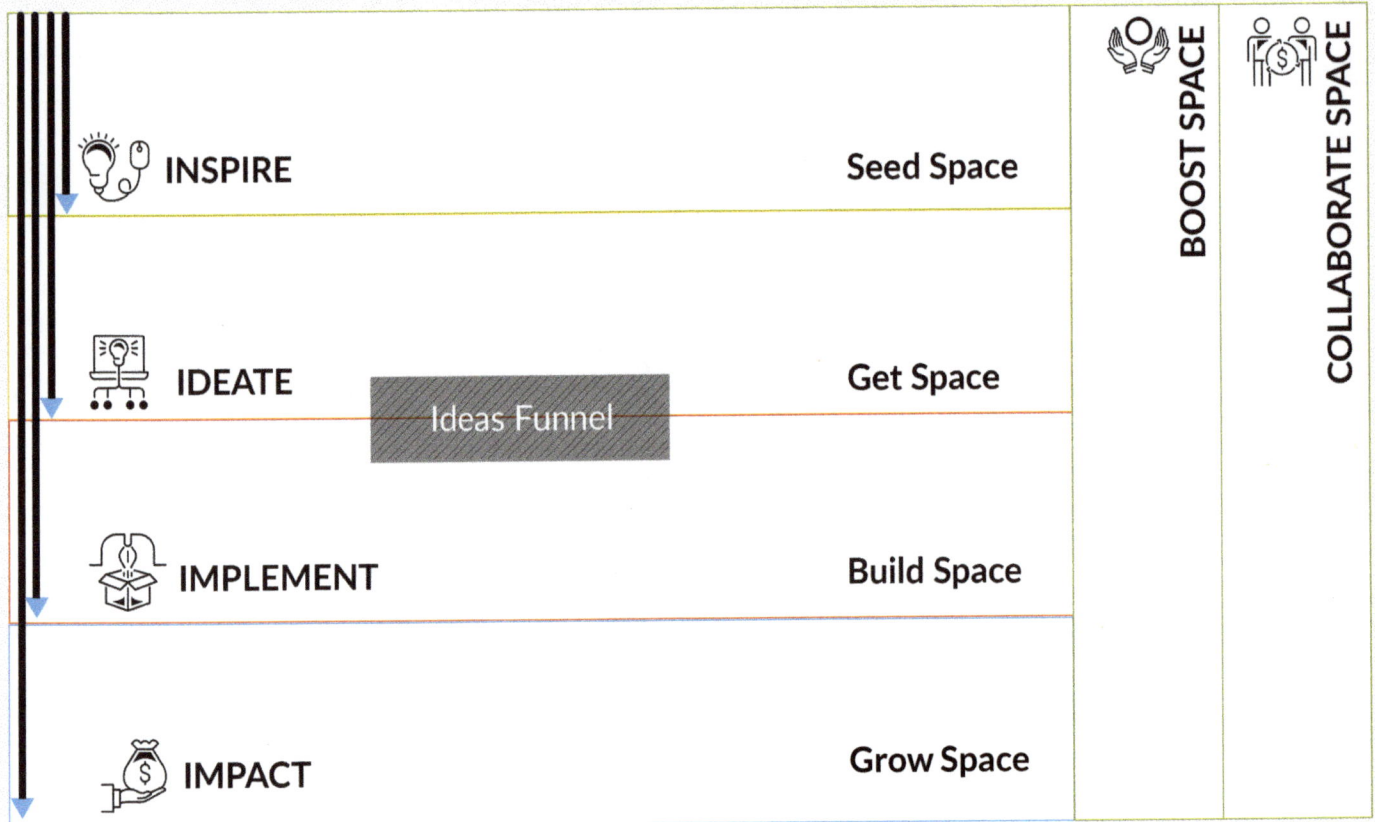

		BOOST SPACE	COLLABORATE SPACE
INSPIRE	Seed Space		
IDEATE	Get Space		
	Ideas Funnel		
IMPLEMENT	Build Space		
IMPACT	Grow Space		

Designed by: Motaz Agamawi
www.theinnovativedinosaur.com

THE
INNOVATIVE
DINOSAUR

Enterprise innovation initiatives interactive design canvas provides a single view for all of the enterprise's innovation programs and initiatives. The canvas is divided into different spaces, each one designed to represent initiatives with various natures. The objective of the enterprise's innovation strategies, initiatives, programs, and frameworks is to create new products, features, and processes that heighten its overall competitive edge. What we need to achieve and ensure is that all of the enterprise's investments and activities will lead to an increased number of ideas entering the ideas funnels. Following that, we can then focus on maturing those ideas, transforming them into services, products, or features that yield a stronger competitive position. Throughout this process, we must ensure that the puzzle pieces are correctly situated and efficiently managed, thus leading the enterprise to its desired goal and objective.

GOALS

Together, the end goal of the enterprise's activities is to achieve a commercially successful and competitive offering. To do so, we must devise strategies that lead to different internal and external initiatives and programs.

These initiatives and programs are integrated to accumulate new ideas for the ideas funnel, to bring the most competitive concepts to the development stage, and to then take another set of the most developed ideas to grow and reach impact. But, first, we must design innovation boosters while also collaborating externally with the various ecosystem stakeholders.

The enterprise innovation interactive design canvas is designed to ensure that our strategies and initiatives are mutually exclusive yet integrating

together to achieve our targets and objectives. This canvas gives us a single view for all of the initiatives, programs, and activities that help us foster, grasp, and achieve impact from our innovation management investment. This is done through placing each and every initiative in the proper space with the clearly defined input and output. The goal of each space can be summarized as follows:

- **Seed space:** the output of this space includes information, insights, knowledge, expertise, exposure, and a means of formulating the organization's internal and external intelligence and roadmaps.
- **Get space:** the output of this space includes ideas that are structured, sorted, analyzed, evaluated, and ready to be placed in the organization's ideas funnel or pipeline.
- **Build Space:** The output of this space is IPs, published papers, POCs (proof of concepts), mock-ups, simulations and working models.
- **Grow Space:** The output of this space is MVP (minimum viable product), BD (business model), pre-commercialized version, initial customers

THE
INNOVATIVE
DINOSAUR

acquisition/adoption and/or internal/external fund allocation.

ɕ **Boost space:** aims to boost all other spaces. The space includes infrastructure, methods, tools, platforms ,organization structures, policies, processes & leadership.

ɕ **Collaborate space:** aims to open the pipeline with the external world, the creation of different gatekeepers.

ɕ **Ideas funnel:** is our ideas repository where we get, build and grow our ideas to reach successful commercialization.

How to Use

The enterprise innovation initiatives interactive design canvas is used in pivoting nature. At the early stage of the enterprise innovation management system design, the canvas is used to structure and guarantee the coherent nature of the overall enterprise initiative's design. To guarantee that all initiatives are in the proper place and integrated all together to achieve the desired impact. At the later stage, and as our model is designed to follow the PDCA (Plan, Do, Check, and Act) cycle in a continuous manner, we refer to the canvas to make sure that we are on the right track and have modified what is needed based on the assessment result.

The enterprise innovation initiatives interactive design canvas should have the following prerequisites in place:

ɕ Completed the enterprise innovation audit
ɕ Finalized audit analysis through the usage of the enterprise innovation maturity evaluation grid
ɕ Formalized enterprise innovation maturity roadmap, including the final approved resources, budgets, implementation timeframe, and agreed upon objectives, goals, and KPIs.

At that stage we can start working on the design of the enterprise innovation initiatives interactive design canvas with a clear objective to make sure that all initiatives are placed on the proper space with the intended initiative objectives. After finishing the design of the enterprise innovation initiatives interactive design canvas, we move directly to design each initiative at the proper planned time through the usage of the innovation initiative design canvas for every initiative with all the needed details.

On the whole, the canvas is designed to give a single holistic and integrated view for the enterprise's innovation initiatives and activities. Further, the framework is designed with a consideration for the PDCA cycle in a pivotal continuous manner, so the canvas is used to design the enterprise initiative and also is used in a continuous pivotal manner correct, improve the original design whenever needed based on the continuous assessment results.

**THE
INNOVATIVE
DINƆSAUR**

Seed Space includes all process, policies, and initiatives that inspire and support the ideation process. It is regarded as an inspiring, preparing, supporting, and structuring space, and it also includes some of the required prerequisites. The output of this space is information, insights, knowledge, expertise, exposure, & a means of formulating organization internal and external intelligence and roadmaps.

Get Space includes all process, policies, and initiatives that generate ideas and support the organization's ideation process. Accordingly, it is regarded as an idea production space. The output of this space is ideas that are structured, sorted, analyzed, evaluated, and ready to be placed in the organization's idea funnel or pipeline.

Build Space includes all process, policies, and initiatives that aim to realize and implement the selected ideas. Regarded as the realization or the prototyping space, its output of is IPs, published papers, proof of concepts (POCs), mockups, simulations, and working models. Implementation, which realizes ideas in different maturity stages. The desire is to swiftly acquire customer feedback and validation.

Grow Space includes all processes, policies and initiatives that aim to grow the output of the build space and reach the desired impact. Regarded as the acceleration space, its output is minimum viable product (MVP), (business model), pre - commercialized version, initial customer acquisition /adoption and / or internal / external fund allocation.

Boost Space aims to boost all of other spaces. It includes infrastructure, methods, tools, platforms & organization structures, policies, processes and leadership.

Collaborate Space aims to open the pipeline with the external world for the creation of different gatekeepers, from academics, suppliers, to customers (e.g., crowd sourcing). It is regarded as `an open innovation space.

The Idea Funnel is our concept - filled repository, where we get, build, and grow our ideas to reach successful commercialization. The objective of the Enterprise Innovation Initiative Interactive Design Canvas is to follow a structured framework for designing your internal innovation initiatives with the main target being the proper management of the idea lifecycle through its different development and maturity stages.

THE
INNOVATIVE
DINOSAUR

EXAMPLE OF ENTERPRISE INNOVATION INITIATIVES

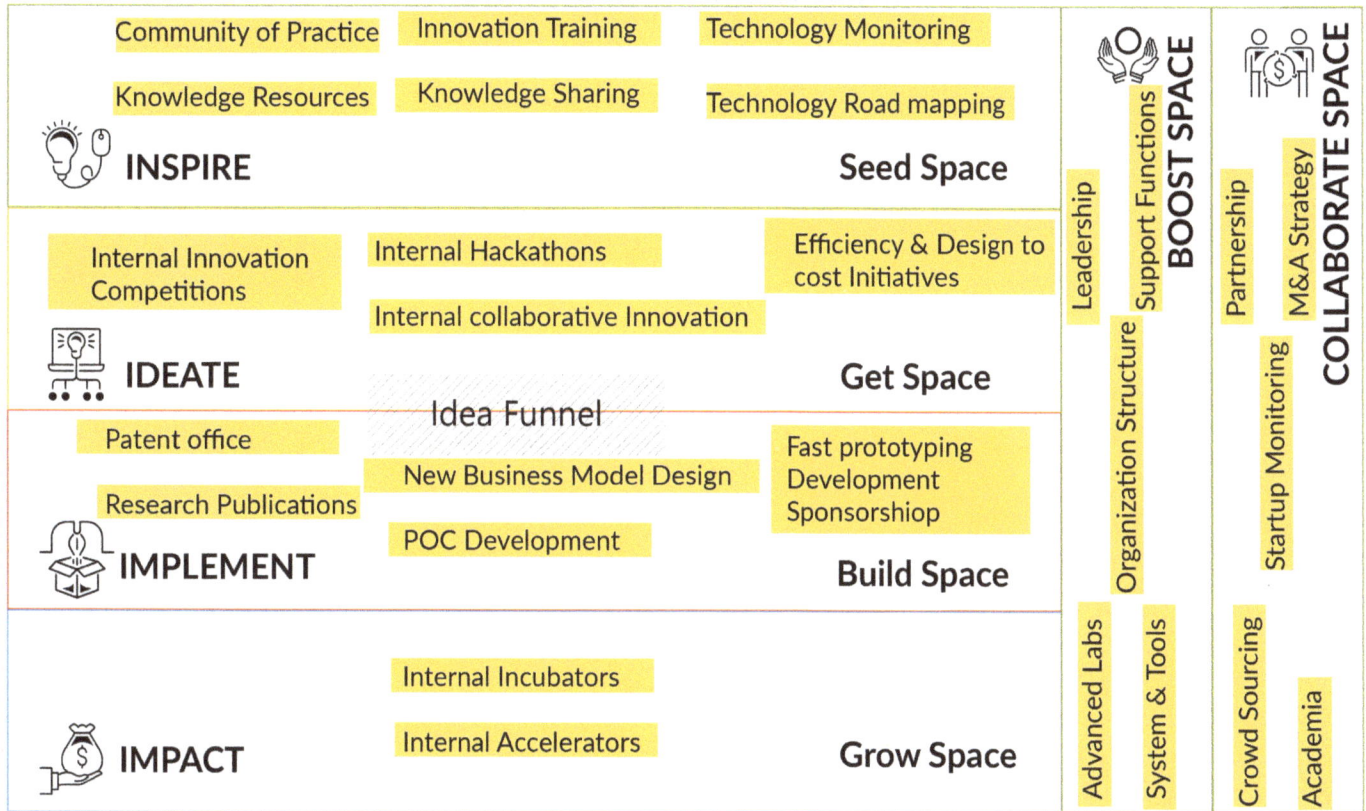

			BOOST SPACE		COLLABORATE SPACE	
Community of Practice	Innovation Training	Technology Monitoring				
Knowledge Resources	Knowledge Sharing	Technology Road mapping				
INSPIRE		**Seed Space**	Leadership	Support Functions	Partnership	M&A Strategy
Internal Innovation Competitions	Internal Hackathons	Efficiency & Design to cost Initiatives				
	Internal collaborative Innovation					
IDEATE		**Get Space**		Organization Structure		Startup Monitoring
Patent office	Idea Funnel	Fast prototyping Development Sponsorshiop				
Research Publications	New Business Model Design					
	POC Development					
IMPLEMENT		**Build Space**				
	Internal Incubators		Advanced Labs	System & Tools	Crowd Sourcing	Academia
	Internal Accelerators					
IMPACT		**Grow Space**				

Designed by: Motaz Agamawi
www.theinnovativedinosaur.com

THE INNOVATIVE DINOSAUR

INNOVATION INITIATIVE
DESIGN CANVAS

Description:

Start Date:

Duration:

Target Segment:

Serving Pillar(s):

Type:

Motive and Positioning:

Dependency:

Frequency:

Communication Plan (Activit level):

Stakeholders Alignment Strategy:

Stakeholders:

Experience and Process:

Budget: $

Talent Allocation:

Platforms, methods, tools and Activities:

Supporting Team:

THE INNOVATIVE DINOSAUR

The innovation initiative design canvas is a trial to structure, quantify, and visualize all of the elements needed for the success of the initiative in a single place. It is a tool that can be customized and tailored according to the nature of the initiative and the objectives behind it. The most important thing is to guarantee that all elements are covered, considered, and planned ahead of time. Additionally, it is used to ensure that all of the related stakeholders are on the same level in terms of understanding and commitment.

GOALS

⊂ The goal of the canvas is to guarantee — in a structured manner — that all of necessary elements for a specific initiative are considered, established, budgeted, and planned in an optimal fashion to achieve the desired objectives and goals.

HOW TO USE

The initiative design canvas offers a high-level details for the planning needs of each initiative. The canvas covers the following main planning elements:

⊂ **Description:** Each initiative needs to have a brief description with a clear mission and objective to achieve.

⊂ **Target Segment:** Each initiative is targeting a specific segment(s) based on the enterprise team inventiveness persona. Identifying the segment is crucial for ensuring the suitable targeting.

⊂ **Motive and Positioning:** Based on the identified segment, the suitable motive and positioning for such a segments will be designed. This will directly impact the initiative process, give and gets.

⊂ **Communication Plan:** Each initiative must have a clear internal — or external, in case of open innovation — communication plan, which includes the communication strategy, communication channels, and the necessary campaign intensity.

⊂ **Stakeholders Alignment Strategy:** Based on the type of the initiative must be identified. Clear alignment strategy must be in place. As we need to agree that in many cases we have important stakeholders (like first line supervisors or manager or even in some cases department heads or directors) who are not directly involved in the initiative. But those influencers or stakeholders are key for the success. Finding the clear wins, making sure that they believe in the direct and indirect value of the initiative and achieving the needed alignment level is always important. Also, stakeholders may include different organization supporting functions as the HR, Finance, Purchase or others, identifying them and what is needed from each of them from the beginning will secure the efficient and effective operations of the initiative.

THE
INNOVATIVE
DINOSAUR

- **Experience and Process:** Identifying the target segment level of experience is of utmost importance. Designing a clear, transparent, and detailed process is one of the key elements for securing target segment involvement.
Platforms, Methods, Tools and Activities: Any initiative, even the simplest ones, must be supported by a set of platforms, methods, tools, and activities
- **Start Date:** Selecting the right start date is another one of the major elements of success. Thus, many factors must be considered, including seasonality of the enterprise activities, major industry events, major deliveries, and annual vacation seasons.
- **Duration:** Based on the nature of the initiative, the suitable duration must be laid out with a clear balance between the needed effective doze to achieve the objectives of the initiative's activities.
- **Serving Pillar:** As each initiative is designed to achieve a specific enterprise innovation maturity level for a specific pillar. The identification of each serving pillar is important. Please refer to the enterprise innovation audit pillars and sub-pillars.
- **Dependency:** Dependencies may include time allocation, a specific competency, or change in a specific organizational process.
- **Frequency:** Each initiative must have a planned frequency, either as a one-time initiative or a regular initiative that will be repeated within a specific frequency.
- **Stakeholders:** The key internal and external stakeholders must be listed.
- **Budget:** Total dollar value — in many cases out-of-pocket investment — must be identified.
- **Talent Allocation:** The needed time investment to be allocated for the organization's team members across different departments must be budgeted.
- **Supporting Teams:** The needed activities, budget, and resources from the different enterprise supporting teams (including HR, Finance, Admin, facility, safety) must be identified.

ENTERPRISE INNOVATION
4I APPROACH

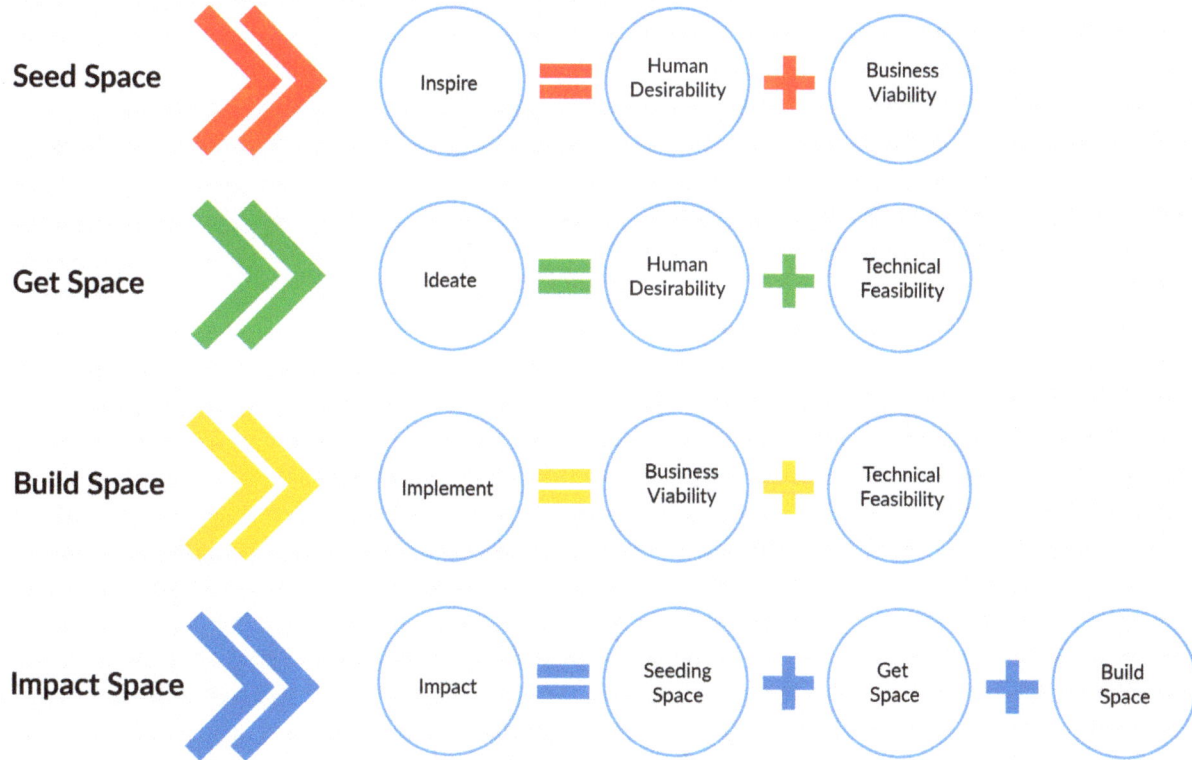

Seed Space ⟫ (Inspire) = (Human Desirability) + (Business Viability)

Get Space ⟫ (Ideate) = (Human Desirability) + (Technical Feasibility)

Build Space ⟫ (Implement) = (Business Viability) + (Technical Feasibility)

Impact Space ⟫ (Impact) = (Seeding Space) + (Get Space) + (Build Space)

Designed by: Motaz Agamawi
www.theinnovativedinosaur.com

THE INNOVATIVE DINOSAUR

The 4I approach — Inspire, Ideate, Implement, Impact — summarizes the main concepts for the enterprise innovation fostering strategy through the linkage of the innovation fostering people-centric approach and the enterprise innovation interactive initiative design canvas spaces.

GOALS

Seizing the full potential of people talent and competencies is the cornerstone of fostering the innovation culture within an enterprise.

The 4I approach is designed to support the design of human-centric enterprise innovation management initiatives. This approach links the innovation fostering people-centric approach, the enterprise innovation interactive initiative design canvas spaces, and our understanding of the different team personas categorized in the team inventiveness persona distribution curve.

The main goal is to guarantee that all the necessary prerequisites are in place at the appropriate time. This is achieved by linking up the pillars of the 4I approach with the different enterprise innovation space as follows:

- Inspire is linked to the 'seeding space.' Inspire is the result of human desirability combined with business viability.
- Ideate is linked to the 'get space.' Ideate is the result of human desirability combined with technical feasibility.
- Implement is linked to 'build space.' Implement is the result of business viability combined with technical feasibility.
- Impact is linked to 'impact space.' Impact is represented in the total sum of the output from the three spaces: seeding space, get space, and build space.

HOW TO USE

Inspire

The inspire phase can be mapped directly to the seeding space in the interactive innovation initiative design canvas. The seeding space includes all process, policies, and initiatives that inspire and support the ideation seeding process; it is regarded as an inspiring, preparing, supporting, and structuring space. Also, it includes some of the required prerequisites for building the innovation culture. The output of this space is information, knowledge, expertise, exposure, and a means of formulating organization internal and external intelligence and roadmaps.

Ideate

The ideate phase can be mapped directly to the get space in the interactive innovation initiative design canvas. The get space includes all process, policies, and initiatives that generate ideas and support the organization's ideation process. Accordingly, it is regarded as an idea production space. The output of this space is ideas that are structured, sorted, analyzed, evaluated, and ready to be placed in the organization's ideas pipeline.

Implement

The ideate phase can be mapped directly to the get space in the interactive innovation initiative design canvas. The get space includes all process, policies, and initiatives that generate ideas and support the organization's ideation process. Accordingly, it is regarded as an idea production space. The output of this space is ideas that are structured, sorted, analyzed, evaluated, and ready to be placed in the organization's ideas pipeline.

Impact

The impact phase can be mapped directly to the grow space in the interactive innovation initiative design canvas. The grow space includes all process, policies, and initiatives that aim to expand the output of the build space and reach the desired impact. Regarded as the acceleration space, the output of this space is minimum viable product (MVP), business model, pre-commercialized version, initial customers acquisition / adoption and / or internal/external fund allocation.

Inspire Results

To reach the maximum result, we need to consider the enterprise team inventiveness persona. With a special focus on 'geeks,' researchers, and multipotential personas motive. So we need to consider what such personalities are looking for:

- Challenges
- Self-esteem
- Realization of Dream
- Opportunity to Implement Own Ideas
- Prove Individual Capabilities
- Recognition & Reward
- Appreciation & Support
- Encouragement & Support
- Culture of Accepting Failure

THE INNOVATIVE DINOSAUR

Implement Results

To reach the maximum result, we need to consider the availability and implementation of the following:

- Team to include diversified discipline
- Supporting multi-site diversified team formulation in case of global operations
- Fast Prototyping Methodology
- Availability of Equipment and lean purchase process
- Guidance, best practices and mentorship network establishment
- Develop POCs and Prototypes through
- Acceleration like environment
- Early customer validation (Go Out of the building mind set)
- User centric, design thinking approach and focusing on user experience
- Design the education and competency increase means and experience
- Commitment to take competitive ideas to next level (patenting and new product development)
- Recognition of success and creation of enterprise wide role models
- Delivery to your teams more than what you have promised

Inspire Results

To reach the maximum result, we need to consider designing a robust, unambiguous, and clear enterprise innovation KPIs, and targets. Such KPIs and targets need to cover the innovation from a 360-degree perspective, including:

- Internal Cultural Fostering engagement and participation level Output of the internal fostering strategy in a tangible form including number of ideas, number of generated patents, number of POCs, published papers and so on.
- Innovation output in the form of newly offered products, services and differentiation factors including new production capabilities, design to cost and better pricing and/or profitability, quality differentiation capabilities and/or production capacity and/or delivery time.
- Innovation Economical impact measures must be set which may include % of new product development compared to total sales or order intake. % of profit margin increase, market share increase and also existing customer share of wallet must be considered.

ENTERPRISE TEAM INVENTIVENESS DISTRIBUTION

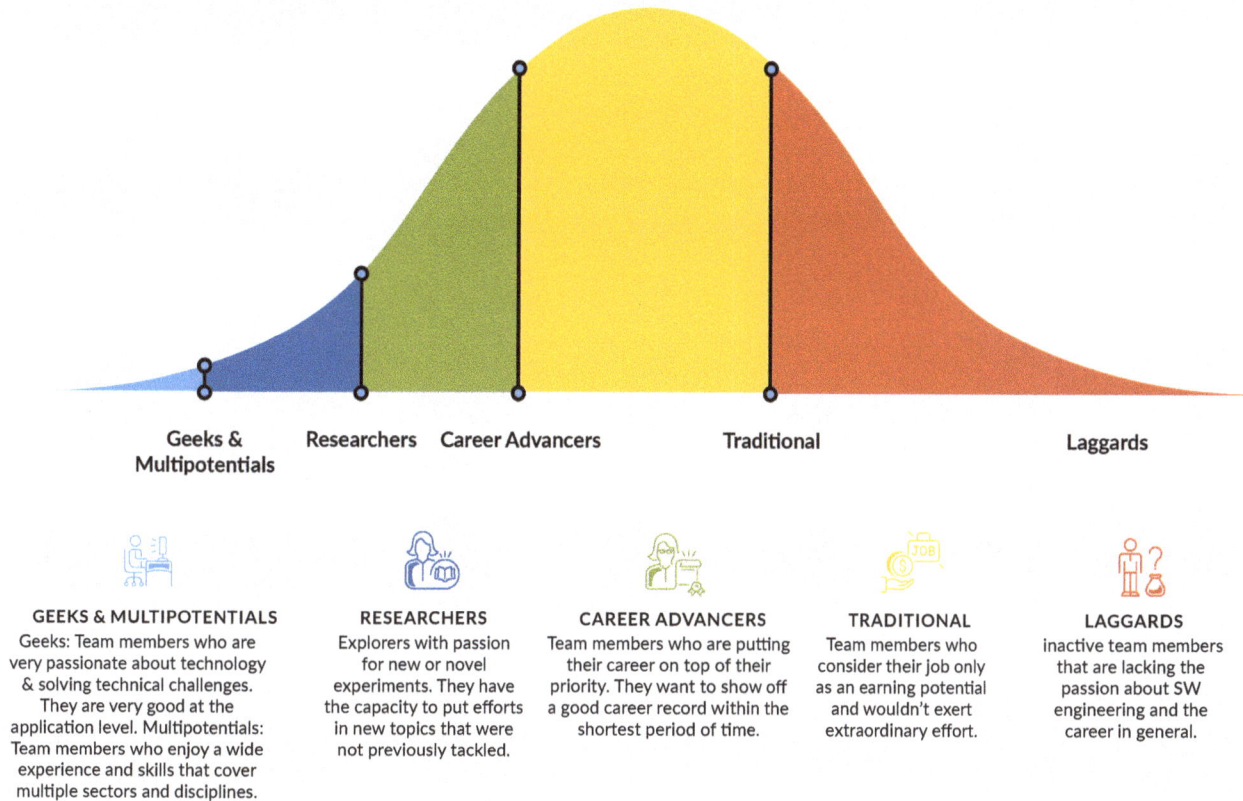

Geeks & Multipotentials — **Researchers** — **Career Advancers** — **Traditional** — **Laggards**

GEEKS & MULTIPOTENTIALS
Geeks: Team members who are very passionate about technology & solving technical challenges. They are very good at the application level. Multipotentials: Team members who enjoy a wide experience and skills that cover multiple sectors and disciplines.

RESEARCHERS
Explorers with passion for new or novel experiments. They have the capacity to put efforts in new topics that were not previously tackled.

CAREER ADVANCERS
Team members who are putting their career on top of their priority. They want to show off a good career record within the shortest period of time.

TRADITIONAL
Team members who consider their job only as an earning potential and wouldn't exert extraordinary effort.

LAGGARDS
inactive team members that are lacking the passion about SW engineering and the career in general.

THE INNOVATIVE DINOSAUR
WHAT IF DINOSAURS WERE INNOVATIVE

Designed by: Motaz Agamawi
www.theinnovativedinosaur.com

THE INNOVATIVE DINOSAUR

Enterprise Team Inventiveness distribution is an essential tool for understanding the enterprise team members' motives, needs, and readiness. By conducting this exercise, the internal innovation initiative designer can guarantee the usage of the proper tool, the initiative type, and the internal readiness of the enterprise.

The distribution of team personas is different for an enterprise to another. This difference is based on multiple factors, including:

ϵ The nature of the business
ϵ The nature of R&D, along with the percentage of R&D activities and team size compared to manufacturing and operations
ϵ The enterprise's culture and leadership style
ϵ The enterprise's policies, processes, methods, and tools
ϵ The nature of competition in the target market
ϵ The core competencies and talent readiness

By understanding the enterprise team inventiveness distribution curve, the innovation management can better understand the target population and thus:

ϵ Set priorities for the enterprise's innovation management strategy
ϵ Grasp the motives of the target population and then design the target enterprise innovation initiatives
ϵ Guarantee with greater precision the percentage of engagement and alignment with the different stakeholders

HOW TO USE

Understanding the motives, needs, aspirations, and objectives of each group will be of great value when it comes to designing and launching the proper initiative at the right time. Each of the abovementioned groups have a unique method and approach for determining and/or actualizing the initiative's nature, motives, rewards program design, and communication strategy. The distribution percentage of each of the groups within the organization varies according to many parameters, including the enterprise's size, hierarchical structure, industry type and nature, internal culture, complexity of team members' competencies and skills, management style and type, as well as the geographic location of the operations. All of these parameters and factors directly impact the enterprise team inventiveness personas distribution curve. So, for example, the different internal organizations or site locations of the same enterprise could have a completely different distribution curve. The curve may differ from manufacturing site to R&D site and headquarters to global offshore center. Therefore, before an enterprise inventiveness personas curve is established it is necessary to assess the different enterprise organizations, functions, and even sites. At the end this process, we will consolidate and aggregate the results to arrive at the average of the enterprise consolidated inventiveness personas curve.

Career Advancers	**Recognition, Benefits, Lifestyle, Learning**
Geeks	**Challenge, Appreciation, Idea Realization, Learning**
Researchers	**Exploration, Learning, Sense of Achievement**
Multipotentials	**Proof of Capacity, Learning**

**THE
INNOVATIVE
DINOSAUR**

Geeks & Multipotentials

Geeks: Team members who are very passionate about technology & solving technical challenges. They are very good at the application level.

Multipotentials: Team members who enjoy a wide experience and skills that cover multiple sectors and disciplines.

Researchers

Explorers with passion for new or novel experiments. They have the capacity to put efforts in new topics that were not previously tackled.

Career Advancers

Team member who are putting their career on top of their priorities. They want to show off a good career record within the shortest period of time.

Traditional

Team members who consider their job only as an earning potential and wouldn't exert extraordinary effort.

Laggards

Inactive team members that are lacking the passion about SW engineering and the career in general.

INNOVATION INITIATIVES VS INVENTIVENESS PERSONA COVERAGE

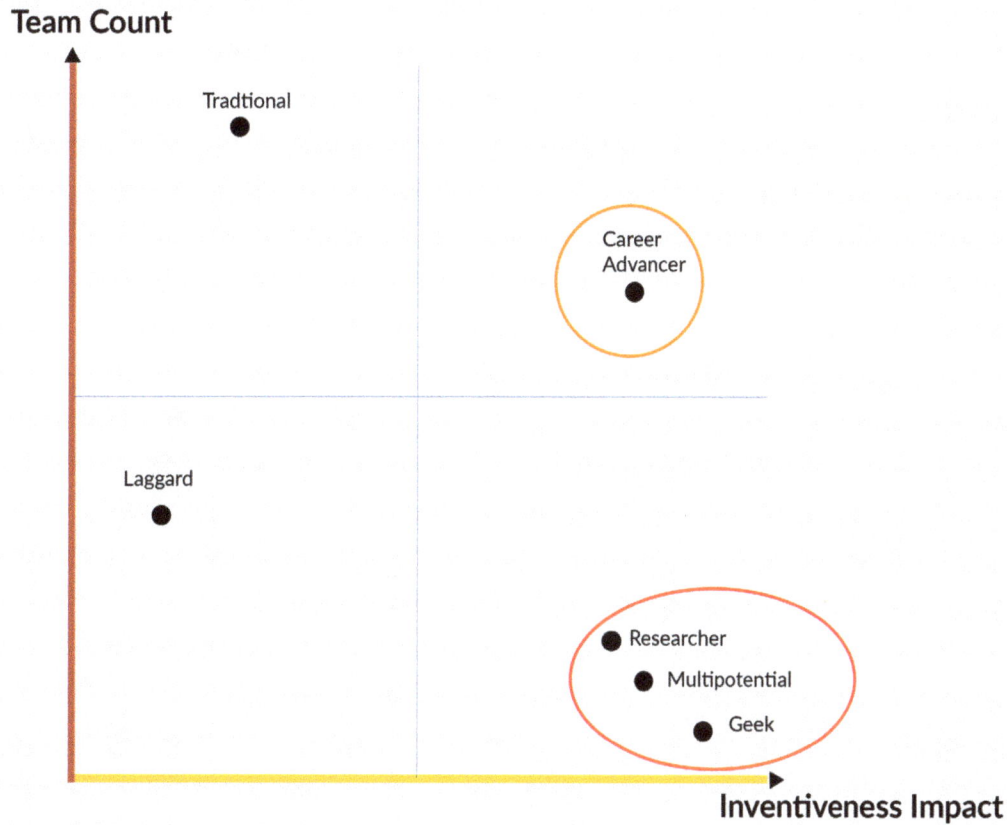

Designed by: Motaz Agamawi
www.theinnovativedinosaur.com

THE
INNOVATIVE
DINOSAUR

The enterprise innovation initiative versus inventiveness coverage graph is designed to help in mapping out the internal initiative or programs that target population size and anticipated inventiveness impact.

The graph comprises four quadrants:

€ The first quadrant (bottom left) represents the initiatives that serve the laggard group, which is characterized by a medium-sized team and low impact.

€ The second quadrant (top left) represents the initiatives that serve the traditionalist group, which is characterized by a large team and low impact.

€ The third quadrant (top right) represents the initiatives that serve the career advancer group, which is characterized by midsize to large team and medium impact.

€ The fourth quadrant (bottom right) represents the initiatives that serve the geek, multipotential, and researcher groups, which are characterized by a small team and high impact.

The decision of targeting which persona group depends on several factors, including:

€ The stage of internal innovation maturity
€ The objective of the internal innovation strategy or program
€ The degree to the enterprise's innovation culture fosters readiness

Generally, when establishing the internal enterprise's innovation culture, we recommend:

€ In the early stage, start with the first quadrant (geeks, researchers, and multipotentials), as this group's readiness is clear from a competency perspective and motive; these group members will usually be made into innovation ambassadors and influencers.

€ In the intermediate maturity stage, approach the third quadrant three (career advancers), as this group holds a clear motive and is usually competent, with a larger team size and high interpersonal skills as promoters.

€ As the internal innovation culture maturity increases, approach the second quadrant (traditionalists), followed by the first (laggards); the more team members the enterprise attracts and engages from those two quadrants, the more you can consider that the transformational objectives have been achieved.

**THE
INNOVATIVE
DINCSAUR**

CHAPTER 9:
MANAGING
THE IDEA FUNNEL

One of the most challenging tasks and objectives of any innovation management or new product development management team is to increase the success rate of ideas-turned-products that have a high economic impact and reward for the organization. Let's agree that the actual cost of the new product development is the result of all the associated investments that an enterprise has made to reach a successfully commercialized product, including all failure costs associated with all the other unsuccessful product ideas. In other words, the cost of a successful commercialized product equals the sum of all investments made for the full number of ideas within the idea funnel across its different stages, plus the cost of the successfully commercialized product.

Accordingly, the cost of innovation failure directly affects the overall efficiency and impact of the enterprise's innovation performance. The core concept behind the ideas funnel is "fail fast, win fast," which aims to minimize the final innovation failure costs as much as possible. Starting from the idea stage and passing through the funnel, the proper selection of the most competitive ideas decisively influences the final cost structure while minimizing the cost of innovation failure and increasing the organization 's economic performance overall.

In this chapter, we will focus on idea funnel lifecycle management, as ideas management and its associated success rate are among the most pressing challenges of the enterprise's internal innovation management. Ideas are the beating heart of products and services, thus our goal is to achieve superior or, at the very least, competitive products and services that yield a high economic return.

**THE
INNOVATIVE
DINOSAUR**

LIST OF TOOLS, DIAGRAMS, AND ILLUSTRATIONS

1. TID Illustration: Ideas Funnel
2. TID Illustration: Ideas Funnel - The Get Phase
3. TID Illustration: Ideas Funnel - The Build Phase
4. TID Illustration: Ideas Funnel - The Grow Phase
5. TID Illustration: Ideas Funnel VS Activity VS Maturity
6. TID Illustration: Ideas Funnel Investment & Resources per Phase
7. TID Illustration: Ideas Funnel - Success Rate
8. TID Illustration: Ideas Funnel –Team Roles over Different Phases

CHAPTER'S SECTIONS

- ϵ The Ideas Funnel
- ϵ Ideas Funnel VS Activities VS Maturity
- ϵ Ideas Funnel Investment & Resources Per Phase
- ϵ Ideas Funnel Success Rate
- ϵ Ideas Funnel –Team Roles over Different Phases

LIST OF REFERENCES & EXTRA READINGS FOR THIS CHAPTER

1. Crossing the Chasm, by Geoffrey A. Moore
2. Winning at new product development, by Robert Cooper
3. 101 Design Methods, by Vijay Kumar
4. Sprint, by Jake Knappwith with John Zeratsky and Braden Kowitz
5. The Design of Everyday Things, by Don Norman
6. The Four Steps to the Epiphany, by Steve Blanck
7. How to Lead in Product Management, by Roman Pichler
8. Strategize, by Roman Pichler
9. Agile Product Management with Scrum, by Roman Pichler
10. Ideo University
11. Hasso Plattner Institute
12. Stanford Design School
13. Product Development and Management Association
14. Agile Project Management
15. Project Management Institute
16. International Institute of Business Analysis
17. International Council on Systems Engineering (INCOSE)
18. Scrum Alliance

THE IDEAS FUNNEL

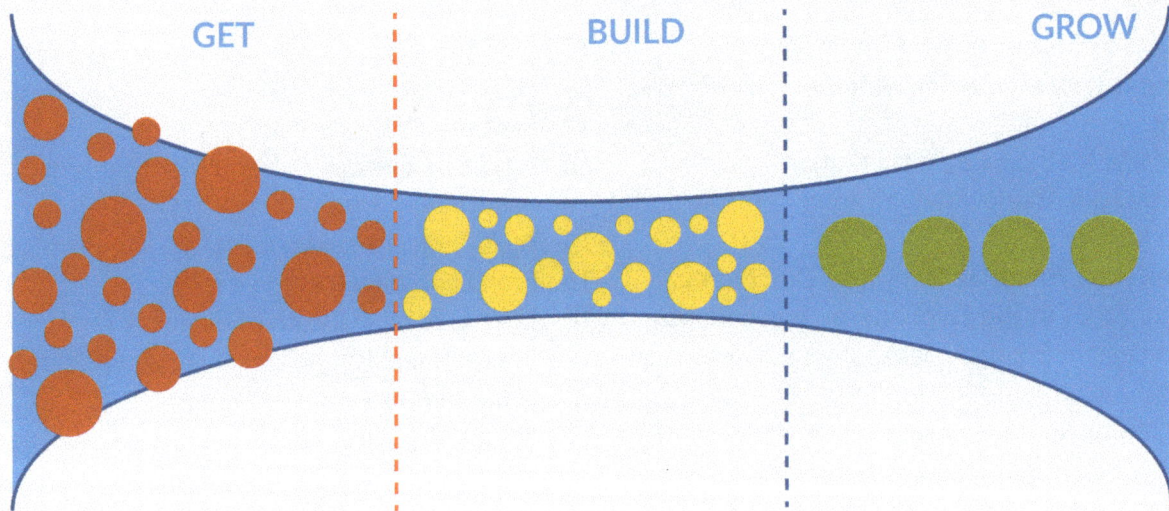

GET

BUILD

GROW

Designed by: Motaz Agamawi
www.theinnovativedinosaur.com

THE INNOVATIVE DINOSAUR

The ideas funnel is divided into three principal stages. The first is the Get stage, where in the main challenge is to get as much as possible competitive ideas. The second is the Build stage, wherein the main challenge is to guide promising ideas down the path of product development; such a path will include various checkpoints for guaranteeing the effectiveness and efficiency of the new product's development lifecycle. And the third is the Grow stage, wherein the main challenge is to successful productize and commercialize our ideas into diffused products and/or services with high economic impact.

The ideas funnel's lifecycle introduces a visual aid, or guide, for the different maturity stages of an idea. Further, it provides an overall view of the distinct nature of each stage along with the necessary activities, maturity, competencies, and lifecycle management approach.

THE
INNOVATIVE
DINOSAUR

IDEAS FUNNEL –
THE GET PHASE

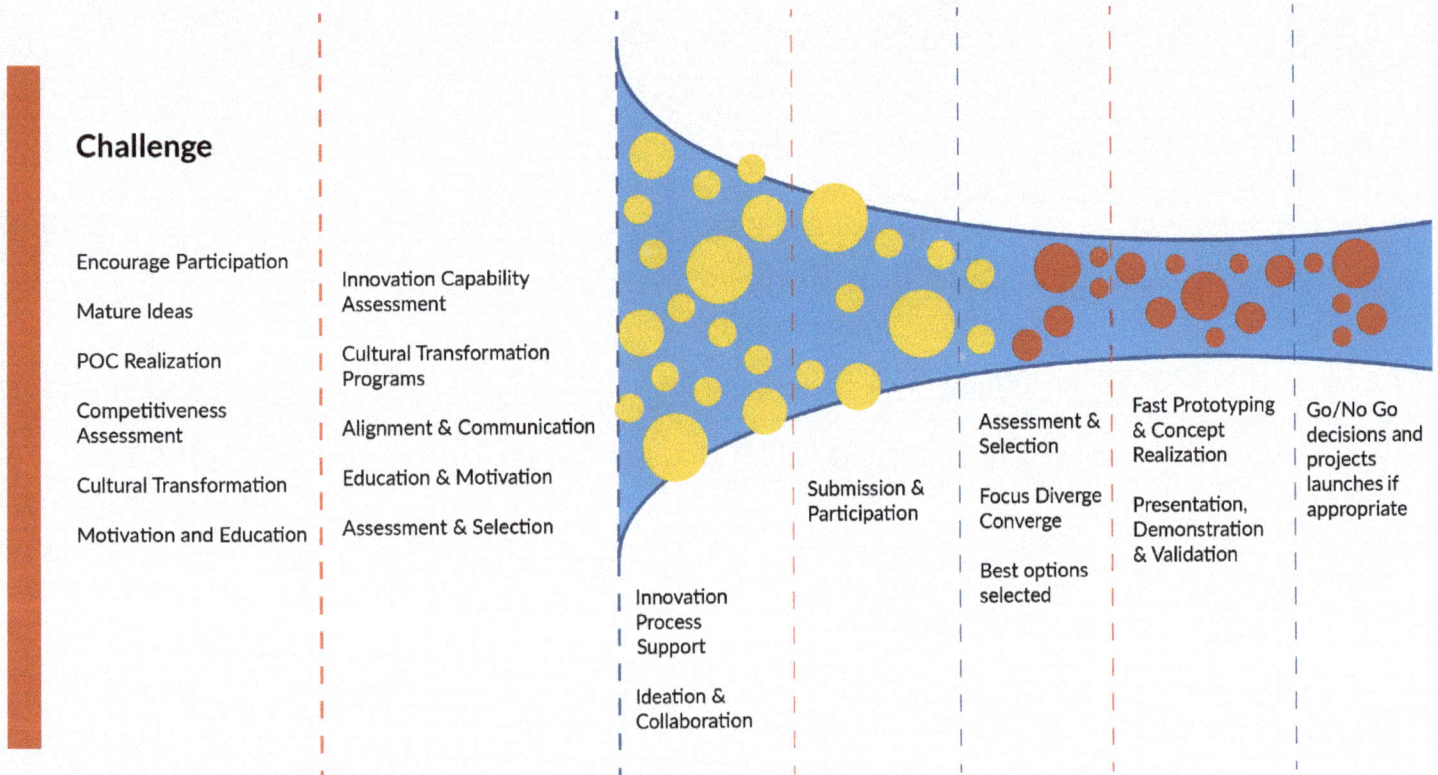

Challenge

Encourage Participation

Mature Ideas

POC Realization

Competitiveness
Assessment

Cultural Transformation

Motivation and Education

Innovation Capability
Assessment

Cultural Transformation
Programs

Alignment & Communication

Education & Motivation

Assessment & Selection

Submission &
Participation

Innovation
Process
Support

Ideation &
Collaboration

Assessment &
Selection

Focus Diverge
Converge

Best options
selected

Fast Prototyping
& Concept
Realization

Presentation,
Demonstration
& Validation

Go/No Go
decisions and
projects
launches if
appropriate

Designed by: Motaz Agamawi
www.theinnovativedinosaur.com

**THE
INNOVATIVE
DINOSAUR**

The main focus of the Get Phase is to capture as many ideas as possible from the enterprise's various team members.

In this phase, the most instead challenges are:

- Encouraging participation
- Enriching Maturity of ideas
- Identifying and supporting competitive ideas to reach POC realization
- Assessing competitiveness
- Conducting and implementing cultural transformation objectives
- Motivating and educating different team members

In this phase, the following set of activities and initiatives should be carried out:

- Cultural transformation
- Alignment and communication
- Encouragement and education of team members
- Assessment and selection
- Ideation and collaboration
- Ideas collection and submission
- Fast prototyping and concept realization
- Presentation, demonstration, and validation
- Go/no go decisions (to continue to the phases to follow)

IDEAS FUNNEL – THE BUILD PHASE

Challenge:

Keeping the commitment and motivation of the inventors

Turning the POCs to more mature Prototypes

Protecting the IPs

Evolving the Prospect Customer in the Product Definition as early as possible

Time to Market with first MVP

Securing the Proper Competencies, funds and GTM strategies

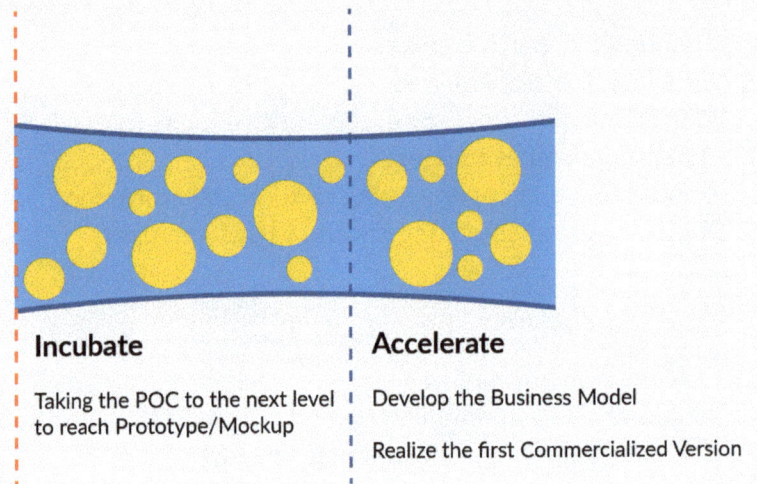

Incubate

Taking the POC to the next level to reach Prototype/Mockup

Accelerate

Develop the Business Model

Realize the first Commercialized Version

Designed by: Motaz Agamawi
www.theinnovativedinosaur.com

THE
INNOVATIVE
DINOSAUR

In the Build Phase, the most competitive ideas that have been selected in the Build Phase are included. Here, to "build" is to focus on increasing the maturity of the selected ideas. Generally, ideas enter this phase with a POC, and mockup or early-stage prototype.

The challenges of this phase include:

- Securing both the commitment and motivation of the inventors
- Turning the POCs into more mature prototypes
- Protecting the IPs
- Involving prospective customers in the product features definition as early as possible
- Time to market with first minimum viable product (MVP)
- Securing the necessary competencies, funds, and go-to-market strategies
- Reaching a customer desired product features and benefits from a fast and competitive positioning

The stages of the Build Phase

- The first is the incubation stage, wherein we must focus on developing the MVP feature and a high-level business model design as well as initial customer validation (CV) and feedback.
- Then we conduct another selection which lead to choosing the most competitive ideas. Such selected ideas start a new wave in the lifecycle through acceleration stage. In the acceleration stage, we must focus on implementing and establishing a deeper CV, feedback, detailed business model design, and the development of the pre-commercialized product version.

THE INNOVATIVE DINOSAUR

IDEAS FUNNEL – THE GROW PHASE

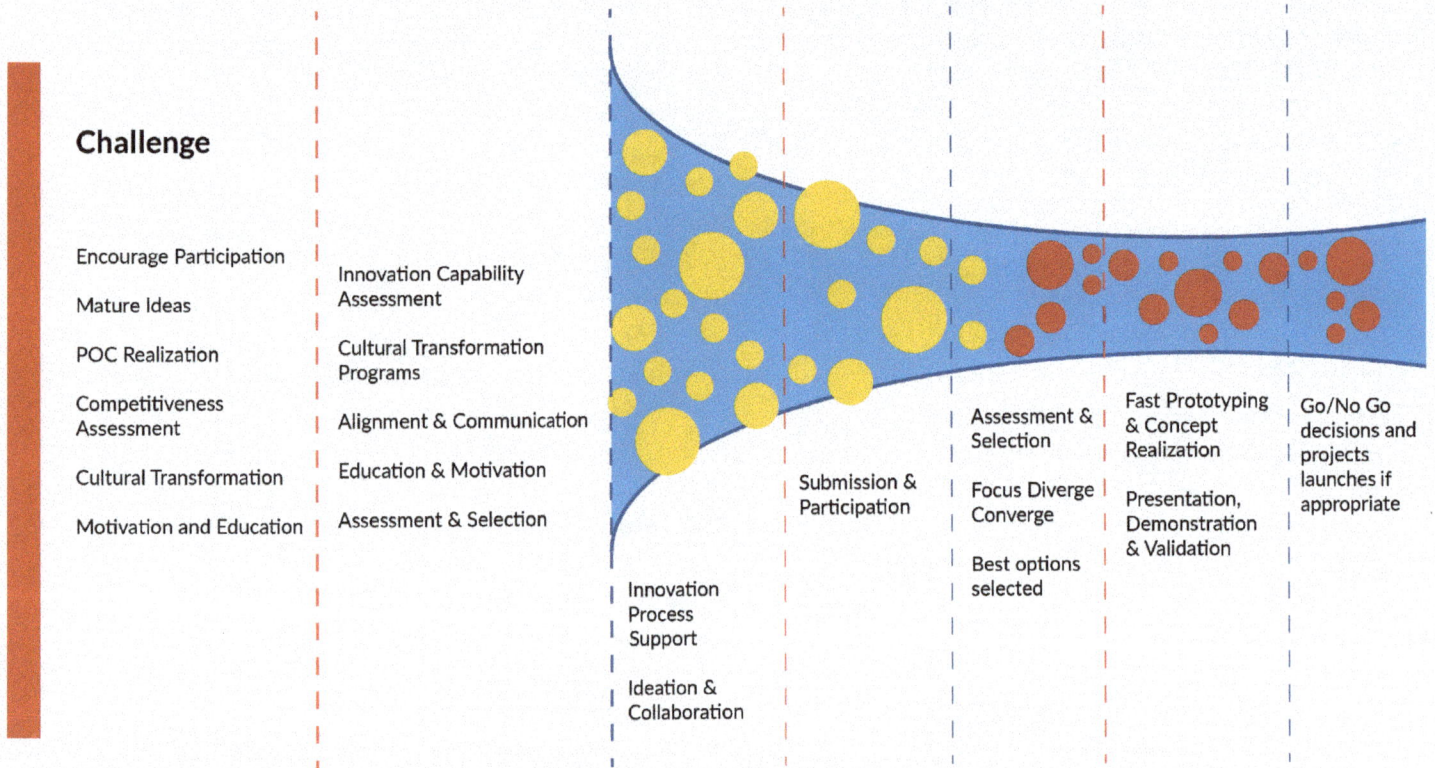

Challenge

Encourage Participation

Mature Ideas

POC Realization

Competitiveness
Assessment

Cultural Transformation

Motivation and Education

Innovation Capability
Assessment

Cultural Transformation
Programs

Alignment & Communication

Education & Motivation

Assessment & Selection

Innovation
Process
Support

Ideation &
Collaboration

Submission &
Participation

Assessment &
Selection

Focus Diverge
Converge

Best options
selected

Fast Prototyping
& Concept
Realization

Presentation,
Demonstration
& Validation

Go/No Go
decisions and
projects
launches if
appropriate

Designed by: Motaz Agamawi
www.theinnovativedinosaur.com

THE
INNOVATIVE
DINOSAUR

In the Grow Phase, the main focus is on the commercialization and impact of the most competitive ideas. In this phase we compile the business architecture, including enterprise business model, revenue model, and demand capture through the early adopters identification and acquisition. Further, this phase is concerned with scaling, manufacturing readiness, securing a value chain, and generic growth management strategies.

The challenges of this phase include:

- Acquiring early adopter customers
- Securing adequate funds
- Establishing productization and operational needs
- Industrial-scale delivery
- Grow revenue and profit
- Securing value chain stakeholders

THE
INNOVATIVE
DINOSAUR

IDEAS FUNNEL VS
ACTIVITIES VS MATURITY

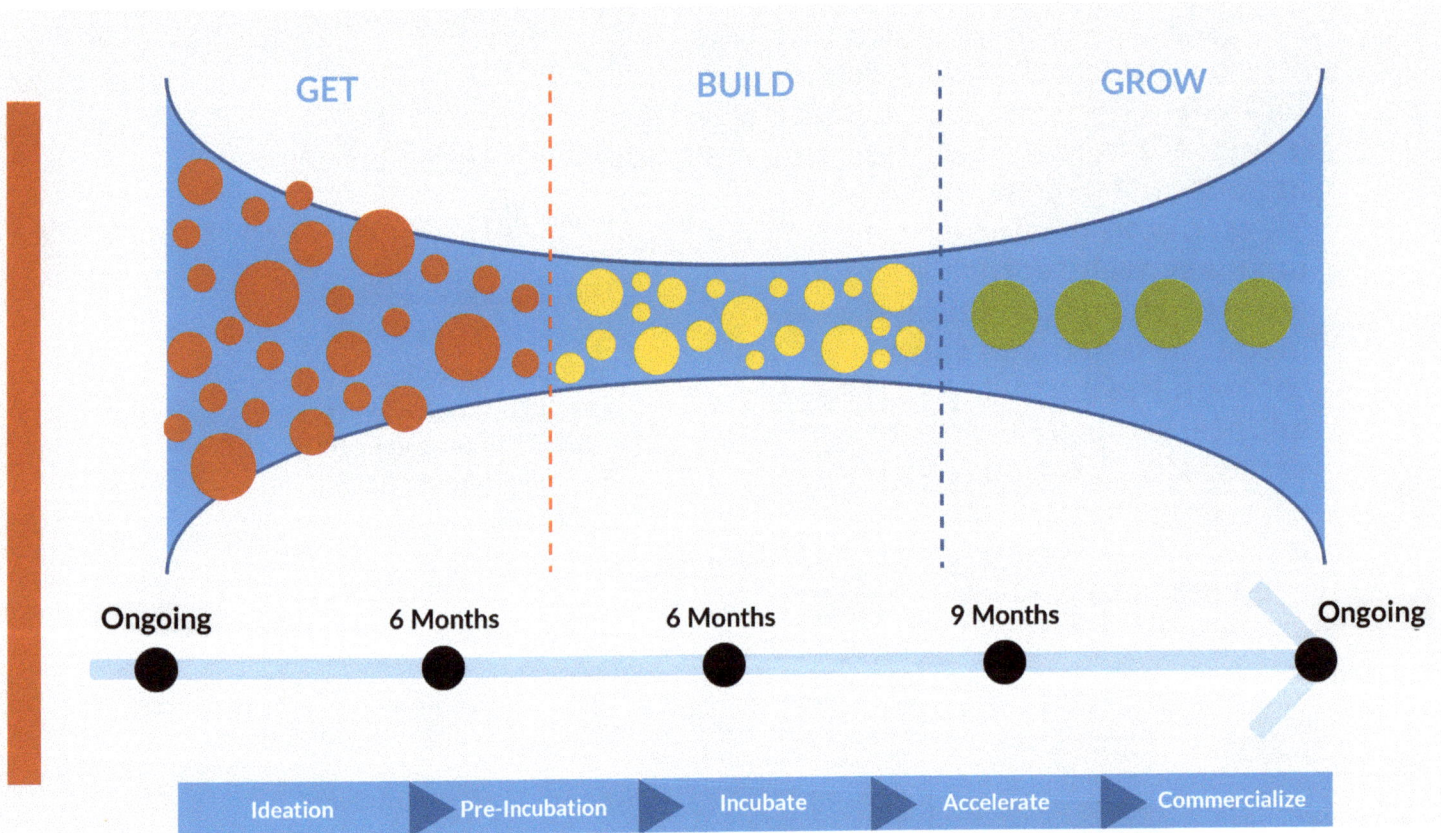

GET   BUILD   GROW

Ongoing   6 Months   6 Months   9 Months   Ongoing

Ideation   Pre-Incubation   Incubate   Accelerate   Commercialize

THE
INNOVATIVE
DINOSAUR

The ideas funnel represents the flow of ideas through the different stages of maturity. At each stage, we have a predefined maturity level, starting from having an idea alone, which will then go through a defined selection process before moving to the next level, and ideally reaching the highest maturity level of commercialization readiness. For each phase and maturity level, we must undertake a specific activity to help mature the idea, thus elevating it to the next level of the product development maturity. The above diagram illustrates the relationship between the activity and the maturity of each idea in the funnel, which aims to help us identify the most suitable course of action for each phase.

IDEA FUNNEL PHASE VS. ACTIVITY

When we mention activity, it is better to refer to the enterprise innovation initiatives interactive design canvas and then link the activities to each of the six spaces. This way, we will have a more visualized understanding of each activity versus the idea funnel phase and the Enterprise innovation initiatives interactive design canvas related space.

The Innovation Culture Fostering activities primarily concern the activities of the Seeding Space, possibly including:

- ∈ Community of practice
- ∈ Knowledge resources and sharing
- ∈ Innovation training
- ∈ Technology monitoring
- ∈ Technology Road mapping

The Stimulating new ideas activities primarily concern the activities of the Get Space, possibly including:

- ∈ Design sprints
- ∈ Internal hackathons
- ∈ Efficiency and design-to-cost (DTC) initiatives
- ∈ Internal innovation competitions
- ∈ Internal collaborative innovation

THE
INNOVATIVE
DINƏSAUR

The activities that build up innovation capacities primarily concern the failed activities and/or initiatives of the Build space, Boost Space, and Collaborate Space, possibly including:

Build Space
- € Patent office
- € Research publications
- € POC development sponsorship
- € New business model design
- € Fast prototyping development sponsorship

Boost Space
- € Advanced labs
- € System and tools
- € Organization structure
- € Leadership
- € Support functions

Collaborate Space
- € Mergers and acquisitions (M&A) strategy
- € Partnership
- € Startup monitoring
- € Academia
- € Crowdsourcing

The activities for realizing new ideas and pushing for their adoption primarily concern the activities and/or initiatives of the Grow Space, possibly including:

- € Internal or external incubators
- € Internal or external accelerators
- € Enterprise spin-off initiatives
- € Enterprise intrapreneurship platforms

THE INNOVATIVE DINESAUR

Ideas Funnel Vs. Maturity

At each phase of the ideas funnel, the ideas have different maturity levels. which are increasing all over the life cycle. The idea funnel maturity levels can be summarized as follows:

Ideation Maturity Level:

During the ideation stage, the ideas are at very early stage of maturity, including idea briefs, initial incomplete thoughts, initial technical feasibility, business viability, and customer desirability assessments. Generally, it is an outcome of brainstorming and initial assessment exercises, and in most cases it ends with a concept paper, pitch presentation, and/or business case.

Preincubation Maturity Level:

During the preincubation stage, the ideas are initially validated, and technical feasibility is assessed through high level mockups, initial POCs, and/or prototypes. Further, initial business model thoughts and a customer desirability assessment are usually conducted.

Incubation Maturity Level:

During the incubation stage, the ideas are often elevated to the next level following the completion of an initial customer desirability exercise, with a clear need, demand, and problem or solution validation through professional assessment. Ideas are converted from POCs and prototypes to a more mature version through the development of MVP features, which is in turn expected to suit target customers' needs, wants, and demands and is competitive enough when compared to competition and substitute offerings.

Acceleration Maturity Level:

During the acceleration stage, the MVPs are thoroughly tested with the target customers. Customer desirability is validated. Business model, value proposition, revenue streams and pricing are designed, validated and tested. Based on the output, the pre-commercialized version is then developed, before manufacturing processes are designed and validated.

Commercialization Maturity Level:

At the commercialization stage, all of the needed business elements are in place: detailed plans are compiled and tested, first set of customers including early adopters are identified, product and its packaging are in order, manufacturing is geared up, and value chain agreements are secured. The primary concerns of this stage include customer acquisition, revenue stream generation and growth hacking.

THE INNOVATIVE DINƆSAUR

IDEAS FUNNEL INVESTMENT & RESOURCES PER PHASE

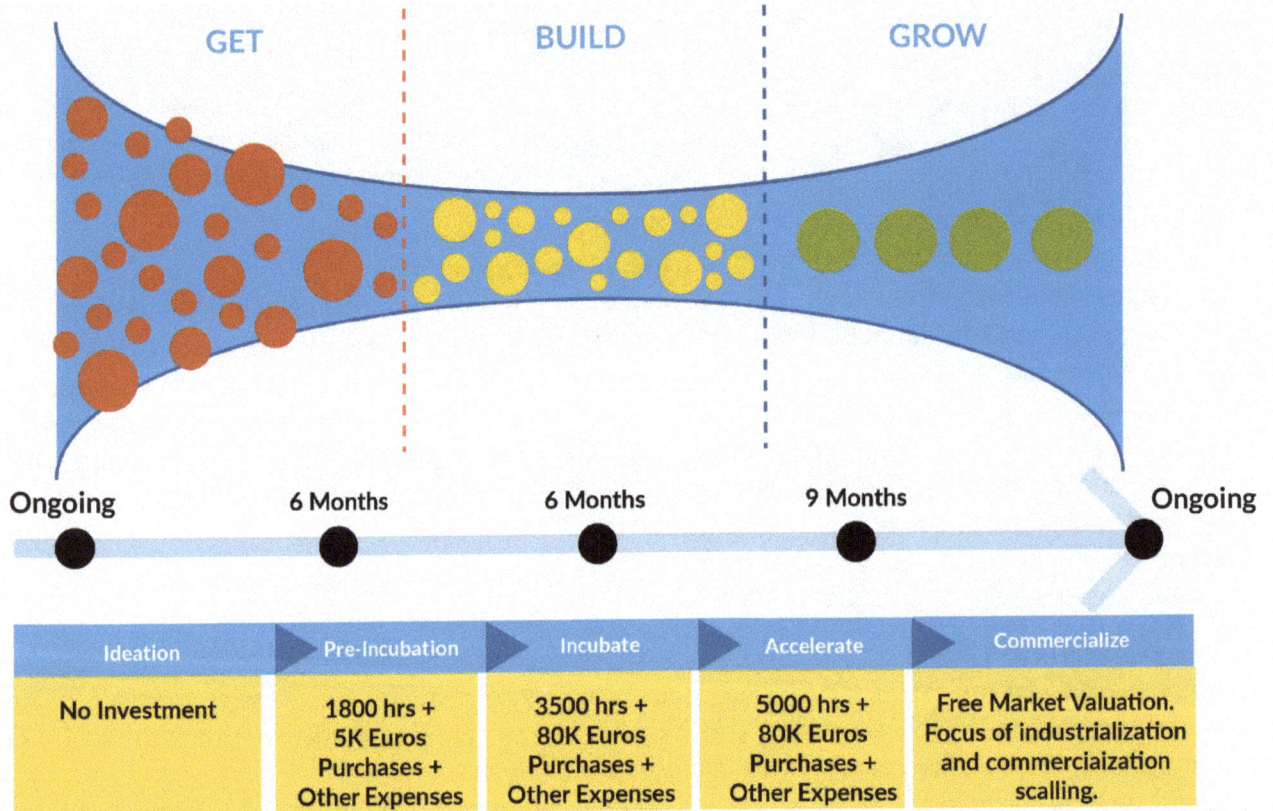

Ideation	Pre-Incubation	Incubate	Accelerate	Commercialize
No Investment	1800 hrs + 5K Euros Purchases + Other Expenses	3500 hrs + 80K Euros Purchases + Other Expenses	5000 hrs + 80K Euros Purchases + Other Expenses	Free Market Valuation. Focus of industrialization and commerciazation scalling.

Designed by: Motaz Agamawi
www.theinnovativedinosaur.com

THE INNOVATIVE DINOSAUR

For each phase of the ideas funnel, we must plan the appropriate needed investment. The investment required per phase and per idea is directly related to the idea maturity level. For more details about each phase needed activities and its related level of idea maturity, please refer to the "Idea Funnel Vs. Maturity Vs. Activity" section.

In comparison to the idea maturity level, the idea funnel investment and resources can be summarized as follows:

Ideation Maturity Level:

At this level, we can consider zero direct investment since most of the activities are generic organizational-based initiatives Additionally, it is usually recommended that the intrapreneurial team members are encouraged to invest their own time and efforts to generate their competitive ideas in this phase.

Preincubation Maturity Level:

At this level, the main cost will be allocated for the development of mockups, initial POCs, or prototypes. The cost element will be mainly dedicated to the time that will be granted to the intrapreneurial team members as well as another minimum budget to be allocated for any needed equipment or license purchases. Typically, we can consider 1,800 working hours over a six-month period, with a minimum of two and maximum of six team members, along with an average purchasing budget of 5,000 Euros.

Incubation Maturity Level:

At this level, the main cost will be allocated for the development of -Minimum Viable Product features - MVP. The cost element will be mainly dedicated to the time that will be granted to intrapreneurial team members as well as another budget to be allocated for any needed equipment or license purchases. Typically, we can consider 3,500 working hours over a six-month period, with minimum of three and maximum of eight team members, along with an average purchasing budget of 20,000 Euros.

Acceleration Maturity Level:

At this level, the main cost will be allocated for the development of the pre-commercialized version. On average, and based on the target product domain and industry nature, if we consider a new product with a large SW component, we can consider 5,000 working hours over a nine-month period, with a minimum of three and maximum of eight team members, along with an average purchasing budget of 80,000 Euros. Additionally, consultancy services may be included either for business management-related services, online marketing, manufacturing sampling and/or commercialization marketing activities.

Commercialization Maturity Level:

At this level, now that all the business elements are in place, the associated commercialization cost will vary according to many parameters, including the product nature, target customer segment, full-scale manufacturing, competition nature versus marketing strategy investment, distribution and channels needed for investment, and growth management strategy. Here, we are focusing on scaling, demand capturing, operational steadiness, and fulfillment readiness.

IDEAS FUNNEL
SUCCESS RATE

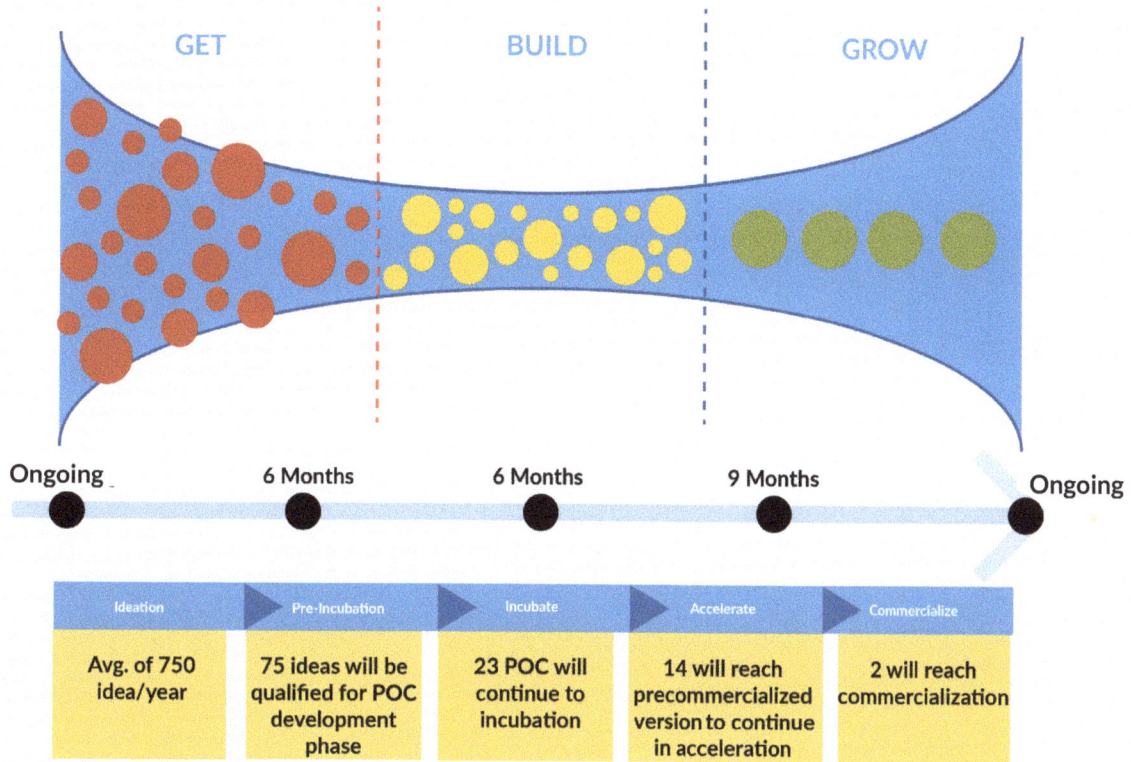

Designed by: Motaz Agamawi
www.theinnovativedinosaur.com

One of the most challenging tasks and objectives of any innovation management or new product development management team is to increase the success rate of ideas-turned-products that have a high economic impact and reward for the organization.

Now, let's agree that the actual cost of the new product development is the result of all the associated investments a firm has placed to reach a single successfully commercialized product including all the failure cost associated from all the other unsuccessful product ideas. In other words, the cost of a successful commercialized product equals the sum of all investments made for the full number of ideas within the ideas funnel across its different stages, plus the cost of the successfully commercialized product.

THUS, THE COST OF INNOVATION FAILURE DIRECTLY AFFECTS THE OVERALL EFFICIENCY AND IMPACT OF THE ENTERPRISE INNOVATION PERFORMANCE.

Based on various statistics, reports, and the general opinions of innovation and new product development experts, the success rate for newly developed products is an average of one out of seven. Thus, for every seven products that are introduced, only one achieves the desired economic impact. If we calculated the average from the beginning of the funnel, or the ideation stage, then, passing through POC and MVP before reaching commercialization, it will be clear that the success ratio is complex and its associated cost is enormous.

The main concept behind the ideas funnel is to apply the "fail fast, Win Fast" concept to minimize the final innovation failure cost as much as possible. We all accept the concept that failure is more often than not an unavoidable fact of the innovation management domain. Starting from the idea stage and passing through the funnel, the proper selection of the most competitive ideas directly impacts the final cost structure and minimizing the cost of innovation failure while increasing the overall organization economic performance.

Each of the three stages of the idea funnel has its own selection criteria, evaluation techniques and different selection committee members profiles. For example, selecting an idea from the Get Stage to be included in the Build Stage to be furtherly developed as a POC, we can depend more on the internal organization team members. But, if we are designing a selection criterion for moving an idea in the Build stage from preincubation to incubation or from incubation to acceleration, then we must have more weight for the customer validation and external expert feedback. As much as we can engage target customers during the concept validation as early as possible, thus the greater our success rate may be.

IDEAS FUNNEL – SPACE BETWEEN HYPHEN AND "TEAM"TEAM ROLES OVER DIFFERENT PHASES

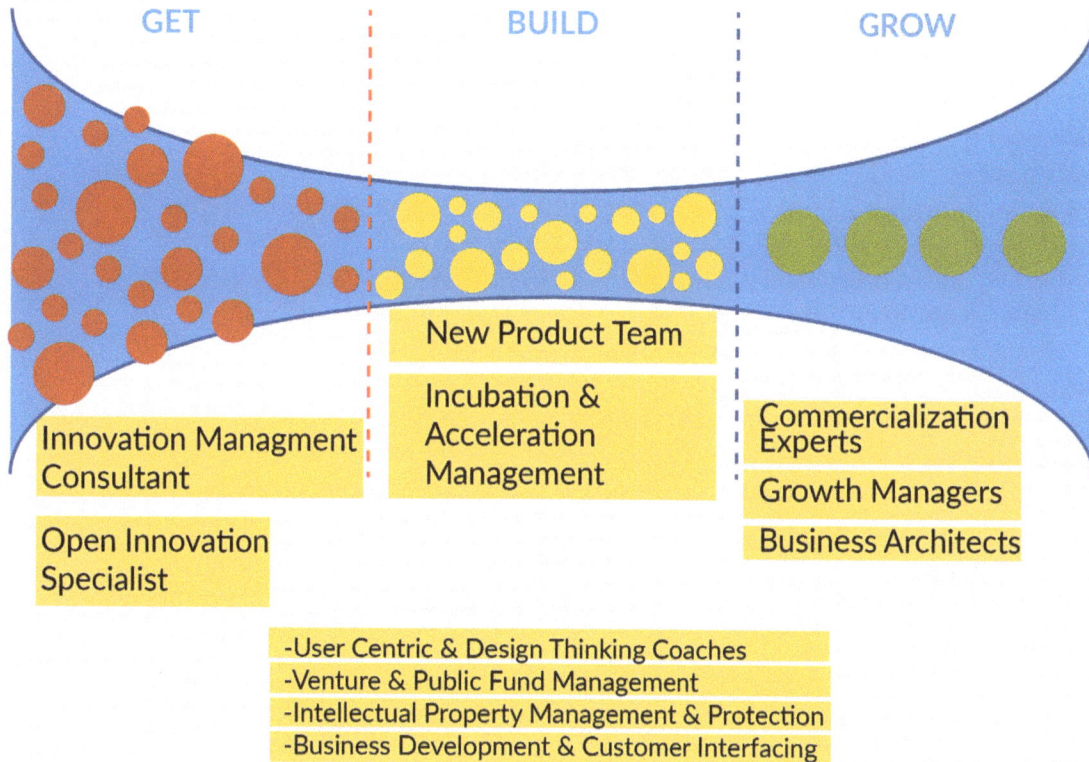

GET

BUILD

GROW

New Product Team

Incubation & Acceleration Management

Innovation Managment Consultant

Open Innovation Specialist

Commercialization Experts

Growth Managers

Business Architects

-User Centric & Design Thinking Coaches
-Venture & Public Fund Management
-Intellectual Property Management & Protection
-Business Development & Customer Interfacing

Designed by: Motaz Agamawi
www.theinnovativedinosaur.com

THE INNOVATIVE DINOSAUR

Through its three phases — Get, Build, Grow — the idea funnel represents the different activities and thus the range of necessary competencies and skill-sets of the innovation organization team. Accordingly, we can use the idea funnel to identify the required competencies and skills based on the nature of each phase. In the Get Phase, we must direct our focus on innovation management and open innovation management knowledge and skills. In the Build Phase, our main focus is on new product development management, incubation, and acceleration management. In the Grow Phase, our main focus is toward technology commercialization, growth hacking, and business architecture. Across the three phases, we have areas of common knowledge that can either be replicated as a required skill set for each phase or a cross-functional team can provide it. This skill set includes user-centric and design thinking processes, intellectual property management, venture and public funding as well as business development and customer interfacing.

TEAM COMPETENCY BUILDING GUIDE

In the table we list some courses, certificates and training workshop focusing on developing the needed skills and competencies needed over the different phases of the ideas funnel.

COURSE	DOMAIN	LEVEL	BODY
HELLO DESIGN THINKING	Design Thinking	Intro	ideou.com
POWER OF PURPOSE	Design Thinking	Intro	ideou.com
INSIGHTS FOR INNOVATION	Design Thinking	Intro	ideou.com
FROM IDEAS TO ACTION	Design Thinking	Intro	ideou.com
STORYTELLING FOR INFLUENCE	Design Thinking	Intro	ideou.com
LEADING FOR CREATIVITY	Design Thinking	Intro	ideou.com
DESIGNING FOR CHANGE	Design Thinking	Intro	ideou.com
IMPLEMENTING DESIGN THINKING IN ORGANIZATION	Design Thinking	Intermediate	hpi-academy.de
DESIGN THINKING AND ORGANIZATION IMPLEMENTATION	Design Thinking	Advanced	hpi-academy.de

THE
INNOVATIVE
DINOSAUR

COURSE	DOMAIN	LEVEL	BODY
DESIGN THINKING FOR EXECUTIVES	Design Thinking	Advanced	dschool.stanford.edu
NEW PRODUCT DEVELOPMENT PROFESSIONAL (NPDP) CERTIFICATION	NPD	Advanced	pdma.org
LEVEL 1 - ENTRY CERTIFICATE IN BUSINESS ANALYSIS™ (ECBA™)	NPD	Intermediate	iiba.org
LEVEL 2 - CERTIFICATION OF CAPABILITY IN BUSINESS ANALYSIS™ (CCBA®)	NPD	Advanced	iiba.org
LEVEL 3 - CERTIFIED BUSINESS ANALYSIS PROFESSIONAL (CBAP®)	NPD	Advanced	iiba.org
ASSOCIATE SYSTEM ENGINEER PROFESSIONAL (ASEP)	NPD	Intro	incose.org
CERTIFIED SYSTEM ENGINEER PROFESSIONAL (CSEP)	NPD	Intermediate	incose.org
CERTIFIED INNOVATION MANAGER	Innovation Management	Intermediate	ecqa.org
CERTIFIED IMP³ROVE GUIDE	Innovation Management	Advanced	improve-innovation.eu

THE
INNOVATIVE
DINOSAUR

COURSE	DOMAIN	LEVEL	BODY
CERTIFIED IMP³ROVE EXPERT	Innovation Management	Advanced	improve-innovation.eu
GINI CERTIFIED INNOVATION PROFESSIONAL (CINP)®	Innovation Management	Intermediate	gini.org
GINI CERTIFIED CHIEF INNOVATION OFFICER (CCINO)®	Innovation Management	Advanced	gini.org
INCUBATION MANAGER TRAINING	Innovation Management	Intermediate	infodev.org
OPEN INNOVATION WORKSHOP	Innovation Management	Advanced	innovation-academy.co.uk
AGILE PROJECT MANAGER (AGILEPM®)	Agile	Intro	apmg-international.com
PMI AGILE CERTIFIED PRACTITIONER (PMI-ACP)®	Agile	Advanced	pmi.org
CERTIFIED SCRUMMASTER®	Agile	Intro	scrumalliance.org
CERTIFIED SCRUM PRODUCT OWNER®	Agile	Intro	scrumalliance.org

THE
INNOVATIVE
DINOSAUR

COURSE	DOMAIN	LEVEL	BODY
CERTIFIED SCRUM DEVELOPER®	Agile	Intro	scrumalliance.org
CERTIFIED SCRUM PROFESSIONAL®	Agile	Intermediate	scrumalliance.org
CERTIFIED SCRUM LEADER	Agile	Advanced	scrumalliance.org
CERTIFIED INNOVATION STRATEGIST (CINS)®	Strategy	Intermediate	gini.org
AUTHORIZED INNOVATION ASSESSOR (AINA)®	Strategy	Intermediate	gini.org
CERTIFIED CHANGE MANAGEMENT PROFESSIONAL™	Strategy	Intermediate	myccmp.org
STRATEGIC MANAGEMENT PROFESSIONAL	Strategy	Advanced	strategyassociation.org
CERTIFIED KPI PROFESSIONAL	Strategy	Intermediate	kpiinstitute.org
INTRO TO MANAGEMENT OF TECHNOLOGY	MOT	Intro	nu.edu.eg

THE INNOVATIVE DINOSAUR

COURSE	DOMAIN	LEVEL	BODY
INTRO TO TECHNOLOGY FORECASTING & ROAD-MAPPING	MOT	Intro	nu.edu.eg
INTRO TO STRATEGIC MANAGEMENT OF TECHNOLOGY	MOT	Intro	nu.edu.eg
BUSINESS MODEL DESIGN	MOT	Intro	nu.edu.eg
VALUE PROPOSITION DESIGN	MOT	Intro	nu.edu.eg
DESIGN THINKING	MOT	Intro	nu.edu.eg
INTRO TO FAST PROTOTYPING	MOT	Intro	nu.edu.eg
INTRO TO HIGH-TECH MARKETING (CROSSING THE CHASM)	MOT	Intro	nu.edu.eg
INTRO TO INNOVATION MANAGEMENT	MOT	Intro	nu.edu.eg

THE
INNOVATIVE
DINOSAUR

CHAPTER 10:
ENTERPRISE WORKFORCE 3.0, ESTABLISHED

The current business context is moving more and more towards global operations, particularly with organizations that have both an industrial and R&D presence on the international stage. Such a presence either exists to serve specific global market expansion strategies or global capacity and cost efficiency increase. The expansion of global operations brings forth opportunities and challenges alike. Organizations of all sizes must capitalize on their global footprints to guarantee global competitiveness.

The management's ability to establish and expand their footprint based on competency and competitiveness is what guarantees continued success. By way of illustration, relocating a global outsourcing center to achieve being an excellence center, then moving that model towards a global innovation center is when organizations reach the highest level of return on investment. Here, a clear strategy for operations is essential starting on day one, requiring agility and adaptability as the global site's maturity evolves.

In this chapter, we (re)trace the different models, success stories, and methods for Establishing the Enterprise Workforce 3.0, mapping out the context for building global development centers and related explorations of concepts, challenges, and opportunities for remote team management through discussing three models with their different levels of complexity. We begin with the work-from-home policy that is offered by many organizations, and that was heavily utilized during the COVID-19 pandemic, along with explorations of the global distributed team's management challenges, the full remote workforce model, and the crowdsourcing labor model. For small and medium enterprises, new working models are offering a magic solution for the workforce elastic capacity, giving options for professional services and deliveries with bare minimum commitment. For larger enterprise, these models can be perceived as both an opportunity and a threat. If a large enterprise can reach the necessary means, including the methods and processes needed to integrate those models within the overall organization operational model, the enterprise will benefit from the workforce elastic capacity, tapping into the global talent pool, and even more competitive costing structure. On the other side, the enterprise must recognize that an inability to integrate with such models will negatively impact the overall competitiveness of the enterprise.

CHAPTER TEN LIST OF REFERENCES & EXTRA READINGS

CHAPTER TEN SECTIONS:

€ Global Development Center
€ Modern Teams Working Models
€ Crowdsourcing Employment Model

1. ONLINE YOUTH WORK AND E-YOUTH. by Levente Székely, Dr. Ádám Nagy.
2. Personal Knowledge Networks in the Mobile Millennium.by Reddy, Ramana.
3. Knowledge and Information Workers: Who Are They? by White, Colin.
4. Visual Collaboration Tools, *www.Miro.com*
5. Visual Collaboration Tools, *www.Mural.com*
6. Advanced Collaboration Tools, *www.Slack.com*
7. Advanced Collaboration Tools, *www.Trello.com*
8. Project Management Tools, *www.Asana.com*
9. Project Management Tools, *www.SmartSheet.com*
10. Remote Workforce Enterprises, *www.Crossover.com*
11. Remote Workforce Enterprises, *www.Weworkremotely.com*
12. Remote Workforce Enterprises, *www.Buffer.com*
13. Remote Workforce Enterprises, *www.Andela.com*
14. Remote Workforce Tools, *www.Basecamp.com*
15. Remote Workforce Tools, *www.Getharvest.com*
16. Remote Workforce Tools, *www.HackerRank.com*
17. Remote Workforce Tools, *www.debonogroup.com*
18. Remote Workforce Tools, *www.Udemy.com*

THE
INNOVATIVE
DIN€SAUR

19. Remote Workforce Tools, *www.Coursera.org*
20. Remote Workforce Tools, *www.linkedin.com/learning*
21. Remote Workforce Tools, *www.edx.org*
22. Remote Workforce Support Services, *www.Remote.com*
23. Remote Workforce Support Services, *www.Shieldgeo.com*
24. Remote Workforce Support Services, *www.Safetywing.com*
25. Basic tasks crowdsourcing, *www.Mturk.com*
26. Basic tasks crowdsourcing, *www.Microworkers.com*
27. Business or product naming crowdsourcing, *www.Namingforce.com*
28. Business or product naming crowdsourcing, *www.Squadhelp.com*
29. Business or product naming crowdsourcing, *www.available.com*
30. Legal services and advises crowdsourcing, *www.Upcounsel.com*
31. Legal services and advises crowdsourcing, *www.Legalzoom.com*
32. Legal services and advises crowdsourcing, *www.Rocketlawyer.com*
33. Accounting and financial services crowdsourcing, *www.Bookkeeper.com*
34. Accounting and financial services crowdsourcing, *www.Bookkeeper360.com*
35. Accounting and financial services crowdsourcing, *www.Kpmgspark.com*
36. Creative branding & communication crowdsourcing, *www.99design.com*
37. Creative branding & communication crowdsourcing, *www.Hatchwise.com*
38. Generic Professional Services crowdsourcing, *www.freelancer.com*
39. Generic Professional Services crowdsourcing, *www.Upworks.com*
40. Innovation Crowdsourcing, *www.Innocentive.com*
41. Innovation Crowdsourcing, *www.Presans.com*
42. Innovation Crowdsourcing, *www.OpenIdeo.com*
43. Innovation Crowdsourcing, *www.Ideo.com*
44. Crowd funding, *www.Kickstarter.com*
45. Crowd funding, *www.Indiegogo.com*
46. Crowd Equity Investment, *www.Wefunder.com*
47. Crowd Equity Investment, *www.Localstake.com*
48. Crowd Equity Investment, *www.Circleup.com*
49. Crowd Equity Investment, *www.Peerrealty.com*
50. Crowd Equity Investment, *www.Fundable.com*
51. Crowd Equity Investment, *www.Crowdfunder.com*
52. Crowd Equity Investment, *www.Gofundme.com*
53. Crowd Equity Investment, *www.Patreon.com*
54. Crowd shipping, *www.flexe.com*
55. Crowd shipping, *www.flexport.com*
56. Crowd shipping, *www.Piggybee.com*
57. Crowd shipping, *www.roadie.com*
58. Crowd shipping, *www.Convoy.com*
59. Crowd shipping, *www.Cargomatic.com*
60. Crowd shipping, *www.Flex.Amazon.com*
61. Crowd shipping, *www.Doordash.com*
62. Crowd shipping, *www.flexe.com*
63. Crowd shipping, *www.Sparefoot.com*
64. Crowd Supporting NLP, *www.Definedcrowd.com*
65. Crowd Supporting NLP, *www.Scale.com*
66. Crowd Supporting NLP, *www.Appen.com*
67. Crowd Supporting NLP, *www.Cloudfactory.com*
68. Crowd Supporting NLP, *www.Sama.com*
69. Crowd Supporting NLP, *www.clickworker.com*

THE
INNOVATIVE
DINCSAUR

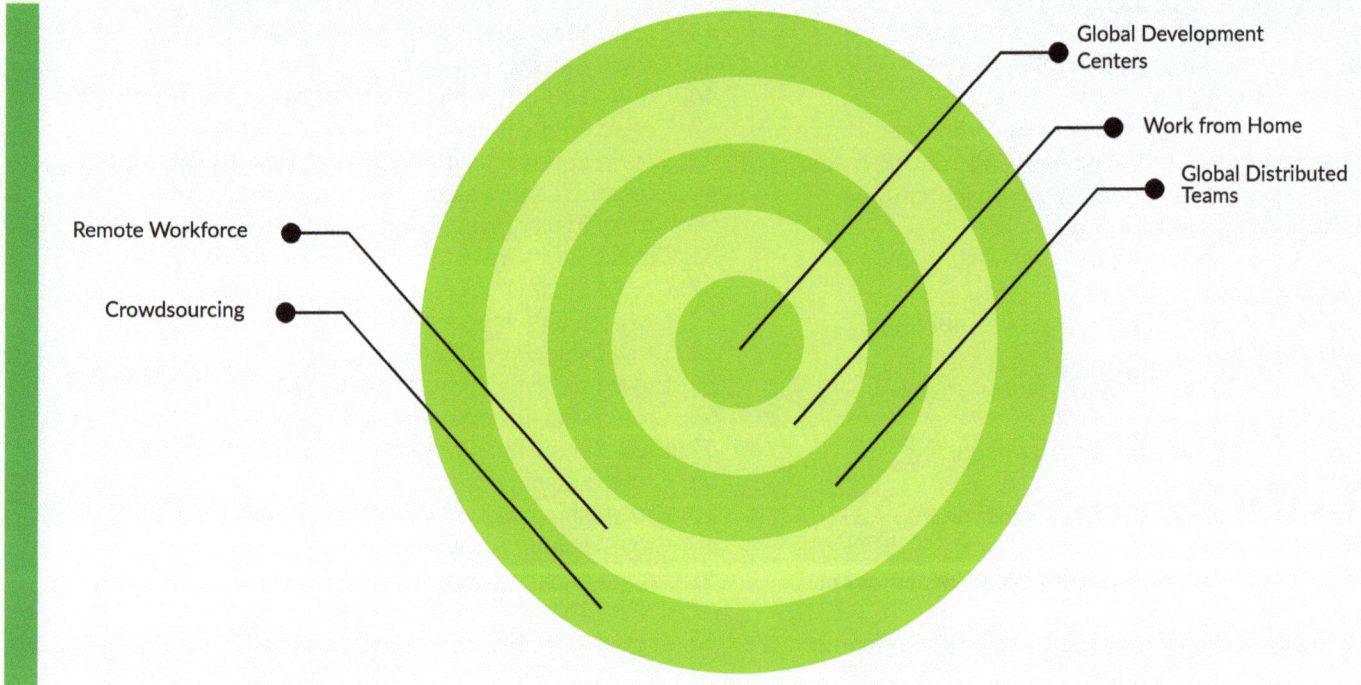

Global Development Centers

Work from Home

Global Distributed Teams

Remote Workforce

Crowdsourcing

Designed by: Motaz Agamawi
www.theinnovativedinosaur.com

THE INNOVATIVE DINOSAUR

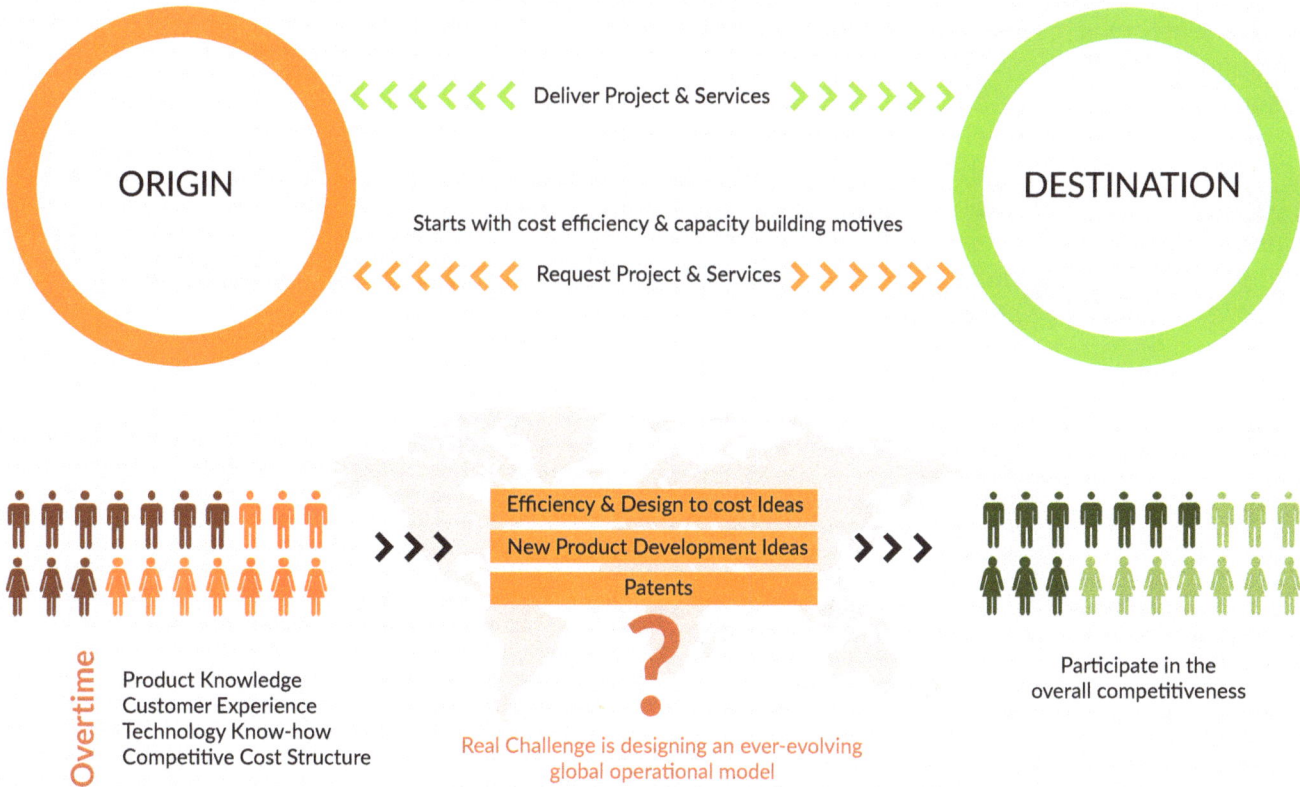

ORIGIN

Deliver Project & Services

Starts with cost efficiency & capacity building motives

Request Project & Services

DESTINATION

Efficiency & Design to cost Ideas

New Product Development Ideas

Patents

?

Overtime

Product Knowledge
Customer Experience
Technology Know-how
Competitive Cost Structure

Real Challenge is designing an ever-evolving
global operational model

Participate in the
overall competitiveness

Designed by: Motaz Agamawi
www.theinnovativedinosaur.com

THE
INNOVATIVE
DINOSAUR

Today, due to globalization, and other global integration factors, many businesses are either outsourcing or insourcing part(s) of their business activities. Outsourcing occurs when part of the development lifecycle is assigned to a third-party supplier, either to achieve cost efficiency or acquire specific know-how, even benefit from dynamic capacity. Insourcing is also a popular practice in which enterprises establish an offshore remote technical center to achieve the same objectives of the former outsourcing model but within the organization's boundaries. Cost efficiency and increased capacity are the common drivers behind the adoption of outsourcing or insourcing frameworks. The initial questions that interested enterprises must explore usually relate to the type of services, tasks, scope, development (either task-based or ticket-based), business model (either fixed cost or time and material), and management structure. These explorations help the organization establish the part within the value chain should be rerouted to outsourcing or insourcing. Enterprises generally begin this practice by guiding the basic parts of the value chain into a more cost competitive geographical location. The long journey of outsourcing and/or insourcing integration is packed with challenges and opportunities. In essence, every challenge presents an opportunity, and vice versa.

After the organization management team decides upon their route into the future, the journey is then initiated by a group of middle management members. But before they commence, they must understand the mindset and perception of the two different parts of the equation: the "outsourcing origin," or team from the mother company employs outsourcing model; and the "outsourcing destination," or the team that executes outsourcing services.

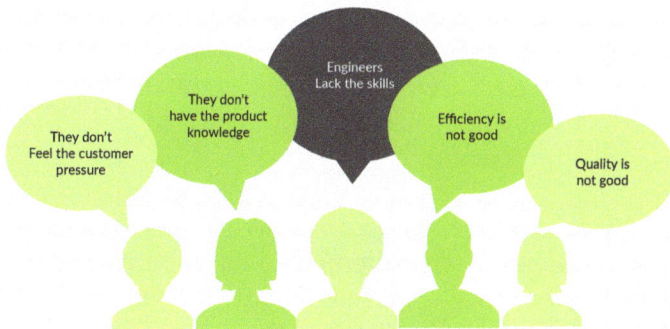

ORIGIN TEAM CLAIMS

They don't Feel the customer pressure

They don't have the product knowledge

Engineers Lack the skills

Efficiency is not good

Quality is not good

DESTINATION TEAM CLAIMS

We do not have enough tools

We are disconnected from the industry

We are trapped in a very limited scope

We may be low cost but high competency

We are not given the room for innovation

Unable to win proper work scope

Unable to win business

No value creation to global team

First Center to close with the next restructure

OUTSOURCING MANAGEMENT PRESSURE

Unable to attract the right talents

Unable to retain your good people

Can't grow your business

Unable to realize the economies of scale

Lose your competitive edge

THE INNOVATIVE DINOSAUR

Origin teams usually have a predetermined perception with respect to the above-described equation. Such organizations educate their employees on how the outsourcing approach will offload repetitive tasks that do not require highly-skilled labor to a cost-effective destination, creating the necessary space for the origin team to engage in high value activities. In many cases, the origin team cultivates an image that suggests they are more skilled than their counterpart, the destination team, and thus in a position of seniority or superiority. Sometimes this leads to a customer-supplier relationship, even within the insourcing model, which results in a disconnected teams within the same enterprise. Another set of common perceptions within outsourcing origin teams includes that the team in the other part of the world is immune to customer pressure , do not have product knowledge or customer needs understanding, and although outsourcing destination teams are cost effective but there output deliverables are less efficient and with lower quality standards.

Destination teams usually have a predetermined perception, too. Such organizations communicate to their employees where they fall on the value chain, and that if they prove their capabilities, their roles will be expanded, be it through a wider scope of participation, or more complex tasks and assignments. In many cases, the destination team cultivates an image that suggests the other team is dealing with a superiority complex and refuses to cooperate, and consequently a set of common concerns and issues rolls in: we are disconnected from the industry, and the technology trends; we are not allowed to propose innovative ideas related to processes and/or new product features or ideas; we do not have customer interfacing, and we do not have enough training investments; we are the more cost-effective and efficient model; we are disconnected from the mother company, and we are less valued than our colleagues in the other part of the world.

As the bridge between two perspectives, the enterprise's management faces continual, even immense, pressure. From the global team perspective, the following obstacles may appear in the origin team's path: the inability to attract and retain the right talent, challenges in growing the destination team, which leads to the inability to realize the economy of scale and then a lost opportunity for the enterprise to increase its overall competitiveness. On the other side, the outsourcing destination is facing another set of challenges: the inability to attract the proper activities scope, which leads to the inability to attract sizable businesses and less value creation for the global team, perhaps posing a threat to their jobs and operations.

Over the course of my nearly two-decade-long career, I have stood on both sides of the equation: as a customer and supplier, and as part of an insourcing origin global team and a destination team.

This journey has taught me an indispensable series of best practices, including the following insights:

ⴹ There are two approaches to establishing our global insourcing strategy: build the insourcing team as either an internal supplier or an extension of the global team, which physically exists in a different geographical location. In my professional experience, the latter approach has proven to be better in the long-term. This cannot be achieved without a clear commitment from the enterprise's leadership teams.

ⴹ Terms like "Low-Cost Countries" and "High-Cost Countries" may come with in-built biases attached, and if misused by the management, may lead to the establishment of a toxic working culture for both teams, origin and destination.

ⴹ Providing the outsourcing destination with comparable facilities, equipment, benefits, processes, methods, tools, and the enforcement of a shared corporate culture, widens the scope for creative solutions, while closing destructive gaps.

ⴹ Quality is a culture, and it is not enforced by simply implementing proper processes and methods. Outsourcing destination teams must have the same quality of facility, benefits, services, and tools as the team based in the mother company. If we compromise the quality of our outsourcing destinations, then the quality of output will be also impacted. We provide our outsourcing destination teams with the comparable production and development gears, both in terms of quality and quantity. In short, if the same gear is needed to best conduct a certain task, then shouldn't teams in all geographical locations have access to it, leveling the globally-driven playing field?

ⴹ Best practices depend upon the best choice of leadership team members for the outsourcing destination; we cannot have one without the other. Therefore, globally-minded professionals, with strong work ethics and problem-solving skills, are our backbone in this journey. Finding a balance of power and access between the different leadership teams will involve an open dialogue on the mother company and outsourcing destination cultures — it is the leader's job to ensure that conversations precipitate changes and consensus.

ⴹ Ensure that the corporate mission, vision, strategy and yearly plans are thoroughly communicated to the outsourcing destination teams. Direct top management engagement with the destination teams is of utmost strategic importance. This can be achieved through annual roadshows, regular workshops, and continuous engagement across the organization, the industry, and, more and more, the world.

ⴹ Opening the pipelines between the different organization functions in the mother company headquarters and its outsourcing destination counterpart is of great benefit to the overall culture and implemented processes on ground.

ϵ To keep a dedicated eye out for talents and fast-trackers, is to be mindful of the future. Creating global opportunities for the outsourcing destination team members guarantees the retention of the talents and motivates other team members to expand and reach their career aspirations.

ϵ Respect the local context, including the cultures, challenges, and needs, by granting autonomy to the local management of the outsourcing destination, and working hand in hand with them.

ϵ Opening the doors and opportunities for inter-company relocation from outsourcing destinations to the global teams, and vice versa, gives our enterprise a competitive edge, as talent- and knowledge-sharing models yield greater organizational outreach with different but connected markets and cultures.

ϵ Establishing the proper pipeline to receive innovation ideas and process improvement initiatives from the outsourcing destination, along with the proper means of implementing what makes sense, is of great value to future-facing enterprises.

ϵ Cultural awareness and sensitivity workshops are an asset for origin and destination teams alike, as they foster an interconnected, or bridged, workplace culture.

ϵ Outsourcing destination teams must work on acquiring projects, customers, and product knowledge to be able to increase the value of their contributions within the overall product and service delivery.

ϵ To create the necessary time and space for leveraging local talent and higher workplace value, the destination teams must prioritize efficiency improvement and standardization — meaning, follow the industry's quality standards with no quality compromises.

ϵ A smart budget accommodates the continuous development of hard and soft skills for the outsourcing destination teams.

ϵ When members of the origin and destination teams travel to one another on organized trips, the cross-team pollination of ideas and knowledge dissemination not only accelerates, it diversifies.

ϵ Designing functional organization structural links between both teams, and supporting them with the informed organizational objectives, is essential to mitigating enterprise silos and eliminating customer-supplier relations by embracing team culture.

☐ Build the insourcing team as an extension of the global team, which physically exists in a different geographical location.

☐ Do not use the terms like "Low-Cost Countries" and "High-Cost Countries."

☐ Quality is a culture, providing the outsourcing destination with comparable facilities, equipment, benefits, processes, methods, tools.

☐ Enforcement of a shared corporate culture, widens the scope for creative solutions, while closing destructive gaps.

☐ Choice of leadership team members for the outsourcing destination; globally-minded professionals, with strong work ethics and problem-solving skills.

☐ Finding a balance of power and access between the different leadership teams will involve an open dialogue on the mother company and outsourcing destination cultures.

☐ Ensure that the corporate mission, vision, strategy and yearly plans are thoroughly communicated to the outsourcing destination teams.

☐ Opening the pipelines between the different organization functions in the mother company headquarters and its outsourcing destination counterpart.

☐ Creating global opportunities for the outsourcing destination team members.

☐ Respect the local context, including the cultures, challenges, and needs, by granting autonomy to the local management.

THE
INNOVATIVE
DINOSAUR

☐ Establishing the proper pipeline to receive innovation ideas and process improvement initiatives from the outsourcing destination.

☐ Cultural awareness and sensitivity workshops are an asset for origin and destination teams alike.

☐ Outsourcing destination teams must work on acquiring projects, customers, and product knowledge to be able to increase the value of their contributions.

☐ The destination teams must prioritize efficiency improvement and standardization — meaning, follow the industry's quality standards with no quality compromises.

☐ A smart budget accommodates the continuous development of hard and soft skills for the outsourcing destination teams.

☐ Designing functional organization structural links between both teams, and supporting them with the informed organizational objectives, is essential to mitigating enterprise silos and eliminating customer-supplier relations.

THE INNOVATIVE DINOSAUR

Upon the implementation of the listed tips and recommendations,

our operations will have an elevated probability of success, followed and supported by a more competitive structure. Such successes may give life to an outsourcing team, whose members will participate in more and more projects, products, and service deliveries, year after year. The teams in the outsourcing destination are gaining greater experience and exposure, maturing over time in terms of size and capabilities. At a certain stage, the outsourcing destination will move from basic outsourcing center toward excellence center. Over time, the outsourcing destination center will start to have expertise in specific domains, rising up the value chain, with more responsibilities and a wider scope of service delivery. With each project and delivery, each failure and success, each customer interfacing and customer complaint, the handling of the outsourcing destination team's maturity, know-how, and experience is increases as the overall competencies are being built. It is undeniable that the value creation and contribution of the outsourcing teams are contributing to the mother company overall competitiveness. Through this journey of evolution within the value chain, the leaders of the destination team have been moving from basic outsourcing scope to excellence and, in time, may make a direct contribution to the organization's overall innovation capabilities. Each stage of the maturity lifecycle, from the challenges to opportunities, is synonymous with change. The complexities of managing the competitive industries of today must be addressed and dissected in an effective manner when the leadership sees fit. Some of these complexities can be summarized as:

⊂ Increases in the maturity of the outsourcing destination, increases the value to the mother company. Simply, gain more with less cost.

⊂ During the different maturity stages of the outsourcing destination, the mother company's management team must evolve at the same speed, often by way of providing greater autonomy, changing up the management style, and creating opportunities to increase the scope of activities done within the outsourcing destination, consistent with increases in team competency.

⊂ Over time, many jobs will be transferred from the origin team to the outsourcing destination. In some cases, upon achieving high maturity

THE INNOVATIVE DINOSAUR

in the outsourcing destination, most activities — sometimes all — are transferred to the outsourcing destination teams. The mother company team becomes disconnected from the reality of how things are done. At this stage, top management must be aware, ensuring that the organization's managerial levels are professionally designed without bias towards other geographical locations.

€ As more and more positions and task scopes are being transferred to outsourcing destinations, job security fears and issues commonly emerge within the origin teams, and sometimes morph into forms of friction between the two teams. Management must dialogue with the conflicting parties, answering their different concerns and designing a strategy that utilizes the competitive advantage of each geographical location.

€ The increase of competencies and experiences in the outsourcing destination, directly increases the talent retention competition. The outsourcing destination team members become more and more attractive for other organization including competition. During this stage, the talent competition becomes more global and thus less limited to the outsourcing destination's local context, for instance, the front office opportunities available to the outsourcing destination teams. Accordingly, outsourcing destination centers are not only competing for financial benefits, but also for changes in traditional working modes, like having greater access to challenging and complex assignments — from increased customer interfacing and engagement in new product development, to increased global career progression, and participation in shaping the future through clear engagements within research and innovation activities. Completing all of this amounts to the creation of a light at the end of the tunnel for the teams working in the outsourcing destinations.

€ The mother company's top management must realize that wisdom is not located in the headquarters alone, and that the global expansion and presence of the organization in different parts of the world will lead to the existence of talents in different geographical locations. It is unacceptable to find organizations operating in scores of countries, while all of its top management come from a single nationality, which, in most cases, will be the nationality where the headquarters is located. A common example of this gap in representation is an organization establishing 50 to 70 percent of its production sites in China, and 50 percent of its research and development in either India, Egypt, or Eastern Europe, while its management team does not include a single team member from any of those countries. From top management to the headquarters' team, diversity of leadership ensures a stronger global management performance. Clear examples of strength in diversity can be found in digital- and software-based companies, like the Indian-born CEOs of Microsoft, Google, Adobe, and previous CEO of MasterCard.

€ Managing the global outsourcing destination's cost structure presents another pressing challenge. The mother company's top management must accept that moving up the value chain and creating more value will lead to an increase of the personnel cost structure of the outsourcing destination. Methods for evaluating the cost should include the return on investment, not just monitoring an absolute value. The cost should be evaluated through comparisons with the output and considerations related to the in-house know-how gained. This requires a special handling, particularly when such outsourcing destinations work on research and development as part of a traditional manufacturing enterprise. As talent output and personnel cost employ other means of evaluation, the standard costing methods of traditional manufacturers lose grip on the industry. Squeezing the outsourcing destination's cost structure will yield a lower quality in terms of final deliveries in combination with less competitiveness when attracting ideal or promising talent. Furthermore, talent retention formulas and targets should be designed and monitored based on brainware industry standards, not those set by traditional organizations.

Increase of destination Maturity	The mother company's management team must evolve at the same speed, often by way of providing greater autonomy.
Transfer most activities to destination entity	The mother company team becomes disconnected from the reality of how things are done. At this stage, top management must be aware, ensuring that the organization's managerial levels are professionally designed without bias towards other geographical locations.
Rise of job security fears	Management must dialogue with the conflicting parties, answering their different concerns and designing a strategy that utilizes the competitive advantage of each geographical location.
Increase of competencies & experiences in the outsourcing destination	At this stage, outsourcing destination employee's retention packages are not the competing element, but also working modes like complex assignments, engagement in new product development, to increasing global career progression, and engagements within research and innovation activities. Targeting the creation of a light at the end of the tunnel for the teams working in the outsourcing destinations.
Global Top Management representation	The mother company's top management must realize that wisdom is not located in the headquarters alone, and that the global expansion and presence of the organization in different parts of the world will lead to the existence of talents in different geographical locations.
Change of cost structure	The mother company's top management must accept that moving up the value chain and creating more value will lead to an increase of the personnel cost structure in the outsourcing destination. The cost should be evaluated through comparisons with the output and considerations related to the in-house know-how gained.

Moving a global outsourcing center to achieve being an excellence center, then moving it towards a global innovation center, is when organizations reach the highest level of return on investment. Starting from day one, this necessitates a clear, well-defined strategy of operations, which must be agile and continuously evolving along with the global site's maturity level. Management's ability to build a global footprint based on competency and competitiveness is what guarantees continued success.

THE
INNOVATIVE
DINOSAUR

A few years ago, I was assigned to design and manage a global innovation cultural transformation program. The scope covered both industrial and R&D entities located in more than 18 countries and targeting more than thirty thousand team members in 40 globally-distributed centers and manufacturing facilities. We decided to launch a global internal innovation competition that included a well-defined educational experience designed for the target population.

The experience was thrilling and fulfilling, leaving me with a series of lasting lessons, some of which include:

- We designed a weekly hour-long educational pulse session for a period of six weeks. For the industrial sites, the sessions were designed to start in between the change of shifts on the workshop floor. For R&D sites, the sessions followed the same sequence, but the location was left for the participating entity to determine. Attendance was not deemed mandatory, and each session was divided into two equal parts: the first was designed to disseminate a specific aspect of the organization's overall mission, vision, and objectives, which were covered over the different weeks; and the second was designed to explore one of the concepts of the new product's development and innovation.

- The weekly attendance in both industrial and R&D centers in the developed economies of France, Germany, and the United States, proved to be considerably lower than that of their developing counterparts in China, India, and Egypt. The commitment of the management team, including regional directors, R&D directors, general managers of factories, and first-line supervisors, in less developed countries was notably higher than that of the developed ones.

- The number of ideas received from China, India, and Egypt were the highest in both industrial and R&D centers. Over one-hundred and seventy patent ideas were generated and submitted — with not one qualified idea from the sites located in France, Germany and the US.

- We offered a five percent bonus evaluation score for ideas, including team members with diversified experience (i.e., members coming from different domains). The quality level of ideas coming from teams with diversity of experience demonstrated a greater maturity level.

- We offered another five percent bonus evaluation score for ideas, including team members from various geographical locations. The geographically diversified teams' submissions also demonstrated a greater maturity level.

Within the different stages of the competition, we conducted several surveys and interviews to dig into the root causes of some of the findings:

- Teams located near the headquarters are less eager to participate, as they hold a general feeling that they're closer to the decision-making process and do not need to prove their capabilities to become part of the creative and innovative development activities.

ↄ Teams working on sites located in more developed countries are not eager to walk the extra mile to prove their capabilities or stand within the crowd — although the junior population in sites located in the more developed countries were interested in participating by sharing their voice with the management team.

ↄ Teams located in sites beyond the headquarters, particularly in less developed countries, were eager to prove their capabilities and have the chance to deliver their voices, deeming such initiatives as an opportunity for an increased scope, which creates a greater sense of purpose.

To conclude, our current business context is moving more and more towards global operations, with many organizations having both an industrial and R&D presence globally. This combined presence either exists to serve specific global market expansion strategies or global capacity and cost efficiency increases. Such global operational expansion efforts carry opportunities and challenges alike. Organizations of all sizes must capitalize on their global footprint to guarantee global competitiveness. When the maturity of the organization's global sites increases, it is the top management's duty to grasp this maturity for the benefit of the organization. Moving a global outsourcing center to achieve being an excellence center, then moving it towards a global innovation center, is when organizations reach the highest level of return on investment. Starting from day one, this necessitates a clear, well-defined strategy of operations, which must be agile and continuously evolving along with the global site's maturity level. Management's ability to build a global footprint based on competency and competitiveness is what guarantees continued success. Upon reaching heightened levels of maturity in the global outsourcing development centers, management should begin dividing the scope, roles, responsibilities, and activities between the teams according to competitiveness. Teams located in the front office, near the customers, may concentrate on ideation, customer validation, and design thinking, while teams in the other part of the world delve into development and project management. In time, the product design and system architecture may be shared, and after that, the global outsourcing destination may start to see greater participation in the ideation process (even if this representation- and access-driven dynamic still exists within the bounds of the local geographical site). Following that, a true global team with a scope definition based on competency, not geographical divisions, must come into primary focus. The ability to mature global outsourcing centers to become involved in the process of new product development and innovation is considered the highest level of success. Such involvement will lead to a higher ability to grasp the power of global operations through more competitive development cost structure and thus lower cost of innovation failure which leads to better overall organization competitive positioning.

THE INNOVATIVE DINOSAUR

MODERN TEAMS
WORKING MODELS

In the previous section, we discussed the challenges of having global development centers following either the outsourcing or the insourcing models. Now, in this section, we will dig deeper into the concepts, challenges, and opportunities of the remote team's management. Accordingly, three models covering different levels of complexity for the remote team management will be explored, starting with the work-from-home policy, which is offered by many organizations and has been heavily utilized during the Covid-19 pandemic. Following that, we will examine the challenges facing the global distributed team's management. And finally, we will discuss the complete remote workforce model.

WORK-FROM-HOME
MODEL

The work-from-home policy is not new. Software- and digital-based organizations in particular started this trend longtime ago, offering their teams the option of working remotely, be it part- or full-time, based on the activity and nature of the assignment for each team member. This trend is present in the businesses that mostly employ team members who within white collar categories. Industrial-based organizations that mostly employ team members from blue collar categories, have been reluctant to offer such a model, even for their white collar R&D teams. The reasons behind such reluctance are perhaps justified based on the vast majority of the team's nature within such organizations are blue collars. The human resources department of those companies argue that they are seeking equality between the organization's different teams, and that they will not be able to extend such a policy to the teams within the factories, as machines cannot be relocated to the team members' homes. Even in some case, they argue that embedded software development teams require the sensors, actuators, and measurement devices to be physically close to the development teams, which cannot be transferred to the team members homes. When the coronavirus pandemic became a household name, in the early 2020, most of those organizations — if not all — shifted to the work-from-home model, and many of the previous challenges were resolved, and solutions were offered.

THE
INNOVATIVE
DINOSAUR

Organizations and policy makers in the different levels of the decision-making process must understand the needs, the competition landscape, and the psychometric analysis of today's workforce, global talent acquisition opportunities and challenges, and technological infrastructure capabilities that are opening the doors of unprecedented possibilities. As our societies and businesses continue to shifting more and more towards knowledge-based economies and digitally-enabled organizations, industry leaders must recognize such key changes in workforce needs, wants, motives, and desired modes of operation.

Back in chapter one, we discussed the needs of the Generation Y — millennials — and how they have different expectations and motivations. In return, organizations must cater to these needs and avail the policies, tools, and infrastructure necessary for achieving the desired working environment of this new generation that will represent the vast majority of workforce in coming five to ten years. Simply, millennials are seeking the same experiences of their personal lives within the professional sphere: a flexible work-life balance and efficient working environment in which they are satisfied with — or, at the very least, convinced by — the decisions of the organization's leadership. So, when it comes to the work-from-home model, millennials believe that it is the more convenient and productive framework, as they do not need to waste time commuting to work and they believe that all the of technological elements are currently available to support this change.

From the organization's point of view, many benefits can be achieved by widely implementing the work from-home model. Let's imagine the potential savings to be had from simply applying a shared seating plan policy instead of the standard office setup of rigid seat assignments. An office space that is designed to fit a team of one hundred can accommodate at least three times the members, and the space that is designed to accommodate two thousand can fit a thousand or two more than that. Savings in office rental costs, along with other associated operational costs, will have direct impact on the organization's profit and loss statement (P&L), which can be measured by millions of dollars yearly. Elevating the comfort and convenience of the teams' working environment will have a direct impact on productivity, which will, in turn, positively influence the organization's overall performance. Other examples of such benefits include savings in transportation costs, other overheads, and organization support functions cost.

From a nationwide economical perspective, the work from home model having many benefits as reducing the load over the transportation infrastructure which will lead to saving and less CO_2 emission which will lead to pollution reduction, better social bonding between family members and opening opportunities to remote location workforce to be engaged within more available employment opportunities which will reduce the impact of remote areas unemployment and immigration to other locations.

Without a doubt, organizations may have other issues and prerequisite investments to be addressed before rerouting itself as described above. Some organizations are concerned with productivity and efficiency levels, their ability to monitor and control the workplace, the readiness of their technological infrastructure, and the loss of human-centered relations upon applying the complete work-from-home model. Some of these concerns will be examined in this section, and others will be addressed in the sections to come.

☐	**Access of Enterprise information systems**	HR services, finance information, Customer Relationship Management (CRM), Product Information Management (PIM), and other related administrative systems.
☐	**Technical teams must have full access to the required tools**	Product Lifecycle Management (PLM), CAD Tools needed for the designs, Project Management Tools, Software Development IDE, Compilers, Configuration Management Tools and CI-Continuous Integration and CD- Continuous Development/Delivery.
☐	**Corporate Security and Compliance Consideration**	Readiness and availability of access from outside the organization's firewall in an efficient and secured manner. Predefined access rights for all applications including the needed set of privileges and permissions. Corporate VPN capabilities need to be in place. Even corporate on premise and on cloud server infrastructure must be made accessible from outside the organization's firewalls.
☐	**Information Worker and Sharing Tools**	Information worker productivity tools, like as spreadsheets, word processors, and email systems, must be available, supporting collaborative interactions and versioning management capabilities. Cloud-based drives, from Google Drive to Microsoft OneDrive, are recommended for better collaboration.
☐	**Corporate Intranet**	Availability of a mutually exclusive and collectively exhaustive corporate intranet, including all the essential information from policies, procedures, organization structures, product information, news and ability to push communication messages , and updates.
☐	**Virtual Meeting**	Virtual meeting infrastructure must in place with efficiency in mind (e.g., Microsoft Teams, Google Meet, Cisco Webex, and Zoom).
☐	**Virtual Collaboration Tools**	As Miro and Mural are recommended to increase collaboration and productivity.
☐	**Laptop**	Employees must be equipped with high quality laptops that are supported by robust corporate operating system and software tools digital image , including all the basic tools from operating systems, security applications, and all the required productivity tools. Continual updates and maintenance for those laptop images are mandatory, and the information system teams must have all the needed IS operational tools to access and push software updates for the population as needed.

THE INNOVATIVE DINOSAUR

The organization's information technology readiness is key when implementing the work-from-home model, as are its information systems readiness and availability of access from outside the organization's firewall in an efficient and secured manner.

Team members must be able to access the needed information from the different enterprise management information systems, whether it's for HR services, finance information, Customer Relationship Management (CRM), Product Information Management (PIM), and other related administrative and operations systems. Technical teams must have full access to the required tools within the Product Lifecycle Management (PLM), CAD Tools needed for the designs, Project Management Tools, Software Development IDE, Compilers, Configuration Management Tools and CI-Continuous Integration and CD- Continuous Development/Delivery. The necessary applications, platforms, and tools should be made accessible to all of the team members as based on a predefined set of privileges and permissions. Corporate VPN capabilities need to be in place, from both implementation and capacity perspectives. Even corporate on premise and on cloud server infrastructure must be made accessible from outside the organization's firewalls. Information worker productivity tools, like as spreadsheets, word processors, and email systems, must be available, supporting collaborative interactions and versioning management capabilities. Cloud-based drives, from Google Drive to Microsoft OneDrive, are recommended for better collaboration. One of the most important elements is the availability of a mutually exclusive and collectively exhaustive corporate intranet, including all the essential information from policies, procedures, organization structures, product information, news and ability to push communication messages, and updates. Virtual meeting infrastructure must in place with efficiency in mind (e.g., Microsoft Teams, Google Meet, Cisco Webex, and Zoom). Employees must be equipped with high quality laptops that are supported by robust corporate operating system and software tools digital image, including all the basic tools from operating systems, security applications, and all the required productivity tools. Continual updates and maintenance for those laptop images are mandatory, and the information system teams must have all the needed IS operational tools to access and push software updates for the population as needed. More tools and concerns will be covered in the sections to come.

☐ Organizational HR processes and policies	Must be tailored and adapted to the model's needs and nature. Attendance policies, procedures, and systems may require an overhaul, from conceptual and implementation perspectives. Digital Sign-in/out for managing daily attendance should be implemented.
☐ Working Hours	A flexible working hours process , one with a clear definition of core hours to guarantee the needed intersection between the teams within a minimum number of hours.
☐ Team Availability Management	Digitally-driven tools for managing the team's availability — including who is in training, who is on sick leave or vacation, and who is working from the office or from home
☐ Space Management	Shared space policy must be defined, clearly communicated, and digitally managed, along with a seating booking system must be in place
☐ Organization Meetings	HR should revisit the design of the organization's standard structure for meetings to accommodate the new model.
☐ Talent Development	The talent development methods and tools must also be revisited, factoring in the advantages of having a greater dependency on online trainings.
☐ Remote Management	Special trainings and mentorship programs for the management teams, particularly on how to manage remote teams and operate within the new model, must be designed, disseminated, and monitored, as managers of all levels will need to communicate more frequently and through various digital means.
☐ Talent Acquisition	Talent acquisition criteria, processes, methods, and tools must be reshaped accordingly, reflecting the new requirements and needs at hand and into the future. A simple impact here will be the implementation and deployment of virtual hiring and interviewing tools .
☐ Communication	Managers of all levels and needs have to adapt their management styles, techniques, and paradigms, including a greater emphasis on communications, and the utilization of different means and tools to maximize outreach.
☐ Performance Monitoring & Evaluation	Performance monitoring techniques should be lean and objectively measured, and performance evaluations should be based on results and supported by data, as increased digital capabilities assists in achieving what was previously unavailable.
☐ Promotion Management	Promotion and change of assignment techniques need to be modified based on clear, transparent, and measured matrixes.

The human resources wing of the organization plays a crucial role in the success of the work from-home model. Many organizational processes and policies must be tailored and adapted to the model's needs and nature. Attendance policies, procedures, and systems may require an overhaul, from conceptual and implementation perspectives. Digital sign-in/out for managing daily attendance should be implemented in an easy and efficient way to satisfy both corporate requirements and user expectations. A flexible working hours process, one with a clear definition of core hours to guarantee the needed intersection between the teams within a minimum number of hours, should also be implemented. In this day and (Internet) age, digitally-driven tools for managing the team's availability — including who is in training, who is on sick leave or vacation, and who is working from the office or from home — are critical to success, and such information should be made digitally accessible for ease of collaboration between the different team members. Any shared space policy must be defined, clearly communicated, and digitally managed, along with a seating booking system must be in place and designed to provide the same user experience as the systems used by the shared working spaces providers.

Further afield, HR should revisit the design of the organization's standard structure for meetings to accommodate the new model. The talent development methods and tools must also be revisited, factoring in the advantages of having a greater dependency on online trainings. Targeted or special trainings and mentorship programs for the management teams, particularly on how to manage remote teams and operate within the new model, must be designed, disseminated, and monitored, as managers of all levels will need to communicate more frequently and through various digital means. The talent acquisition criteria, processes, methods, and tools must be reshaped accordingly, reflecting the new requirements and needs at hand and into the future. A simple impact here will be the implementation and deployment of virtual hiring and interviewing tools.

On the other end, managers of all levels and needs have to adapt their management styles, techniques, and paradigms, including a greater emphasis on communications, and the utilization of different means and tools to maximize outreach. Performance monitoring techniques should be lean and objectively measured, and performance evaluations should be based on results and supported by data, as increased digital capabilities assists in achieving what was previously unavailable. Promotion and change of assignment techniques need to be modified based on clear, transparent, and measured matrixes. As for the corporate managers, it's advisable for them to move from their parental chairs and push for the concept that everyone is responsible for their own career journeys — meaning, encourage the pace that best suits the individual's own preferences, capabilities, and goals.

GLOBAL DISTRIBUTED TEAMS MODEL

In today's business landscape, challenges related to globally distributed teams are on the rise, day after day, and disruption by disruption. The team's distribution is applied to all organizational functions, especially the supportive ones, from HR, finance, and supply chain to research and development, and production and industrial activities.

A project related to the production of a new parking assistant system within a new vehicle illustrates the complexities of this globally-geared model:

- The vehicle architecture is designed by an original equipment manufacturer (OEM) headquartered in Germany.
- The OEM selected the rear camera from a US-based supplier with their research team based in California and production facility in China.
- The OEM selected a tier-one supplier who will supply ultrasonic sensors and the system integration services provider from a France-based supplier with their main R&D center in Paris, mechanical designers in India, electronics designers in China, software development team in Egypt, and system team in Germany, in addition to production facilities in both France and China.
- All parties agreed to assign a third-party testing and validation supplier based in Ukraine.
- The electronic control units (ECUs) are supplied from a US-based supplier with production facilities in India.
- The final in vehicle integration will be completed in Germany, and the OEM will produce the final vehicle using their production facilities located in Germany, Morocco, and China.
- The project manager from the OEM side is based in Germany, the tier-one supplier project manager in France, and the rest of the suppliers' project managers are positioned in the same location as the headquarters.

The above-described setup is not unique to the automotive sphere and can be found in many other industries. The above example includes multi-geographical locations, domain of expertise with different natures, complex production value chain, and activity types with completely different natures, needs and requirements. We have teams that must work together, on the same playbook page, regardless of where each member is coming from, be it a completely different frame of reference or, in many cases, a completely different corporate culture. If we observe the software part of a company, we can easily recognize the complexity level of managing such a project, especially if we consider the number of features that are needed in a mid-size project, as is the one mentioned in the above. If the project manager decided to manage such an endeavor by following the usual project management principles, we can guarantee the complete failure of the project.

Today's project management for distributed teams is more complex by nature. The question here concerns the readiness of the traditional manufacturing organization to manage such complexities efficiently and successfully. The answer hangs in a balance. Accordingly, the organization of today must adopt lean and agile project management practices complete with the support of advanced project management and collaboration platforms. The project managers' agile practices must be integrated into the traditional manufacturing enterprise and with a level of tailoring that does not dilute the essence of the agile methodology. The complex system should be broken down into subsystems through smart system designs, and then the agile sprint, release, and backlog management can be implemented. Defining interfaces between the subsystems is a critical to success.

Skilled and qualified project managers, from all stakeholders, must be selected, and their team's roles, responsibilities, and scopes should be defined during the early stages of the project. The empowerment of the team with solid experience, technical skills, and, perhaps most importantly, soft interpersonal skills, is key. An enterprise should focus on the knowledge and skill levels of their teams rather than laying emphasis on increasing their resources capacity regardless of competency. Unfortunately, many traditional enterprises tackle such projects with the same concept of production line capacity in mind, believing that by adding many team members — "resources as they name it" — the faster the project will be delivered. In short, the paradigm must be shifted from the quantity of team members to the quality of the team members.

Advanced collaboration tools and platforms must be established to guarantee the success of globally distributed projects. As the next level of advancement of virtual meeting tools, visual collaboration tools are not optional to manage globally distributed teams. Tools such as Miro.com and Mural.com are essential for ensuring that teams are aligned, synergized, and equipped with proper communication capabilities. Also, advanced collaboration tools like Slack.com and Trello.com help boost the collaboration performance of teams. Project management tools including Asana.com and SmartSheet.com, help leverage the capabilities and performances of the managers. In-office smartboards and interactive audiovisual capabilities inspire team-building interactions.

Enforcing a mechanism and policies that guarantee continued communication between the teams is crucial for survival and growth, including regular team meetings (Sprint Planning, Retrospectives, Daily Standups), and management and customer status updates. Defining the proper escalation paths for guaranteeing the appropriate interference timing is important along with well-defined arbitration levels. Designing frequent face-to face meetings and workshops with the different team members is also advisable. For instance, by hosting three- to five-day-long face-to-face bootcamps for the teams once every six months to a year, based on the project duration, we will surely strengthen the synergy between the different team members.

☐	**Agile Practice**	The project managers' agile practices must be integrated into the traditional enterprise and with a level of tailoring that does not dilute the essence of the agile methodology.
☐	**System & Components Management**	The complex system should be broken down into subsystems through smart system designs, and then the agile sprint, release, and backlog management can be implemented. Defining interfaces between the subsystems is a critical to success.
☐	**Distributed Teams**	The empowerment of the team with solid experience, technical skills, and, perhaps most importantly, soft interpersonal skills, is key. An enterprise should focus on the knowledge and skill levels of their teams rather than laying emphasis on increasing their resources capacity regardless of competency.
☐	**Team Capacity**	The paradigm must be shifted from the quantity of team members to the quality of the team members.
☐	**Visual Collaboration Tools**	Visual collaboration tools are not option to manage globally distributed teams. Tools such as Miro.com and Mural.com are essential for ensuring that teams are aligned, synergized, and equipped with proper communication capabilities.
☐	**Advanced Virtual Collaboration Tools**	Advanced collaboration tools like Slack.com and Trello.com help boost the collaboration performance of teams.
☐	**Modern Project Management Tools**	Project management tools, including Asana.com and SmartSheet.com, help leverage the capabilities and performances of the managers.
☐	**In Office Collaboration**	In-office smartboards and interactive audiovisual capabilities inspire team-building interactions.
☐	**Communication Mechanisms & Policies**	Enforcing a mechanism and policies that guarantee continued communication between the teams is crucial for survival and growth, including regular team meetings (Sprint Planning, Retrospectives, Daily Standups), and management & customer status updates.
☐	**Definition of Escalation Path**	Defining the proper escalation paths for guaranteeing the appropriate interference timing is important along with well-defined arbitration levels.
☐	**Face to Face Meetings**	Designing frequent face-to-face meetings and workshops with the different team members is also advisable. For instance, by hosting three- to five-day-long face-to-face bootcamps for the teams once every six months to a year.

THE
INNOVATIVE
DINOSAUR

THE
INNOVATIVE
DINOSAUR

REMOTE WORKFORCE MODE

Now it is time to extend our discussion into the domain of the full remote workforce. Over the past few years, we have started to hear more and more about companies that are embracing that domain, offering complete remote distributed teams. They have no dedicated physical office space, according to the traditional definition. Their teams are distributed globally, and serve customers around the world. Most, if not all, of their taskforce team members follow the work-from-home model, and they provide their services with the help of white collar members. The vast majority of these companies operate in industries like high-tech, digital, information technology, and software related service providers, consultants in various fields, creative agencies, as well as electronic learning and training services. Diversity helps (re)shape their teams, constructing bridges between different nationalities, languages, educational backgrounds, and genders, that lead to personal, professional, and collective growth in the workplace, even in life. Even though the headquarters of such companies are usually incorporated in a specific city and country, they are still widely perceived as a globally-connected, "Internet-based" organization regardless of the size of their teams or revenue. This model is not the same as the crowdsourcing model discussed earlier, so it will be covered in greater detail in the coming sections — in fact, the difference is that the remote workforce employment model follows the standard full-time, or even part-time standards, a model that is followed by the organizations of today; the only departure is that it offers a remote working environment rather than the traditional office-based organizations and hiring is not limited to geographical locations.

In the beginning, there were many doubts about this model and its probabilities of success. However, at the time of writing, it is clear as day that this untraditional, underdog model is gaining ground and achieving success. Remotive.io has compiled a list of more than two thousand companies that offer remote work vacancies — and many of them are one hundred percent remotely-based organizations. When reviewing the list of available vacancies, we will notice clearly the diversified types of jobs and tasks that are requested. Moreover, by visiting some of those companies' websites, we can navigate and learn how they perceive and position the remote-based workforce, as many of them share their success stories on how this model enhanced their overall competitiveness and operational excellence.

Crossover.com is a prime example of clear success for the fully remote workforce. Established in 2014, and incorporated in the United States, the recruitment platform states on its website that the company headquarters are located in Austin, Texas, but this is just for mailing purposes and legal incorporation

THE INNOVATIVE DINOSAUR

compliance. As of February 2021, Crossover has around 3,500 team members working from a hundred different countries, and all of them serve global clients on a remote basis. Another example is Weworkremotely.com, which claims to be "the largest remote work community in the world," with more than three million visitors to their website per month. Operating since 2013, the workforce hiring service provider boasts a satisfied list of hundreds of companies, offering global remote work opportunities and thousands of satisfied workforce team members. Others include Buffer.com, an "intuitive social media management platform," with a fully distributed team of 85 people living and working in 15 countries around the world and 11 different time zones, as well as Andela.com, a New York-based startup that offers a remote workforce mixed with a defined community and societal mission. Launched in 2014 in Lagos, Nigeria, with the objective to empower and avail global opportunities for talents and professionals in Africa, particularly in what it calls, "the African tech landscape," Adela's CEO has stated: "With each successful match Andela delivers, our dream of a world where the most talented people can build a career commensurate with their ability – not their race, gender, or geography – becomes a bit closer to reality." Today, more than 77,000 talents are participating in its learning community, with a thousand engineering talents placed, around 200 customers serve, and the backing of a few reputable investors.

When we begin to dive deeper into such companies, aiming to understand their motives behind embracing the complete remote workforce model, we will find an explicit paradigm of values, benefits, opportunities, and challenges. What is clear is that they are not searching for a more competitive labor cost structure. For instance, when we visit Crossover, we will notice that they're positioned as hiring the top "1% of global talent on long-term, challenging projects in high-paying, 100% remote roles." This precedent is replicated in most of the listed companies offering the full remote workforce model. A visit to the YouTube channel of Basecamp.com will present us with a promotional video (its name is "Remote Work at 37signals") for remote work in which we can listen to the experiences of their team members; from a workforce point of view, their passion, conviction, and the benefits of this model are manifest. These companies have the capacity to identify the opportunities of current advancements in technological infrastructure as well as the global talents with untapped utilization, due to geographical boundaries and distances. They decided to eliminate the geographical barriers through utilizing the available technologies, modifying organizational processes, and shifting the traditional corporate mindset, supported by the readiness of the talents to accept the concept. Many aspects of the traditional organization's structure, processes, methods, and tools must be revisited and adjusted to meet the requirements and nature of the remote workforce model.

Productivity measurement tool for the future of work. As a data-driven solution, it helps managers measure productivity within their teams and assists workers as a personal productivity application.

Advanced project management platform designed specifically for remote workforce teams, providing automatic check-ins, scheduling, message boards, to-do lists, group chats, and instant integration with other information workers productivity tools.

Effective time tracking and management features and capabilities. Although Getharvest.com is not as advanced as the other tools, the beauty of it is the number of pre-set integrations

CrossOver.com
WorkSmart

Basecamp.com
Project
Management

Getharvest.com
Time Tracking

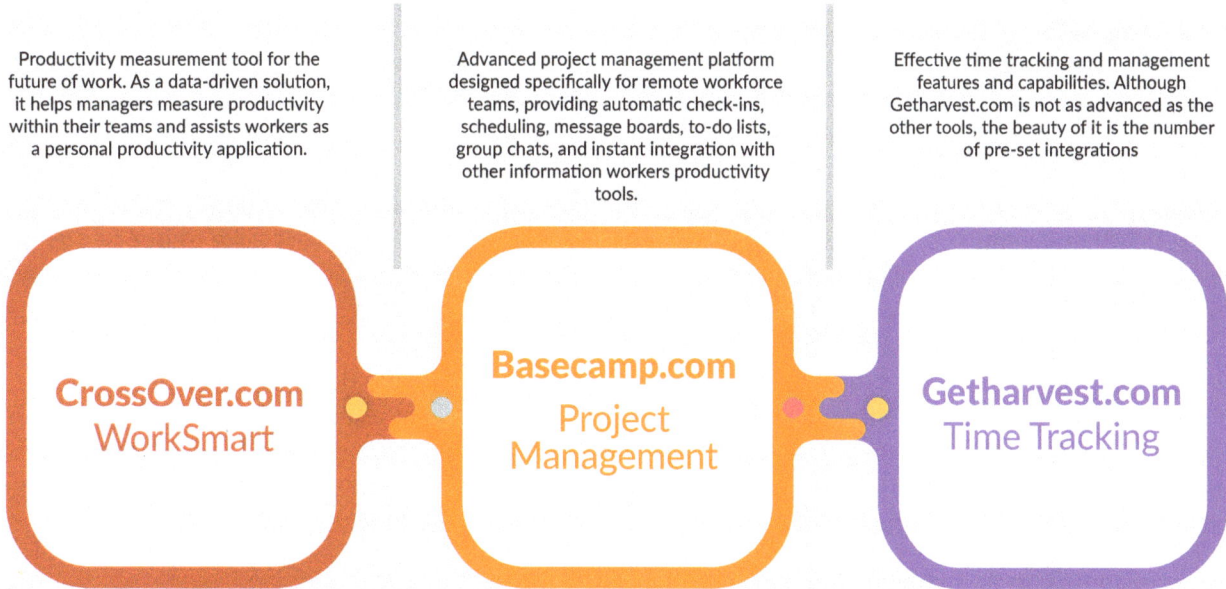

Productivity and Efficiency

THE
INNOVATIVE
DINOSAUR

Now let's tackle this model's first challenge: the productivity and efficiency of the teams in question. Many enterprise managers and executives debate the nature and outlook of having a remote workforce, even how work-from-home models may negatively impacting the overall performance of the workforce. This argument may be true if the necessary tools and environments are incorrectly assembled and merged. To overcome efficiency and productivity issues, several platforms, software solutions, and best practices are available, like Crossover's online productivity platform "WorkSmart," a productivity measurement tool for the future of work. As a data driven solution, it helps managers measure productivity within their teams and assists workers as a personal productivity application. This tool provides several advanced features, like time tracking and logging, while also utilizing some technological features that automatically track keyboard activity, application usage, screenshots, and webcam photos to generate a timecard every ten minutes. Above and beyond that, the tool is provides advanced analytics and AI algorithms that assist workers and employers alike to better plan tasks in a more personalized manner according to each individual team member's patterns, productivity, performance, and preferences. Another example is Basecamp.com, an advanced project management platform designed specifically for remote workforce teams, providing automatic check-ins, scheduling message boards, to-do lists, group chats, and instant integration with other information workers productivity tools, from Google Drive and Drobox to Slack and Asana (for project management to-do lists). For an even simpler time management tool, Getharvest.com offers straightforward and effective time tracking and management features and capabilities. Although Getharvest.com is not as advanced as the other tools, the beauty of it is the number of pre-set integrations that the tool is supporting with hundreds of platforms and applications.

After we overcome the first challenge, the next one concerns our hiring methods and processes for selecting talent. The hiring selection process is already challenging by nature, thus when we move to global remote talent acquisition, challenges will often increase exponentially. The good thing is that we have examples of successful companies to learn from. Again, Crossover provides us with a solid guide for this topic, including a hiring and selection process with around six different stages that each applicant will face before receiving an offer:

1. For the initial resume screening, which is almost the normal traditional screening process that is applied in most organizations, the candidate's resume is reviewed, and if it suits the required qualifications of the job, the process is triggered off.

2. For the five-part online assessment, the candidates who passed the initial screening stage will usually receive a call or email from a recruitment agent informing them that they are enrolled and qualified to continue on in the interviewing cycle.

3. In general, candidates have a deadline of a couple of weeks to start the online assessment. When the candidate is ready, they must allocate around four to six hours to start the five-part assessment, including

   a. **Basic Fit Questions (BFQ):** The candidate will be asked a series of background questions to ensure that they are fit for the specific job vacancy; no special preparations are needed for this step to be completed.

   b. **Criteria Cognitive Aptitude Test (CCAT):** The candidate will complete a fifteen-minute intelligence and aptitude test consisting of fifty questions, in three main sections: logic and math, verbal ability, and spatial reasoning. The CCAT is an easy tool for Crossover to compare candidates with others applying for the exact same position. A standardized score will be received, along with the candidate percentile, and the norms for others applying for the same position across the world.

   c. **English Assessment:** The candidate will complete a two-minute audio recording that will be used to assess their fluency in the required language(s); this stage is of utmost importance, ensuring that the candidate has what is needed to be integrated into a global remote team.

   d. **Subject Matter Expert Questions (SMQ):** The candidate will complete a multiple choice assessment in the area of expertise that they are applying for. Many roles, both technical and non-technical, will face a HackerRank.com assessment. This part may vary from one vacancy to another, but, in general, it should take between 40 minutes and an hour to complete.

   e. **Free Response Questions (FRQ):** The candidate will be presented with a series of project-based, on-the-job scenarios, giving the employer insight into how the applicant would respond in a tangible work situation. Problem-solving scenarios, for instance, are designed to raise the bar and explore how the candidate will perform on their toes. This part has two classifications:

4. **Interview:** The candidates who excel in the previous five stages will receive an email or call with the possible dates for their personal interview, which are usually conducted by hiring managers with the main objectives of forming an impression of the applicant and diving into specific areas related to the assignment's nature. For technical positions, online coding questions may be asked, and online coding may be expected.

   Note: These interviews are conducted in English.

5. **Pre-hire and background check:** A detailed check into and validation of the candidate's past employment and general background; the candidate's internet speed and computer performance are also subject to evaluation at this stage.

THE INNOVATIVE DINOSAUR

6. **Hiring manager interview:** Another interview will be conducted by the hiring manager, but this time the focus will be on the specific job the candidate applied for, in addition to answering any unanswered questions. If both the hiring manager and the candidate are on the same page by this stage, then the hiring process will commence.

7. **Job offer or invitation to join the Crossover Marketplace:** The candidate will either be sent a job offer to join Crossover immediately or invited to join the Crossover Marketplace, a tool that hiring managers can use to select applicants who have already been handpicked and passed Crossover's competitive screening process. This stage allows employers to streamline their own recruitment processes and invite the candidate
to an interview straightaway.

8. **Crossover hiring tournament:** This is not a mandatory step, and it is not included in all vacancy types or even in all announced opportunities. Technical roles may encounter a "hiring tournament" or "hiring marathon," which streamlines the standard hiring process of at least two weeks into a one-day marathon. The candidates who excel in Crossover's tournament will leave with a remote, work-from-home opportunity.

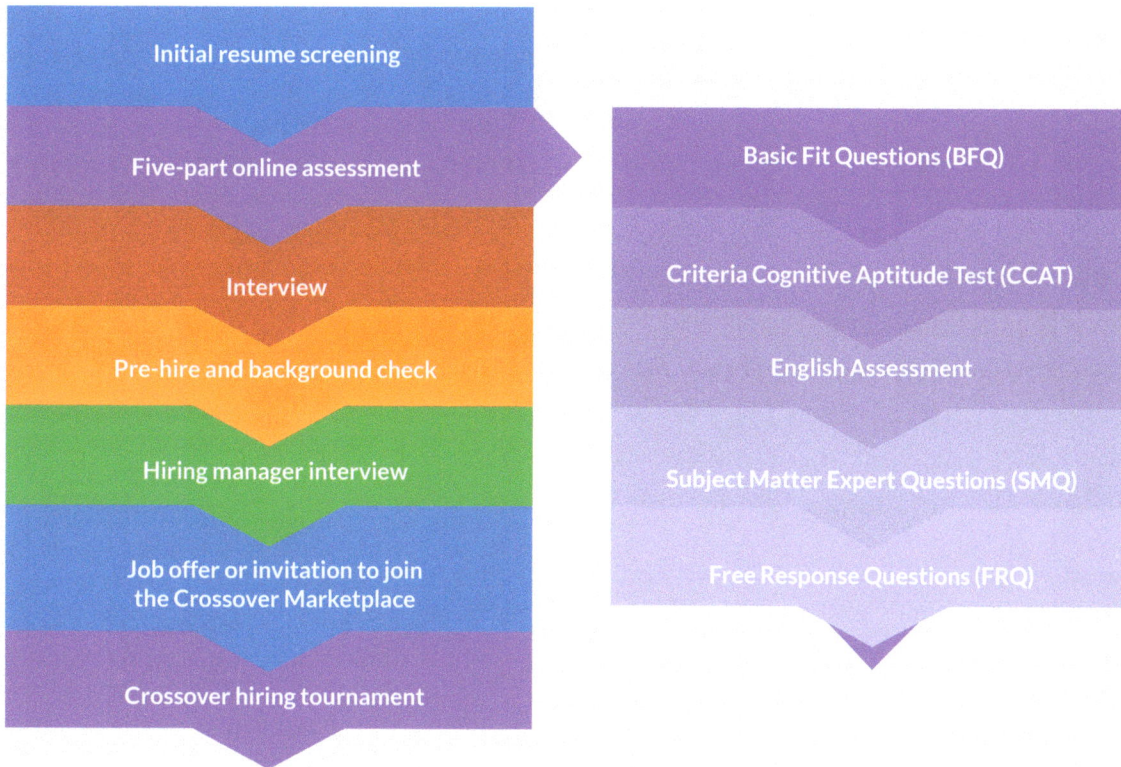

Designed by: Motaz Agamawi
www.theinnovativedinosaur.com

THE
INNOVATIVE
DINOSAUR

Crossover's hiring and selection process may seem overly complex, long, and competitive. But what can be deduced is that such a process guarantees that Crossover is playing a smart, future-facing game and sourcing the top one percent of the global professional caliber pool. Many debate the value of aptitude and personality tests, but without a doubt such types of tests do provide some useful insights about the candidates while enhancing the selection process through more objectivity-anchored evaluation matrixes.

There are several testing types on the market today, including the Criteria Cognitive Aptitude Test (CCAT), the University Clinical Aptitude Test (UCAPT), and the Predictive Learning Indicators (PLI). Many providers and platforms offer the testing services within this domain.

By way of illustration, Good.co is an online psychometric testing platform that classifies individuals into several personality clusters. Also classifies companies based on a vast database of questions and answers provided by employees. One of the platform's most desirable features is the matching algorithm between the individual and the company. Another capability of value is the analysis completed on team bases, including a set of individual team members. Many tools like Good.co are available in the market, but we are providing this specific example here to clearly identify the importance of understanding the personality clusters of our team members, and how they match the organization's culture, as well as to conduct a deeper analysis to ensure that the smaller teams within the organization are formulated correctly, thus expanding, even maximizing, the team's synergy probability.

As another example of psychometric classification, there is the 1985 book *Six Thinking Hats* by Edward de Bono, the Maltese physician who coined the term "lateral thinking," plus many other resources, which can be found on Debonogroup.com. And finally, another exceptionally useful tools for online hiring selection, especially for software- and technology-related hires, is Hackerrank.com, a platform that provides advanced online interviewing features and capabilities. The platform includes thousands of technical software and information technologies questions, so it is of great use within this domain. In other domains, this tool can be used for online remote interviewing, even if we (re) design and add questions related to our domain of business without depending on the platform's predefined question bank.

THE INNOVATIVE DINOSAUR

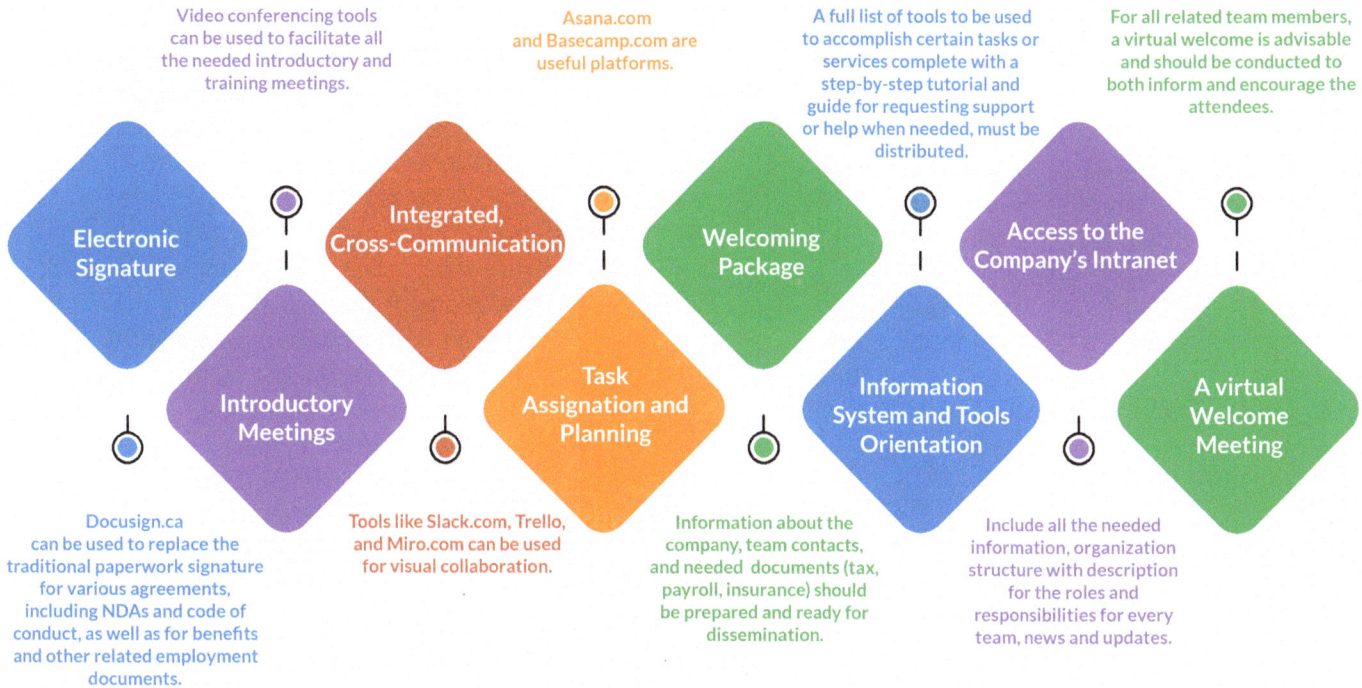

Video conferencing tools can be used to facilitate all the needed introductory and training meetings.

Asana.com and Basecamp.com are useful platforms.

A full list of tools to be used to accomplish certain tasks or services complete with a step-by-step tutorial and guide for requesting support or help when needed, must be distributed.

For all related team members, a virtual welcome is advisable and should be conducted to both inform and encourage the attendees.

Electronic Signature

Integrated, Cross-Communication

Welcoming Package

Access to the Company's Intranet

Introductory Meetings

Task Assignation and Planning

Information System and Tools Orientation

A virtual Welcome Meeting

Docusign.ca can be used to replace the traditional paperwork signature for various agreements, including NDAs and code of conduct, as well as for benefits and other related employment documents.

Tools like Slack.com, Trello, and Miro.com can be used for visual collaboration.

Information about the company, team contacts, and needed documents (tax, payroll, insurance) should be prepared and ready for dissemination.

Include all the needed information, organization structure with description for the roles and responsibilities for every team, news and updates.

THE INNOVATIVE DINOSAUR

Another strategic consideration for achieving a successful remote workforce model is the onboarding process, followed by talent development and competency building. The onboarding process is essential to guaranteeing the productivity, integration, and retention of the company's workforce in general, especially when it comes to the remote workforce and ensuring that everything is in its the proper place. Since in-person interactions are not available, some processes can be streamlined to match the virtual onboarding. Docusign. ca can be used to replace the traditional paperwork signature for various agreements, including NDAs and code of conduct, as well as for benefits and other related employment documents. Video conferencing tools can be used to facilitate all the needed introductory and training meetings.

Integrated, cross-communication tools like Slack.com, Trello, and Miro.com can be used for visual collaboration. And for task assignation and planning, Asana.com and Basecamp.com are useful platforms.

A welcoming package, including information about the company, team contacts, and needed documents (tax, payroll, insurance) should be prepared and ready for dissemination. Information system and tools orientation, including a full list of tools to be used to accomplish certain tasks or services complete with a step-by-step tutorial and guide for requesting support or help when needed, must be distributed. Access to the company's intranet with all the needed information, organization structure with description for the roles and responsibilities for every team, news and updates. This intranet portal must be a main base for all the corresponding information and organizational tools, as if it's a virtual workplace. A virtual welcoming meeting for all the related team members is advisable and should be conducted to both inform and encourage the attendees. For the technical onboarding and orientation, detailed induction training sessions that mix online virtual interactive workshops, seminars, and self-directed studies, lasting for two to three weeks, should be included with the meeting. For junior positions, there is a well-structured competency building program from Andela.com: the Andela Fellowship program is a four-year on-the-job training program in which candidates are part of the global development teams while also taking on training and mentorship opportunities, and growing their careers in the process. The selection criteria of the fully online program is composed of five steps:

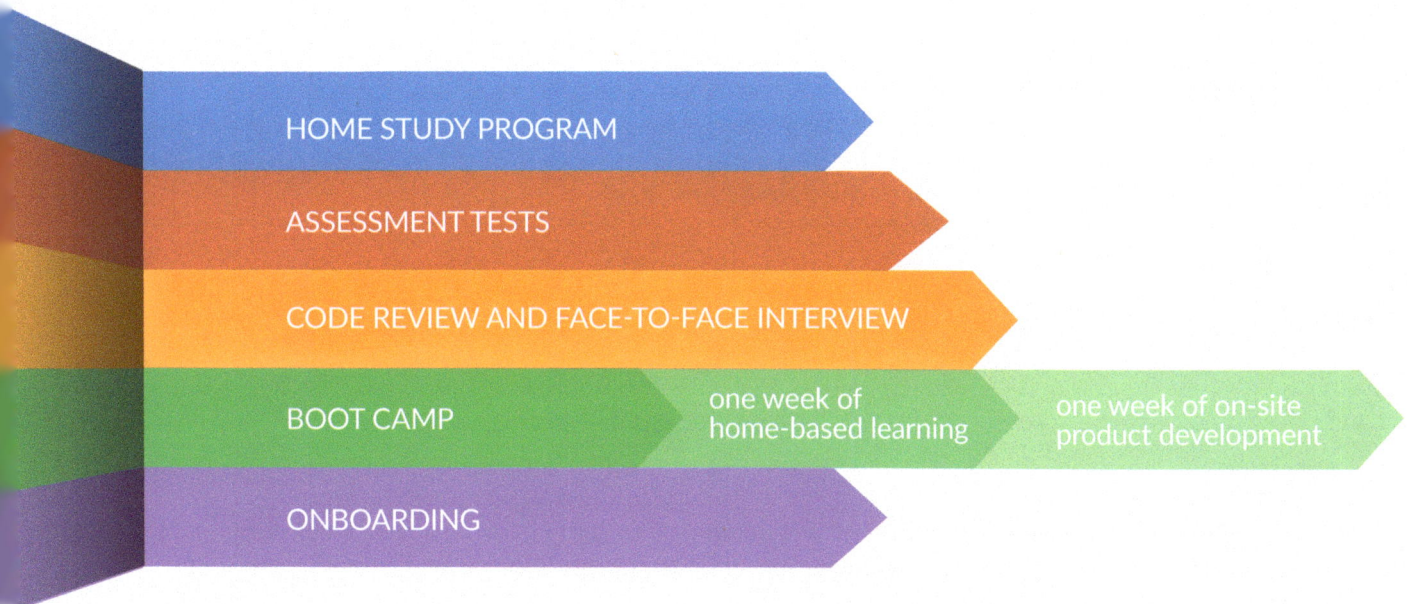

HOME STUDY PROGRAM

ASSESSMENT TESTS

CODE REVIEW AND FACE-TO-FACE INTERVIEW

BOOT CAMP   one week of home-based learning   one week of on-site product development

ONBOARDING

Designed by: Motaz Agamawi
www.theinnovativedinosaur.com

THE
INNOVATIVE
DINOSAUR

HOME STUDY PROGRAM:
An online introduction to the software development curriculum designed by Andela for applicants. The curriculum, which contains material required to grasp the fundamentals of computer science and build a solid foundation in programming, is available for free and applicants can take as long as they need to learn and master the concepts before moving on to the assessment Tests:

ASSESSMENT TESTS:
The first and second online technical exams, plus an online personality test.

CODE REVIEW AND FACE-TO-FACE INTERVIEW:
The candidates who pass the assessment tests will be invited to an in-person interview.

BOOT CAMP:
The candidates who pass the in-person interview will be invited to participate in a two-week-long boot camp, split into two stages: one week of home-based learning, and one week of on-site product development.

ONBOARDING:
The candidates who scale through the boot camp will be accepted into the fellowship and enter an immersive onboarding process.

Utilizing online knowledge resources and making them available to the team is essential

Availing subscriptions for online libraries of such is of great value to the team

Planning customized development paths per job function and individual is also very important

Utilizing the vast amount of online training providers and courses is crucial

Including a predetermined amount of money that an individual can use to conduct a specific personal development plan within the employment package

Udemy.com

Linkedin.com /learning

Coursera.org

Edx.org

Talent development and competency building for fully remote workforce is not the same as traditional talent development. Utilizing online knowledge resources and making them available to the team is essential, and availing subscriptions for online libraries of such is of great value to the team. Planning customized development paths per job function and individual is also very important. Finding informed ways to utilize the vast amount of online training providers and courses is crucial, whether it's through Udemy.com, Coursera.org, Linkedin.com/learning, Edx.org, or others. Including a predetermined amount of money that an individual can use to conduct a specific personal development plan within the employment package.

THE INNOVATIVE DINOSAUR

Challenge of global compliant contracting, payroll and taxation and administration services which considers the different local laws, rules, and regulations

Remote.com

is an example of a service provider that offers all these services, from a one-stop shop that starts with contracting, to payroll services, onboarding, and IP protection all over the globe.

Shieldgeo.com

is a service provider that offers a one-stop shop for global remote teams to tackle the challenge of securing a medical insurance service for our remote taskforce, which spans the globe.

Safetywing.com

provides a global health insurance service that covers the needs of remote workforces.

THE
INNOVATIVE
DINOSAUR

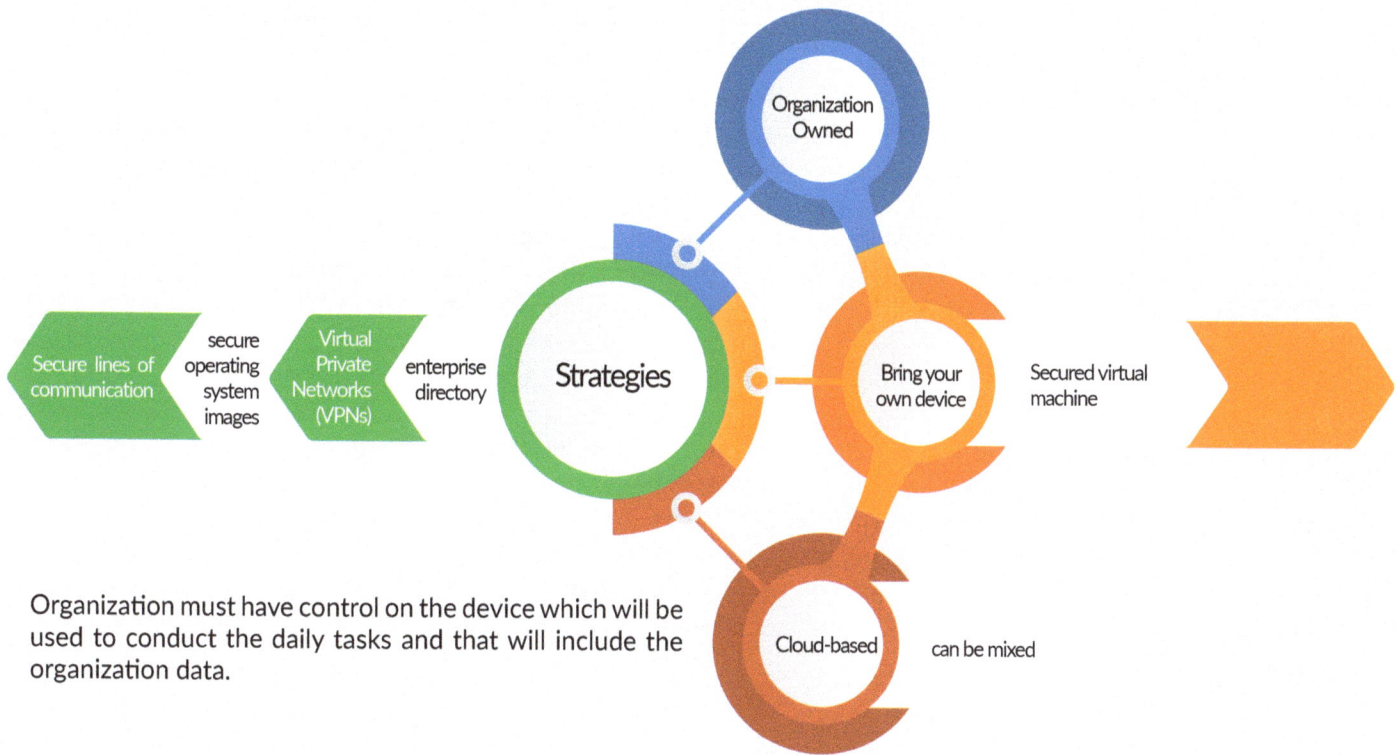

Secure lines of communication

secure operating system images

Virtual Private Networks (VPNs)

enterprise directory

Strategies

Organization Owned

Bring your own device

Secured virtual machine

Cloud-based

can be mixed

Organization must have control on the device which will be used to conduct the daily tasks and that will include the organization data.

THE INNOVATIVE DINOSAUR

Next, we must address the necessary setup for global distributed and remote team members employment packages and benefits including payroll, and administration services. First we start by addressing the challenge of having a global compliant contracting, payroll and taxation and administration services which considers the different local laws, rules, and regulations. Remote.com is an example of a service provider that offers all these services, from one-stop shop that start with contracting, to payroll services, onboarding, and IP protection all over the globe. Another service provider that offers a one-stop shop for global remote teams is Shieldgeo.com. To tackle the challenge of securing a medical insurance service for our remote taskforce, which spans the globe, Safetywing.com provides a global health insurance service that covers the needs of remote workforces. And, for cybersecurity and data protection, a strategic decision must be made: either the organization will provide its global taskforce with the need machinery and equipment, like laptops, telephone over IP (ToIP), and mobile phones, or it will follow the bring-your-own-device model. The needs and investments of the information system and cybersecurity architecture design and software stake infrastructure will differ based on the chosen direction. In the both alternatives, the minimum infrastructure that guarantees the security measures and protection of the organization's data must be implemented, including a corporate enterprise directory, Virtual Privet Networks (VPNs), secure operating system images, and secure lines of communication. The bring-your-own-device alternative will be a valid option only if the organization can compile a secured virtual machine imaged that can be installed on the team member own device. Such images must be installed and deployed on each individual team member's laptop or workstation machine. Additionally, mobile phones and tablets must have a full cyber security stake that can be deployed on each individual team member, securing their devices. Cloud-based technologies and solutions are also available, and they can be mixed with the previously-mentioned solutions. In all cases the organization must have control on the device which will be used to conduct the daily tasks and that will include the organization data.

ORGANIZATION MOTIVE

- acquire top-notch caliber
- more cost-efficient caliber
- increase taskforce capacity
- blend of the three

›››››

CHOICE IMPACT

- financial package
- Induction
- many other parameters

OTHER CONSIDERATION

- costs of a laptop
- predefined internet subscription
- setting up home offices

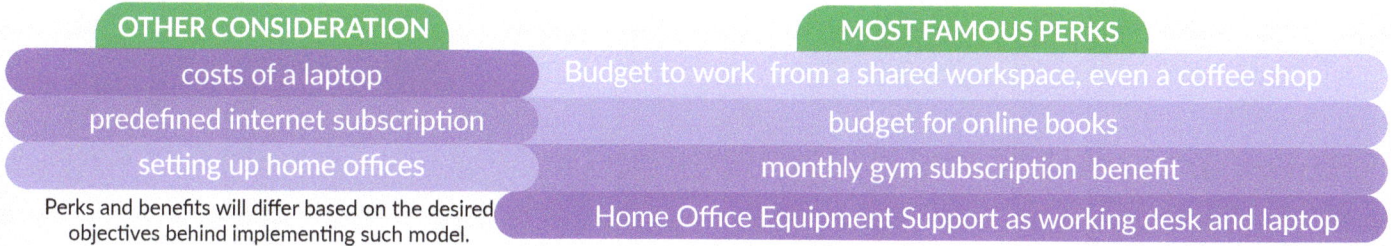

Perks and benefits will differ based on the desired objectives behind implementing such model.

MOST FAMOUS PERKS

- Budget to work from a shared workspace, even a coffee shop
- budget for online books
- monthly gym subscription benefit
- Home Office Equipment Support as working desk and laptop

Designed by: Motaz Agamawi
www.theinnovativedinosaur.com

THE
INNOVATIVE
DINOSAUR

The design of an attractive hiring package is yet another topic that must consider parameters related to the nature of the remote taskforce model. First, the organization must clearly determine the real motive behind their embrace of this model: perhaps it is a desire to acquire top-notch caliber in the different geographic locations, or a more cost-efficient caliber, or to increase taskforce capacity, even a blend of the three. This choice will impact the design of the financial package the induction and many other parameters. For example, Crossover offers international competitive salaries for its workforce regardless of where they're based — meaning, employees in the United States and their remote counterparts in India are paid the same salary. Andela.com, as an alternative, focuses in on the experience, training, and global exposure that they will provide for their team members. Other elements based on the nature of the model must also be taken into consideration, like the costs of a laptop with a defined specification, a predefined internet subscription, and setting up home offices. In their hiring packages, some companies may include a special monthly amount for team members to work from a shared workspace, even a coffee shop, and others a personal development budget for online books, like a monthly gym subscription benefit. Furthermore, a reasonable business travel budget for gathering all of the global team members in one place for face-to-face activities and events, may also be worth considering. Bear in mind that the design of the perks and benefits will differ based on the desired objectives behind implementing such model.

CROWDSOURCING EMPLOYMENT MODEL

The history of crowdsourcing is rooted in the eighteenth century, when the British government conducted a tender for the "Longitude reward" (now known as the "Longitude Prize"); the reward of 20,000 pounds sterling was awarded to any team or individual who could develop a reliable method for calculating the longitude of a vessel at sea. Centuries later, in 2006, an American author and journalist named Jeff Howe introduced the term "crowdsourcing" in his pivotal article for WIRED magazine, "The Rise of Crowdsourcing." Since then, the crowdsourcing model has disrupted all of the smart industries that have utilized it power. The collective knowledge, experience, and wisdom of the crowd has been on the radar of governments, businesses, and the sciences since centuries ago. Today, with the spread of communication and information technology, backed by the easy access of the Internet age, crowdsourcing is now a significant force — to be precise, a game-altering disruptor.

ORGANIZATION MOTIVE
- hiring specific scope of specialization
- hiring for a fixed cost
- hiring for a limited time
- the power of the rating and recommendations provided by previous employers

FREELANCERS
- large demand pool and available opportunities
- easier to be captured through the vast number of available platforms

THE
INNOVATIVE
DINOSAUR

As a labor model, crowdsourcing generates greater leverage for businesses, helping them perform tasks quickly, with cost efficiency at the fore, and, in many cases, with higher quality achieved.

The organization can tap into the global talent pool to ensure that a specific task is met. Businesses enjoy the luxury of hiring the needed specialization for a specific scope for a fixed cost or a limited time, and they benefit from the power of the rating and recommendations provided by previous employers, increasing the quality-of-service providers selection. Labor freelancers benefit from the large demand pool and available opportunities — which become easier to be captured through the vast number of available platforms. Crowdsourcing online digital platforms emerged to help coordinate and regulate the relations between suppliers and buyers. Such platforms are often intermediators with a clear value proposition of creating an online marketplace in which buyers and sellers can find each other and conduct business as a middleperson guarantees customer satisfaction upon delivery of the service and the fulfilment of the service cost to the seller. Many of these platforms provide additional added-value services that leverage and enhance the experience within the project's lifecycle.

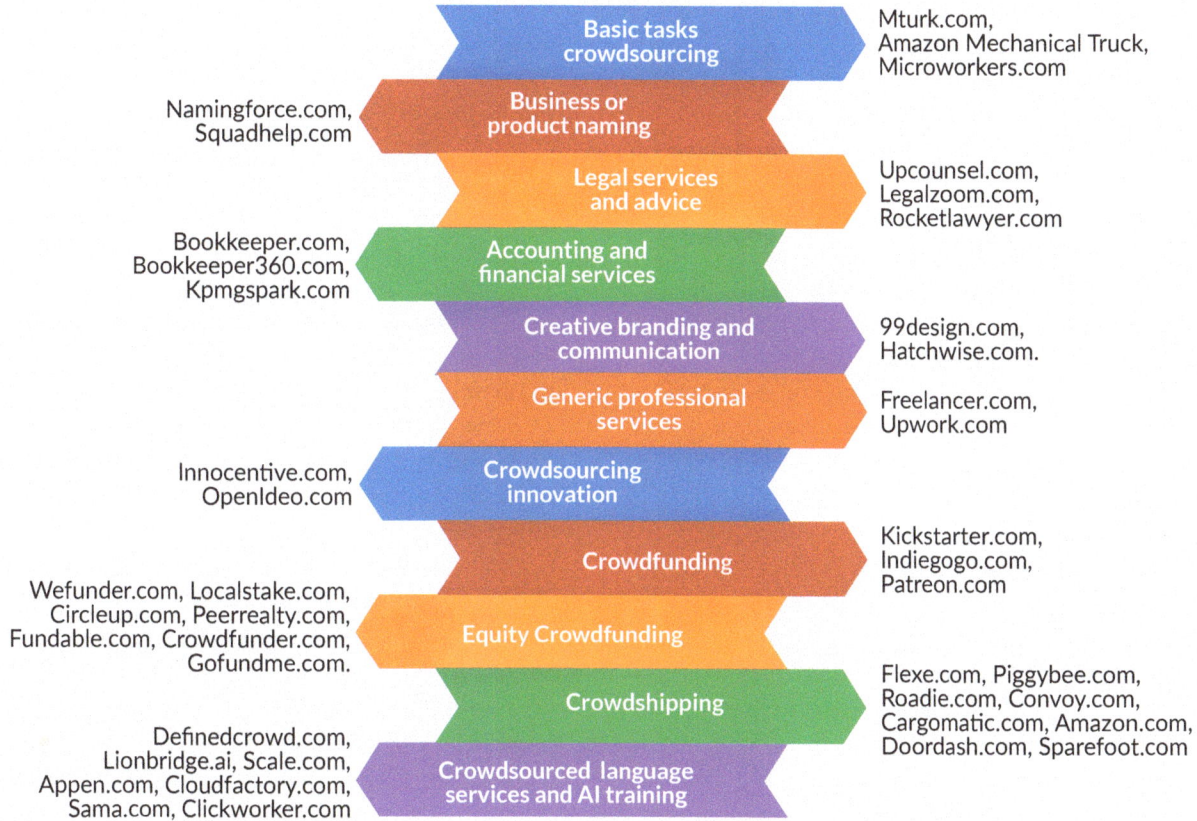

Basic tasks crowdsourcing
Mturk.com,
Amazon Mechanical Truck,
Microworkers.com

Namingforce.com,
Squadhelp.com
Business or product naming

Legal services and advice
Upcounsel.com,
Legalzoom.com,
Rocketlawyer.com

Bookkeeper.com,
Bookkeeper360.com,
Kpmgspark.com
Accounting and financial services

Creative branding and communication
99design.com,
Hatchwise.com.

Generic professional services
Freelancer.com,
Upwork.com

Innocentive.com,
OpenIdeo.com
Crowdsourcing innovation

Crowdfunding
Kickstarter.com,
Indiegogo.com,
Patreon.com

Wefunder.com, Localstake.com,
Circleup.com, Peerrealty.com,
Fundable.com, Crowdfunder.com,
Gofundme.com.
Equity Crowdfunding

Crowdshipping
Flexe.com, Piggybee.com,
Roadie.com, Convoy.com,
Cargomatic.com, Amazon.com,
Doordash.com, Sparefoot.com

Definedcrowd.com,
Lionbridge.ai, Scale.com,
Appen.com, Cloudfactory.com,
Sama.com, Clickworker.com
Crowdsourced language services and AI training

THE
INNOVATIVE
DINOSAUR

In today's world, we can now observe that most functions of any given business have crowdsourcing alternatives. For each type, from the simplest tasks to the most complex or advanced ones, we will easily find different online platforms that provide the services related to the needed service category. Let's explore an example of the various business functions and the corresponding crowdsourcing service providers:

€ **Basic tasks crowdsourcing:** Mturk.com, Amazon Mechanical Truck, and Microworkers.com are crowdsourcing marketplaces that make it easier for individuals and businesses to outsource their processes and positions to a distributed workforce who can perform these tasks virtually.

€ **Business or product naming:** We can benefit — immensely — from the creative power of the crowd, particularly when brainstorming and then selecting our business or product name and trademark. By way of illustration, Namingforce.com and Squadhelp.com both offer packages and services for creating a brand naming context. Start a public dialogue and competition, and there may be a couple hundred, even a thousand, names to choose from. Services, including the available ".com" and ".net" domains, are included, thus eliminating a big part of the hassle. Advanced services like comprehensive trademark search by attorney, linguistics analysis, test audience for names, and NDAs are also available. Such services often come with a price tag of two hundred dollars to a thousand.

€ **Legal services and advice:** Businesses of all sizes require legal services within the different stage of the company lifecycle and, in many cases, specialized legal advises related to their countries of operation. Several crowdsourcing platforms are available, providing services ranging from incorporation and registration filing to trademark and intellectual properly services, patent registration, business operations, and attorney services. Upcounsel.com, Legalzoom.com, Rocketlawyer.com are just a few examples. Note: These examples may not be following the same pattern of the other crowdsourcing ones.

€ **Accounting and financial services:** Bookkeeping, taxation, and payroll services are essential to enterprises of all kinds. Bookkeeper.com, Bookkeeper360.com, and Kpmgspark.com are designed to provide remote support to businesses, larger and small, with a competitive pricing model, and covering a wide range of services, like accounting bookkeeping and taxation, even CFO advice. Furthermore, most of the suppliers offer wide geographical coverage that consider the different countries' regulatory and legal standards.

€ **Creative branding and communication:** Logo design, company profile design, product brochures, presentation decks, company stationary, company website design, creative writing, and technical

THE INNOVATIVE DINOSAUR

product writing, are examples of specializations and talents that are available online through various crowdsourcing platforms. The most famous specialized platforms include 99design.com and Hatchwise.com.

Generic professional services: Both Freelancer.com and Upwork.com offer a wide range of crowdsourcing categories — from highly-skilled software development professionals and creative designers to project managers, scrum masters, product owners, creative writers, marketing experts, communication professionals, legal and accounting experts, and many others. From a platform technology features perspective, both sites are considered highly mature, with diversity of added value services and robust service provider ratings. They also include an efficient escrow mechanism and well-defined arbitration process, in case of any conflict between sellers and buyers.

Crowdsourcing innovation: Innocentive.com is considered a leading platform in the combined field of crowdsourcing and open innovation. Complex challenges are met and solved through this platform: its model has proved that the most tricky problems can be efficiently solved when driven by the collective brainpower of the global crowd. As another example, the platform Presans.com, which offers open innovation for R&D challenges, has been used by companies like Airbus. Also worth mentioning is OpenIdeo.com, a leading collaborative open innovation platform based on their own design-thinking methodology and approach.

Crowdfunding: The power of crowd continuous, from sourcing to funding. Kickstarter.com and Indiegogo.com are leading crowdfunding platforms, which disrupted the industry upon their respective launches, about fifteen years ago. Both platforms empower entrepreneurs and creative professionals with crowdfunding capabilities. The public can engage in the early stages of a new product development by placing pre-orders for products offered by the entrepreneurs. In return, the "backers" in the crowd enjoy a special perk based on the risk they are taking, and the entrepreneurs are able to finance their projects without losing equity.

Equity Crowdfunding: Companies like Wefunder.com and Localstake.com aim to connect individual and institutional investors with previously unavailable investment opportunities. Others, including Circleup.com and Peerrealty.com, act as intermediaries between investors and companies or funds engaged in active fundraising rounds. They typically hold the investors' funds in escrow until the round ends successfully, then the equity is transferred to the company. Further along, we have providers, like Fundable.com and Crowdfunder.com, that offer companies the opportunity to advertise their fundraising efforts to the public. On the other side, we have cause-related and good will-driven fundraising efforts from the crowd itself, perhaps most notably, Gofundme.com. Another increasingly attractive model for creative professionals is Patreon.com, a platform that has helped content creators generate steady monthly incomes directly from their followers since 2013.

∈ **Crowdshipping:** Another revolutionary crowdsourcing model, crowdshipping covers the full spectrum of logistics and the fulfilment of a product and/or service, from across the distance to the last mile. Based on Flexe.com, we can categorize the crowdshipping offering into several categories. Flexport.com offers an international long-haul container shipping service, while companies like Piggybee.com and Roadie.com provide city-to-city shipping services, and Convoy.com and Cargomatic.com, short-haul B2B delivery services. Last-mile delivery services, like Flex.Amazon.com and Doordash.com, move products from retailers, grocery stores, malls, restaurants, and more, directly to the consumers. Flexe.com and Sparefoot.com enable businesses to acquire and expand warehouse space anywhere on demand.

Crowdsourced language services and AI training: Data tagging and annotation benefit from the crowdsourcing model across varied use cases. For instance, Definedcrowd.com is benefiting from more than half a million crowd members who are helping them annotate and train their AI model. Another, Lionbridge.ai, mixes AI with the power of the crowd, including a pool of individual humans specialized in more than three hundred languages. Scale.com is particularly useful for sales call categorization, transcription services, and object tagging for autonomous vehicles. Appen.com offers a wide variety of services to technology companies, including annotation, content moderation, categorization, personalization, transcription, and translation. Cloudfactory.com is a cloud-based crowdsourcing company that provides machine learning, document transcription, and data enrichment services. Sama.com provides hands-on project management for large datasets, with a business model that lifts people out of poverty, and services including categorization, copywriting, and data collection. Clickworker.com is a paid crowdsourcing company that utilizes an online marketplace through which they provide work assignments to over a million individuals, offering categorization, data extraction, copywriting, and data collection.

As stated above, most of the elements that are essential to any business have alternative offerings within the crowdsourcing domain, and the precedent list categorizes some of the available suppliers, though it is not a comprehensive list, just a starting point for what is available and can be utilized. Today, crowdsourcing is still not fully utilized by businesses of different sizes. This model generally offers high elastic capacity for enterprises with no need for long-term commitment between the organizations and the labor force. It also provides the enterprise with the opportunity to select professional services based on needs and to pay-as-you-go. The overhead cost of employment is then directly impacted, giving the organization the ability to extend its workforce as needed and based on demand. Another important aspect here is the ability to acquire specialized knowledge and experience for a given period of time, not to mention, the ability to tap into global talent with greater ease and reach. Finally, governing the relation between supplier and buyers through online crowdsourcing platforms, resolves many concerns for both the buyer and seller.

For small and medium enterprises, the crowdsourcing model offers a magic solution for the variable capacity as well as the ability to receive professional services and deliveries with minimum commitment. For larger enterprises, this model can be perceived as both an opportunity and threat. If large enterprises reach the required means, including the methods and processes for integrating crowdsourcing within the organization's overall operational model, then benefiting from the variable capacity, and even more competitive costing, can be achieved. On the other side, enterprises must recognize that an inability to integrate with such models will impact the overall competitiveness for the means of production. This model sets the stage for small competitors to ideate, design, manufacture, and operate with increased efficiency, which will, in time, give smaller players leverage over the more advanced competitors.

Some crowdsourcing providers offer different means to integrate with medium and large customers. Both Upwork and Freelancer, headquartered in the United States and Australia respectively, provide platforms that caters to the needs, processes, methods, features, and even payment terms, that are sought after by medium to large enterprises which leads that large corporations can easily enter into the beneficial landscape of crowdsourcing. Also concerns related to non disclosure agreements (NDAs) and intellectual property (IP protections are handled and covered by several crowdsourcing platforms. What is not covered properly in this domain are the standardization interfaces between the different providers, thus a customer who wishes to fully leverage the power of the crowdsourcing model will need to navigate between the various platforms

CHAPTER 11:
FOSTERING THE ENTERPRISE'S COLLABORATIVE POWER

Traditionally, companies controlled all aspects related to the delivery of their own products and service offerings. Today, we are moving from industry boundaries to platforms and ecosystems, from single product purpose to connected multi-purpose, from producer and user role to co-creation and product co-creation. Industry 4.0 signals an influx of opportunities for growth, but very few traditional organizations are ready to develop products in an agile and fast time-to-market, either missing or dismissing the necessary pace and/or scope for capturing and seizing the opportunities of today and tomorrow.

Internal and external collaboration presents a multifaceted challenge to enterprises, testing their ability to manage the internal stakeholder collaboration within the innovation process, and to design and create an effective ecosystem of partners, even to participate in the current available ecosystems.

In this chapter, we will unpack the complexities of designing a business and then building a corresponding ecosystem. The process of designing an ecosystem is complex due to the necessity of a holistic system perspective that goes beyond designing the value creation of each stakeholder by also considering the value distribution for various players. Solving the chicken-and-egg problem of creating and attracting a critical mass of partners and customers in a scalable and defendable model while meeting the needs and expectations of each one is a heavy lifting process. We discuss how to establish the proper organizational strategies for creating and/or participating in an ecosystem, covering different approaches, challenges, opportunities, and product design aspects to achieve an ecosystem-ready product.

THE
INNOVATIVE
DINOSAUR

CHAPTER ELEVEN SECTIONS:

- Design for Ecosystem Partners
- Integrating with the existing Ecosystems
- Product Design for Ecosystem Partners
- Foster the Collaborative Innovation
- Summary of Technologies Leading Collaborative Disruption

THE INNOVATIVE DINOSAUR

CHAPTER ELEVEN LIST OF REFERENCES & EXTRA READINGS

1. Conceptual Approaches for Personal and Corporate Information and Knowledge Management. Andrew J. Slade, Albert F. Bokma.
2. The digital consumer: an introduction and philosophy.
3. UK :, DAVID NICHOLAS, IAN ROWLANDS, RICHARD WITHEY, TOM DOBROWOLSKI.
4. Landmarks of Tomorrow, by Drucker, Peter Digital Automation Platforms Comparative Study, ICICT 2020 an IEEE conference
5. Let's DO - Automotive Platform for Interoperability, ICICT 2020 an IEEE conference
6. Automation Platforms, *www.Zapier.com*
7. Automation Platforms, *www.IFTTT.com*
8. Automation Platforms, *www.Integromat.com*
9. Automation Platforms, *www.parabola.io*
10. Automation Platforms, *www.powerapps.microsoft.com*
11. Automation Platforms, *www.powerbi.microsoft.com*
12. Automation Platforms, *www.azure.microsoft.com/en-us/services*
13. Software Ecosystem Aided Tools, *www.instabug.com*
14. Software Ecosystem Aided Tools, *www.Atlasian.com*
15. Software Ecosystem Aided Tools, *www.Github.com*
16. Software Ecosystem Aided Tools, *www.Gitlab.com*
17. Software Ecosystem Aided Tools, *www.Auth0.com*
18. Software Ecosystem Aided Tools, *www.Okta.com*
19. Software Ecosystem Aided Tools, *www.Wso2.com*
20. Software Ecosystem Aided Tools, *www.Apigee.com*
21. Software Ecosystem Aided Tools, *www.Cloud-elements.com*
22. Software Ecosystem Aided Tools, *www.3scale.net*
23. Idea management systems, *www.brightidea.com*
24. Idea management systems, *www.planview.com*
25. Idea management systems, *www.ideascale.com*
26. Idea management systems, *www.crowdicity.com*
27. Idea management systems, *www.untapcompete.com*
28. Idea management systems, *www.f6s.com*

TECHNOLOGY OWNERS

- Enabling Legacy Investment
- Bridging Digital Gap
- Min investment & Higher Efficiency
- Minimizing time to Market
- New revenue source
- Higher Profit
- New business models
  - Subscription
  - Pay as you go...
- Increasing customer loyalty/stickiness

Like: Google, Apple, John Deere

GET IT ON
Google Play $40B 2020 Sales

Download on the App Store $64B 2020 Sales

PARTNER

- Digital Development Experience
- Ease of Use and Efficiency
- Utilizing Technology Owner investment
- Accessing Technology Owner customer base
- Capturing demand
  - Increasing Sales
  - Higher profit

Like: App Developers, Content Producers or Service Providers

JOHN DEERE

100 Connected Software & Tools
- Average customer buy 3 apps
- Customer stickiness increase
- Higher Profitability

CUSTOMER

- Better Experience
- Variety of cases
- Convenience
- Integration with owned products

THE INNOVATIVE DINOSAUR

DESIGN FOR
ECOSYSTEM PARTNERS

Traditionally, companies have controlled all aspects related to the delivery of their own products and services, from analyzing customer needs and leading in-house product development to building external distribution channels and networks. Today, such dynamics are dramatically shifting, from traditional industry boundaries to platforms and ecosystems, single-product purpose to connected multi-purpose, and producer + user roles to co-creation and product co-creation. Industry 4.0 is offering countless opportunities for game-changing growth, but very few traditional organizations are ready to develop products in an agile and fast time-to-market at the necessary pace and scope for truly seizing the potential. A well-developed and managed business ecosystem is now a core element of competitiveness for those who can design and execute well, as customers are demanding digital experience and capabilities within traditional products more and more each day.

Software-based ecosystems involve sophisticated integrations across various stakeholders who each fulfill a well-defined role within the overall system. The value of a given ecosystem is that it brings the collective offerings from multiple stakeholders to create, leverage, and address a specific market, or markets, in a more efficient way than a single organization capacity. Apple iTunes and Google Play are examples of an ecosystem offering. Both of these tech giants offer their pre-developed technologies and platforms to third parties, like developers or content producers, to build use cases and applications to be offered to the target customer segments. This is a win-win relation in which Apple and Google are utilizing their investments and customer base through offering more use cases. The partner's network benefits from the existing customer base and the technology investments of the platform owners. Both technology owners, Apple and Google, enjoy an additional revenue stream, as does the partner network. Customers, too, enjoy new experiences through the partner's offering, competitive pricing, and product quality guarantee. Another example is the American manufacturer John Deere, a traditional player that has built a successful ecosystem around its farm machinery and industrial equipment business. John Deere worked hard to offer such an ecosystem to be able to differentiate its own products in comparison to cheaper competitive offerings. Rather than going down the road of commodity-based competition, the company decided to compete based on value creation, and now sells digital farming solutions and experiences. The partner's ecosystem made this happen in a fast time to market and with less investment from John Deere's side. No company alone can innovate and build such a range of solutions and use cases that are offered based on combining solutions produced and integrated from multiple partners who are eager to seize the opportunity and benefit from John Deere's reputation as a major brand name, along with its customer base and technological investments. This network of partners builds business resilience. Many new product development features, application use cases, and customer requirements have helped the full ecosystem to achieve greater awareness with respect to the needs in a fast time-to-market response serving the evolving needs that are based on customers' demands. Another important element here is the customer lifetime value and recurrent revenue from a single customer, who can purchase an average of three added value applications from the network, covering specific business use case and needs. This dynamic has led to more customer dependency on integrated solutions to manage the business. It became harder for the farmer to switch to another brand, as dependency and stickiness are increasing, leading to a higher barrier to entry for competition. John Deere's business and revenue models have evolved into having the possibility to include digital business models such as subscription based models, even pay-as-you-go, in addition to traditional asset sales models.

SELLING ALLIES are partners who can push ready-to-sell products to a specific target segment. Usually, VARs and Distributors.

DELIVERY CHAMPIONS are partners with an extended delivery capacity that help the organization scale its delivery capabilities.

ECOSYSTEM PIONEERS are partners that often offer a go-to-market based on a customized joint IP solution offering.

COCREATORS are strategic partners that actively collaborate to offer new customer-centric products, solutions, and services.

Based on Deloitte's in-depth 2020 article "Evolving partner roles in Industry 4.0."

THE
INNOVATIVE
DINOSAUR

Based on Deloitte's in-depth 2020 article "Evolving partner roles in Industry 4.0," partners' ecosystem architecture can be classified into four main types: selling allies, delivery champions, ecosystem pioneers, and cocreation. Selling allies are partners who can push ready-to-sell products to a specific target segment in bulk. This type of partnership is focusing on increasing the company's sales reach through a partner that can be considered as an extension to the in-house sales team but with lower cost. Typically, value added resellers (VAR) and distributors are considered selling allies. Delivery champions are partners with an extended delivery capacity that help the organization scale its delivery capabilities in a reduced cost structure. Usually, these partners build complementary skills compared to the core offering and develop extended solutions. Ecosystem pioneers are partners that often offer a go-to-market based on a customized joint IP solution offering. These partners increase the total value creation to the target customer beyond the existing solution. A typical example of ecosystem pioneers is application developers that offer their applications through either the Apple iTunes or Google Play store. And cocreators are strategic partners that actively collaborate to offer new customer-centric products, solutions, and services. Such offerings usually include joint intellectual property, marketing capabilities, and technology expertise. This type brings together differentiation and specialized solutions to address customer's changing needs. Through cocreators, organizations are expanding their knowledge and know-how capabilities.

If designing a business is a challenging marathon, then building an ecosystem is a fairly complex journey to reach the top of Mount Everest. What makes the process of designing an ecosystem complex is the needed holistic system perspective that goes beyond designing the value creation of each stakeholder and considers the value distribution for various players. Solving the chicken-and-egg problem of creating and attracting a critical mass of partners and customers in a scalable and defendable model while also meeting the concerns, needs, and experience of each, is a weighty process. In 2020, Boston Consulting Group published the thought-provoking article, "How Do You 'Design' a Business Ecosystem?", which summarizes this challenge by addressing a set of questions and proposing answers for each of them. The global management consulting firm clearly states that building an ecosystem cannot be entirely planned from the early stages, as new requirements and needs are emerging and thus the adaptability of the design and operating model is one of the major points of strength. To achieve such a dynamic and adaptable model, a set of design decisions must be addressed and answered.

WHAT IS THE PROBLEM THAT YOU WANT TO SOLVE?

Is the problem big enough?
Is an ecosystem the right choice?
What kind of ecosystem do you need?

WHO NEEDS TO BE PART OF YOUR ECOSYSTEM?

What are the players and roles?
Who should be the orchestrators?
How can the orchestrators motivate the other players?

WHAT SHOULD BE THE INITIAL GOVERNANCE MODEL OF YOUR ECOSYSTEM?

How open should the ecosystem be?
What should the orchestrator control?

HOW CAN YOU CAPTURE THE VALUE OF YOUR ECOSYSTEM

Is the problem big enough?
Is an ecosystem the right choice?
What kind of ecosystem do you need?

HOW CAN YOU SOLVE THE CHICKEN-OR-EGG PROBLEM?

What are the players and roles?
Who should be the orchestrators?
How can the orchestrators motivate the other players?

HOW CAN YOU ENSURE THE EVOLVABILITY OF YOUR ECOSYSTEM?

How open should the ecosystem be?
What should the orchestrator control?

Derivative from Boston Consulting Group article, "How Do You 'Design' a Business Ecosystem?", published in 2020

THE INNOVATIVE DINOSAUR

Answering the questions below the firm's proposed steps aids the ecosystem operator or creator in anticipating and designing the model while simultaneously considering the various stakeholders' motives, concerns, and challenges. When designing an ecosystem strategy, we must accept the highly dynamic nature and the needed agility throughout the journey.

What is the problem that you want to solve?

o   First, we must ensure that the problem that the ecosystem is intended to solve is clearly defined, realistic, and large enough to justify the high investment that we are going to place. The size of the opportunity and the clarity of the definition are crucial factors that will impact our ability to secure proper partnerships.

o   The value proposition of the ecosystem will either come from removing an existing industry or market friction (e.g., a legislation, production cost, accessibility, poor quality, limited features or capabilities, and/or lack of trust limitations), or unmet customer needs and demands.

o   Exploring the alternative for building an ecosystem is important. The ecosystem alternative will be more suitable in case we are addressing a market that is unpredictable, dynamic and high modularity of offerings are combined with the need for coordination.

o   The type of ecosystem is either solution-based or transaction-based, or a hybrid.

Who needs to be part of your ecosystem?

o   Mapping the value blueprint between the different ecosystem stakeholders includes defining the flow of information, goods, services, money, and responsibilities between them.

o   We must define and assign the ecosystem platform orchestrator with the approval of all of the ecosystem stakeholders. The orchestrator must have a central role, complete with clear value creation, in the ecosystem.

o   Designing the appropriate incentive program to motivate the different levels of partners is key.

What should be the initial governance of your ecosystem?

o   Ecosystem governance is an important element, as it will define the platform control roles and formulate a sort of constitution for all the relations between the different stakeholders.

o   Governance must cover and strike a balance between the ecosystem value creation and value sharing.

o   The roles must be defined, including who will have access, how each stakeholder will participate, and the commitment level of each participating stakeholder.

o   The level of openness of the ecosystem must also be defined. The degree of openness can vary from a closed ecosystem, like the Nespresso model, to a wide open ecosystem, like Airbnb and the Chinese company Haier, which includes various types of ecosystem stakeholders from home appliances to healthcare and even entertainment. In the mobile industry, ecosystems are competing on the degree of openness; we have the well-known examples of Google versus Apple, in which the first giant offers a more open ecosystem governance.

o The design of the transaction, along with how the platform matches producers and consumers, is another important element: will it be an algorithm matching process, as with Uber and Facebook, or rather based on best offer negotiation, like eBay's model. Once established, curation will be based on platform editors, like Wikipedia, or user feedback, like Airbnb, or algorithms, as with Google searches.

How can you capture the value of your ecosystem?

o Monetization is the next greatest challenge while designing an ecosystems. The ecosystem must maximize the total size of the pie, enable all stakeholders to earn enough profits, and capture the appropriate value for the platform orchestrator.

o The orchestrator revenue model can include a license fee, as with Nespresso, or revenue share, as with Apple and Google mobile stores, or the sales of added value products or services.

o In transaction-based ecosystems, the options are wide ranging. The orchestrator can charge fee for access, additional fees for premium features, and even higher fees for enhanced service level agreement. Crowdsourcing orchestrators like Upwork and Freelancer.com are typical examples of this type of ecosystem.

o Then there is the question of value capturing — in short, who will pay? Orchestrators have several options based on the nature of the ecosystem, either charging all participants or just one type while subsidizing the rest. Sometimes we may find that the orchestrator charges the partners, too. In other cases, the orchestrator charges the customer, not the partners. Others are mixing by having a basic charge for specific stakeholders and offering additional charges for more premium services for another stakeholder. Moreover, others offer a free-of-charge service for all stakeholders while also generating revenue indirectly from other sources, like advertisements.

How can you solve the chicken-or-the-egg problem?

o Achieving a sufficient participation size of both sellers and buyers is critical driver of success for an ecosystem.

o   It is not about being the first to the market, but rather the first with complete solutions. While Apple iTunes was not the first mover, it was the first to offer a complete integrated solution for both music producers and the buyers, with a managed, secured, and disruptive pricing model.

o   The size of the network must not be measured by the number of participants alone; it must include the size and number of transactions that generates value to the different stakeholders.

o   The side of the market to focus on, either supply or demand part, must be determined. Generally, it is exceptionally hard to convince partners to invest in a specific new ecosystem, thus orchestrators must follow different strategies to lower the barrier to entry for the target partners and win them over with the foreseen potential of such an ecosystem.

How can you ensure the evolvability of your ecosystem?

o   In most cases, the ecosystem business model has a high potential in both the supply and demand sides, which leads to positive feedback loop impacting economic scale for both sides.

o   It is important to understand the economic scalability of the ecosystem and design the appropriate ecosystem strategies accordingly.

o   Successful ecosystems have in-built defense characteristics that are formulated around the network scale as ecosystem compete based on the system feature level and not the product feature level. Such characteristics leads to high barrier to entry and prevent competition from the ability to imitate or substitute.

o   The above-mentioned characteristics provide an easier way to achieve scale and harder methods to sustain positioning. Not only do digital technologies offer new ways to leverage network impact and capture different demand levels, but they also provide an easier barrier to entry when compared to traditional business means, like building physical telephone networks.

o   Building a defense strategy to guarantee the evolvability of the ecosystem is incredibly challenging and may include some decisions that strategically impact many other elements. Designing a model in which we can stick the supply part to our platform through following a specific product development standard may increase the supply side dependability, but it can also hinder the participation. Offering incentives and loyalty-based offerings to customers can be considered wisely so the overall profitability is not impacted. Other means to increase the barrier to entry must be considered while designing the ecosystem architecture.

CROWDSOURCING PLATFORMS

DIGITAL SPECIALIZED COMMERCIAL CHANNELS

SOCIAL NETWORKS

ECOMMERCE PLATFORMS

AUTOMATION PLATFORMS

EXISTING PLATFORMS

THE
INNOVATIVE
DINOSAUR

INTEGRATION WITH THE EXISTING ECOSYSTEMS

On the other hand, organizations need to study the possibility of availing their products and services on the existing ecosystem platforms. Today, plenty of platforms exist, covering a vast spectrum of domains and specializations. Studying the available ecosystem options and determining the most suitable ones that an organization can target to make its product and services available and integrated with existing platforms is recommended. We can classify the existing ecosystems as follows:

Ecommerce platforms:

As of today, many online ecommerce and digital marketplaces are available and cover different domains and geographies. This type of ecosystem varies from large international ecosystems, like Amazon and eBay to smaller geographically-focused ones. Such ecosystems provide a clear value proposition built on the large-scale customer base and plenty of platform features and capabilities.

Digital specialized commercial channels,

today we have many specialized online digital stores and platforms with the most famous mobile stores as Apple and Google stores for mobiles and tables as an example. Through this type of store, application developers and content producers can reach a great number of customers. Additionally, there are music stores like SoundCloud and Bandcamp, and film and television series stores like Amazon Premium and Netflix.

Crowdsourcing platforms:

Upwork, Freelancer.com, 99designs, and many other platforms that cover a wide range of services, are suitable for professional service providers, as they achieve a high economical mass of both suppliers and buyers.

Social networks:

Facebook, LinkedIn, and many other related online services offer a wide range of business models, features, and capabilities that an organization can capitalize on by either creating or being part of a business ecosystem powered by digital commercial capacities.

We are also seeing another available alternative on the market that deserves consideration:

Automation platforms, with its unique user experience built around the action trigger-based feature, that do not require programming language skills from the user side in the designing of their own set of workflows through a set of pre-integrated platforms, devices, and applications. By way of illustration, a user can simply set a trigger based action sequence between their home IoT gadget, social network accounts, and email. These platforms automate repetitive human-driven tasks and offer certain types of decision-making capabilities. Today, thousands of applications, platforms, gadgets, and devices are integrated on such platforms.

In 2020, I supervised research on the different available automation platforms, under the title "Digital Automation Platforms Comparative Study," which was published in the International Conference on Inventive Computation Technologies (ICICT), an annual US-based conference run by the Institute of Electrical and Electronics Engineers (IEEE). In this paper for the IEEE Computer Society – "the world's largest technical professional organization dedicated to advancing technology for the benefit of humanity" – we compared the different aspects of automation platforms, including accessibility, usability, UX, license models, performance, and security of such platforms as Zapier, IFTTT, Integromat, Microsoft Power Automate, and Parabola. Zapier, for instance, includes over two thousand pre-integrated digital platforms and applications. It focuses on digital platforms, such as ERPs, CRMs, email providers, and general information worker-related applications, and it provides the widest catalogue in this domain. IFTTT concentrates more on IoT-related gadgets and mobile devices with around 600 pre-integrated applications. Integromat is considered to be the second largest workflow automation platform — after Zapier — in application integration, as it supports over 450 applications. As another example, the main advantage of Microsoft Power Automate is not based on the number of integrated applications, but rather it seen in the full stake of Microsoft technologies that are integrated with the platforms through connecting Power Automate across the entire Microsoft Power Platform (e.g. Power Apps, Power BI, Power Virtual Agents), as well as to Microsoft 365, Dynamics 365, Cognitive Technologies, Robotics Process Automation (RPA), and full Azure Cloud Services support. For Parabola, the main advantage is the supported operation related to data stores that facilitate dealing with databases and tables. The automation platform value proposition is clear as day to the end users based on UX and the vast customization experience that such platforms provide for the non-technical user. For organizations of different sizes such trending platforms provide a clear added value. Organizations are extended there capabilities by availing it products and services through those platforms to cater and leverage their offerings with a considerable number of capabilities and

THE INNOVATIVE DINOSAUR

interoperability that meets the modern user's needs and expectations. An alternative for organizations is to implement such integrations in-house with thousands of platforms and gadgets, and furthermore, to ensure that such integrations are always up-to-date and compatible with any future new versions or software updated that may be offered in future. Imagine an organization wishing to integrate its application or gadget with CRM, ERPs, or social networks, and how many integrations will be carried, and the amount of investment required. Automation platforms provide a clear value through which the integration of your platform will be done once with a specific platform(s) and then you will gain hundreds and thousands of integrations available to your target user out of the box. These platforms also provide a clear cost efficiency, fast time-to-market, and large integration coverage value proposition for organizations. Two concerns must be addressed when deciding to integrate our platform and/or gadget with the automation platforms: the first is related to the cybersecurity design of the integration, and the second is related to the share of wallet that those platforms will represent from the customer sales transaction.

It's worth mentioning that automation platforms have availed new opportunities for developing and catering to many use cases as well as fulfilling customers automation needs and demands. The amount of use cases that can be built and achieved through integrating with those platforms is astronomical and thus an opportunity that needs to be thoroughly investigated and smartly captured. Mailparser.io, an example of a company that was able to seize such an opportunity, is a simple parsing service that can turn any unstructured text stream into a structured format. The service can identify specific fields within a text, such as sender name, or specific financial information, or even a text sequence that can be used as a trigger. Through its integration with an automation platform, this service was able to cater to a range of use cases while serving different user scenarios. Without the integration of various applications — from email and CRMs to social media and others that are available on the automation platforms — the service diffusion would be limited. Many other services and use cases can be achieved in a cost-efficient manner and fast time to market through the automation platforms.

ZAPIER

over two thousand pre-integrated digital platforms and applications. It focuses on digital platforms, such as ERPs, CRMs, email providers, and general information worker-related applications.

IFTTT

concentrates more on IoT-related gadgets and mobile devices with around 600 pre-integrated applications.
It supports over 450 applications.

MICROSOFT POWER AUTOMATE

full stake of Microsoft technologies that are integrated with the platforms through connecting:
Power Apps, Power BI, Power Virtual Agents, Microsoft 365, Dynamics 365, Cognitive Technologies, RPA, full Azure Cloud Services support

PARABOLA

the main advantage is the supported operation related to data stores that facilitate dealing with databases and tables.

Designed by: Motaz Agamawi
www.theinnovativedinosaur.com

THE INNOVATIVE DINOSAUR

PRODUCT DESIGN FOR ECOSYSTEM PARTNERS

Another angle of complexity is related to technological readiness. There are two categories of complexity for an ecosystem-ready product: the first is for a purely software-based product, and the second is for a traditional yet digitally-enabled product . In this section, we will review the challenges and standards for ecosystem capabilities enablement in both categories.

☐ SW Architecture	following a standard pattern, whether it's service-oriented architecture (SOA), virtualization, software-as-a-service (SaaS), or cloud computing.
☐ standard interfaces	RESTful application programming interfaces (APIs), HTTP request, web services, dynamic-link libraries (DLLs), Component Object Models (COMs), or any other means of exposition.
☐ Supported Target Compatibility	including both operating systems and processors.
☐ Supported Programming Language Wrappers	from C# and Java to .NET and Python, and compatibility with different Integrated Development Environments (IDEs) is advisable.

THE INNOVATIVE DINOSAUR

Let's begin with purely software-based products, platforms, and/or solutions, and explore how they can be ecosystem friendly. We need to assume that the software architecture is following a standard pattern, whether it's service-oriented architecture (SOA), virtualization, software-as-a-service (SaaS), or cloud computing.

The software must have an implementation for a standard means for exposing its features through supporting one or more standard interfaces techniques, such as RESTful application programming interfaces (APIs), HTTP request, web services, dynamic-link libraries (DLLs), Component Object Models (COMs), or any other means of exposition. Then comes the software-supported targets, including both operating systems and processors. With the developer experience and convenience in mind, the exposed interface must also be friendly with the commonly-used programming languages, from C# and Java to .NET and Python, and compatibility with different Integrated Development Environments (IDEs) is advisable. Those are the basic minimum standards, capabilities, and design considerations that must be supported by any well-designed software that aims to approach external partners and be ecosystem friendly. To make the software more appealing to the ecosystem community and following the standard developers user experience, the following needs to be covered and considered:

- ☐ The interfaces must follow a standard design pattern. It is recommended to follow the OpenAPI Initiative standard description or the Swagger documentation standard.

- ☐ The interface design and functions parameters (in/out attributes) are recommended to exclude complex objects to guarantee the developer's experience.

- ☐ A comprehensive and clear developer documentation guide must be included and is recommended to feature step-by-step tutorials, deployment instructions, frequently asked questions, and troubleshooting information.

- ☐ Forward and backward compatibility must be supported and governed to ensure that our community investments are secured.

- ☐ Means to capture bugs and runtime issues are preferred to be supported. Services like Instabug provide runtime crash reports, bug reporting, and customer surveying.

- ☐ Software maturity level must be guaranteed and implementing continuous integration (CI) and continuous delivery (CD) as part of the software development lifecycle is essential. Many such platforms are available, including Microsoft CI/CD services, Amazon Web Services Cloud9 (AWS), Google Cloud Platform (GCP), Atlassian, GitHub, and GitLab.

- ☐ Deploying the exposed interfaces over a robust scalable infrastructure is not an option. Cloud solutions like Microsoft Azure, AWS, and GCP are suitable for such applications.

- ☐ Implementing the latest serverless architecture over the cloud is an option that guarantees seamless scalable infrastructure.

THE
INNOVATIVE
DINOSAUR

- [ ] Following a standard secured authentication method, including identity management, either in-house developed or licensed from a third-party supplier, is important. Auth0, Okta, Wso2, or other Identity Authentication Management (IAM) from GCP, AWS, and Microsoft Azure, will guarantee that we are following the latest IAM standards.

- [ ] Guarantee the appropriate cybersecurity defensibility by implementing standard penetration test design consideration and software development standards. We can also assign a third-party supplier to conduct penetration testing services as part of the product or service acceptance testing.

- [ ] Prepare a clear, transparent End User License Agreement (EULA) that includes all the benefits, service level agreement, scope of service, and limitations or liabilities of the different stakeholders. It is recommended to assign the compilation of the EULA to a professional authorized legal counselor.

- [ ] Ensure that data-related compliance measures, like General Data Protection Regulations (GDPR), are followed.

- [ ] Implementing the needed features and capabilities to manage the flow of requests and track the consumer usage is a crucial part of the business model.

- [ ] Implementing the proper means to manage the usage and monetization until invoicing is a must.

- [ ] Supporting cloud microservices is an advanced capability that is recommended to be followed, as it will widen the horizon for various integrations, services, and business models to be offered.

THE
INNOVATIVE
DINOSAUR

- The interfaces must follow a standard design pattern. It is recommended to follow the OpenAPI Initiative standard description or the Swagger documentation standard.
- The interface design and functions parameters (in/out attributes) are recommended to exclude complex objects to guarantee the developer's experience.
- A comprehensive and clear developer documentation guide must be included and is recommended to feature step-by-step tutorials, deployment instructions, frequently asked questions, and troubleshooting information.
- Forward and backward compatibility must be supported and governed to ensure that our community investments are secured.
- Means to capture bugs and runtime issues are preferred to be supported. Services like Instabug provide runtime crash reports, bug reporting, and customer surveying.
- Software maturity level must be guaranteed and implementing continuous integration (CI) and continuous delivery (CD) as part of the software development lifecycle is essential. Many such platforms are available, including Microsoft CI/CD services, Amazon Web Services Cloud9 (AWS), Google Cloud Platform (GCP), Atlassian, GitHub, and GitLab.

  Deploying the exposed interfaces over a robust scalable infrastructure is not an option. Cloud solutions like Microsoft Azure, AWS, and GCP are suitable for such applications.

- Implementing the latest serverless architecture over the cloud is an option that guarantees seamless scalable infrastructure.
- Following a standard secured authentication method, including identity management, either in-house developed or licensed from a third-party supplier, is important. Auth0, Okta, Wso2, or other Identity.
- Authentication Management (IAM) from GCP, AWS, and Microsoft Azure, will guarantee that we are following the latest IAM standards.
- Guarantee the appropriate cybersecurity defensibility by implementing standard penetration test design consideration and software development standards.
- We can also assign a third-party supplier to conduct penetration testing services as part of the product or service acceptance testing.
- Prepare a clear, transparent End User License Agreement (EULA) that includes all the benefits, service level agreement, scope of service, and limitations or liabilities of the different stakeholders. It is recommended to assign the compilation of the EULA to a professional authorized legal counselor.

  Ensure that data-related compliance measures, like General Data Protection Regulations (GDPR), are followed.

- Implementing the needed features and capabilities to manage the flow of requests and track the consumer usage is a crucial part of the business model.

  Implementing the proper means to manage the usage and monetization until invoicing is a must.

€ Supporting cloud microservices is an advanced capability that is recommended to be followed, as it will widen the horizon for various integrations, services, and business models to be offered.

The above is a general list of recommendations and best practices to be followed from a business requirement point of view. Now, if we consider that the above-listed are covered and available, then we need to explore the delivery mechanism for the applications and services interfaces. The standard mechanism and method for offering commercial-ready software interfaces are API Management Systems, which are solutions that provide means to securely manage the distribution of software APIs. Through such systems we can publish our interfaces, manage the access rights, apply the needed security policies, track the customer usage, enforce different revenue models, invoice customers, provide customers with a professional UX, report performance, track our cloud and/or hosting cost structure, and offer a digital online frontend interface to build our own ecosystem or even integrate with other ecosystem platforms. Many alternatives, including opensource and proprietary API management systems, are available. Apigee is a leading API management solution that was acquired by Google to be part of GCP, and Microsoft Azure API management platforms are considered the best. We also have both Cloud Elements and 3scale as other solution alternatives that deserve consideration.

For the open-source alternative, both Tyk and Fusio are featured systems that are available for the community with different deployment options. Upon developing and deploying the above, our products will be ecosystem-ready and thus we can provide our target customers and partners with a professional offering, just like any developer section we can find on an international service provider website.

Now, we can move on to the more complex scenario of recasting a traditional product or service as ecosystem-ready. We will primarily focus on how we can enable a traditional product that has some digital capabilities to be ecosystem friendly — un other words, if we have a sensor, actuator, or gadget that includes digital features, then how we can expose its digital capability to be available for external partners to access and build different use cases. Those sensors, actuators or gadgets can be of any product category: automotive components, healthcare machinery, Industry 4.0 machine, athletic device, personal watch, home appliance (washing machine or oven), home or office automation solution, or even a traditional steel product that includes digital capability.

First, let's agree that most of the traditional industries that are offering digital features within their product offerings are facing some challenges in these times of digital disruption. Such challenges are based on the historical introduction of the software as a late arrival in many traditional industries and domains. The general challenges can be summarized as:

- Non-standard communication protocols, including a CAN, LIN, FlexRay, MOST, OMS, Zigbee, DNP3, DSI, Z-Wave, CIP, MPI, and hundreds of other specific purpose and specific domain protocols are used.
- Longlist of network interfaces; each network interface supplier provides their own driver and thus APIs.
- In most cases, we will find various electronic control units (ECUs) or processors in a single solution. In some cases, products include special purpose ECUs with extremely low capabilities to meet the needed features with a low price range, which increases the complexity and makes the software architecture coupled with the underlying hardware.
- Low level programming languages, like the C language, are usually used. To increase the challenge in large-scale systems many languages may exist.
- Primitive operating systems (OS), and in many cases non-standard OS, are used to meet the ECU limitations.
- Due to the above, in most cases the software design does not consider functional calls through APIs, but rather it depends on message broadcasting architecture techniques.
- In most of cases, the software architecture does not follow the service-oriented architecture (SOA), which hinders the possibility of standard integration with the external world in a cost efficient and timely manner.
- It is likely that the software is designed and developed in a bespoke or tailored manner for a specific functionality delivery without consideration of generic usage, which results in a complex software interface.
- Based on such a closed nature, cybersecurity design considerations and capabilities are not covered, which makes the external world exposition riskier.

The above-mentioned natures and characteristics exist due to many parameters and reasons that have been covered in different sections and chapters of this book. The result of these characteristics is that the traditional methods to integrate a solution, product, or gadget that is following the above described challenging design pattern to the digital world, or even to make it available for external partners or ecosystems, is extremely difficult, time-consuming, and costly.

For more than 4 years, I led a team of research and innovation engineers working on investigating, exploring, and developing a platform to bridge the gap between nondigital traditional systems and the digital world. In March 2020, we published a paper in ICCIT, an IEEE conference under the title "Let's DO - Automotive Platform for Interoperability." In this paper, we propose a novel software platform architecture that increases the efficiency, minimizing the cost and enhancing the time to market for availing a legacy traditional system to communicate and integrate with digital world platforms and applications. Such architecture enables the traditional products to expose its digital capabilities in standard interfaces for external ecosystem stakeholders. Simply, to be able to save the legacy investment and leverage traditionally-designed products to be digitally-enabled, we must think differently. Our proposed architecture can be summarized as follows:

- The concept is based on translating the smart embedded system message frames — generated by ECUs and transmitted over the network — into standardized internet protocol suite (TCP/IP) messages; the latter is in turn transmitted over an IP-based network.
- Following that is the introduction of the concept of nodes, which are the computing devices that consume and/or produce the standard messages. The proposed system architecture includes a set of libraries and software development kit (SDKs) that enable the machines connected to those nodes to process the produced standard messages. Such nodes are compiled to support a wide range of target computing platforms, starting from powerful computing devices such as servers, desktops, or laptops, and passing by specialized computing platforms.
- The framework is based on C++ core API libraries.
- These libraries and SDKs provide the basic functionalities offered by the framework, from connectivity to different networks and publish-subscribe messaging mechanisms to message converters and adapters.
- User applications built using the framework will use the SDK package and may connect to different web services that act as a bridge to digital world platforms and systems and cloud-based platforms.
- Network interfaces libraries are an abstraction layer for controlling different types of network interfaces.
- This layer addresses the challenge of standardizing the network interface controller's access.
- Message-oriented middleware (MOM) libraries: In order to ensure the efficient transfer of messages over the network, we implemented an abstract

publish-subscribe library that enables the developer sending and receiving the messages using various MOM standards, including both brokered and peer-to-peer (P2P) communication, Message Queuing Telemetry Transport (MQTT) protocol, and Data Distribution Service (DDS) protocol.

- ∈ Product abstraction libraries: For each traditional product (e.g. ECUs) or digital world product (e.g. Leap Motion sensors, Logitech pedals), we provide an abstraction library to communicate with the device driver API and convert the device data into standardized messages. Enabling the integration of traditional and digital products on the feature level and abstracting target features allows developers to access both domains without investing much time in learning how to access the various devices.

- ∈ Converter libraries: Special domain message frames contain aggregated data in hexadecimal formats, which is deciphered into meaningful signal information using a communication matrix that defines the message structures for each target platform.

- ∈ Language and platform support: In order to address the previously-mentioned challenges of programming languages and platform support, we deliver the SDK in various programming languages built for various target platforms. To support multiple programming languages, we use automatic code wrapper generator tools that process the C++ library source code and generate respective wrappers for chosen languages.

The above-stated concept achieved a cost reduction of more 60 percent with a 50 percent increase in the time to market within the domain of enabling the integration of traditionally-based products with the digital world applications and platforms. The moral of the story is that even embedded legacy software systems features can be exposed through standard APIs to deal with the digital world standards, thus we have the ability to apply the same business dynamics and models with a cost efficient and fast time to market. Such an approach will bridge the knowledge gap between traditional system developers and digital world developers. Traditional embedded systems developers will be able to communicate and integrate with the digital world architectures with minimum knowledge; the same can be said for the new entrants coming from the digital world to the traditional industries, as they will be able to develop solutions, uses cases, and applications utilizing the existing investments and following the traditional industries architecture limitations. Then, we can claim that the development pace of digitalization and advancements within the traditional industries product development will be accelerated —tremendously. Enabling the traditional industry product with communication interfaces through standard APIs will lead to high impact on the industry in large, whether its automotive or mobility at large, medical or athletic devices, industrial or military machinery, home appliances, or many others, and will have the ability to meet target digital features, capabilities, and UX in a more efficient development lifecycle.

PRODUCT DESIGN FOR ECOSYSTEM PARTNERS

We are witnessing increased complexity in the field of innovation management, particularly in ideas funnel management. At each stage of the funnel, we may have different outputs and milestones. Multiple stakeholders are contributing with a range of engagement levels in development and maturity stages. For instance, we can have an idea in the build space, with a PoC under development, a patent application or application within the patent office filling process, a published paper or papers, and a customer demonstration. All these activities may include the same team members, and in some cases, different team members. Following such idea during the different stages of maturity is an arduous task, as is following all ideas from submission to commercialization. On the other hand, we have other contributors, including jury committees, inventors, innovators, and different types of managers, who participate across the lifecycle. Furthermore, having a 360-degree view for a specific idea across the lifecycle and calculating its return on investment (ROI) by following client interaction through customer relationship management (CRM), or even financial transactions through the enterprise resource planning (ERP) reports, is not achievable in all cases. The current enterprise innovation management challenges can be summarized as:

- Difficulty in assuming a single view for the ideas funnel lifecycle within a given organization.
- This difficulty leads to a high challenges of calculating and reporting the cost and ROI associated with the full lifecycle activities for the ideas funnel.
- Difficulty in compiling a consolidated stakeholders profiles for all of the participating personnel within the enterprise's innovation lifecycle, from inventors, innovators, and researchers to jury committees and management team members, leading to added complexity in terms of managing and tracking skills and competencies development.
- Such missing information views are leading to complications when identifying the bottlenecks and designing improvement strategies.
- Difficulty in standardizing the innovation pipeline and its related processes.
- Difficulty in managing all the related artifacts for a given process.
- Time sensitivity of the innovation process is leading to another level of complexity.
- The diversity of the information management systems that are supporting the innovation lifecycle is also increasing the complexities at hand. We have systems that manage the idea lifecycle, support the filtering and selection of ideas, conduct the patent lifecycle management, handle CRM and technology forecasting

and road mapping, as well as manage design-thinking and collaborative innovation and internal tools related to the various workflow management. Most of these systems are not integrated and do not communicate all together, which is leading to information isolation and the absence of a holistic view to measure the needed KPIs related to the innovation lifecycle and calculating the innovation economic impact precisely.

€ All of the above challenges are leading to inefficient monitoring and reporting, as the aggregation of the needed information is not easily achieved since most of the processes and systems involved in the process are isolated into separate teams and islands.

The current enterprise's organizational structures are increasing the complexity of the enterprise innovation management process. In essence, as the enterprise's size increases, so too does the complexity, mirroring one another. Some organization's team structures separate the R&D teams from the R&I teams, with the former focusing more on project, product, and services delivery, and the latter on new, future-facing product and services developments. This separation presents an array of benefits and challenges, increasing the ideation sourcing, the complexity of collaboration, and the ability to manage the innovation lifecycle.

With the rise of such challenges comes a new domain of information management systems, especially in the past couple of years, under the classification of idea management and enterprise innovation management systems and platforms. In 2018, I led a taskforce that concentrated on benchmarking the different available idea management systems found in the global landscape. The taskforce analyzed the various platforms of different suppliers, including Brightidea, Planview Spigit, IdeaScale, Crowdicity, Untap Compete, and F6S. At the time of research, this list included the top idea management software platforms. Most of these systems have features that are capable of defining different innovation processes pipelines, offering a complete idea lifecycle management from submission to selection, and, in most cases, generating informative reports generated from different pipelines in a consolidated manner, support the tracking of the different stakeholders, supports open innovation and crowd engagement, having in-built features for user recognition and gamification capabilities. The reporting module capabilities for most of the listed platforms support the ability to follow up on the progress of a given idea over different pipelines and maturity stages, analyze the bottlenecks, identify the correlations and profiles of different stakeholder types, manage the standard reward systems, and conduct in-depth studies into the different innovation outputs. The drawback is that almost none of these systems offer the ability to integrate with other systems like CRMs, ERPs, patent management systems, and technology forecasting systems. The integration of different systems is necessary for providing the vital 360-degree view of the innovation management lifecycle.

SUMMARY OF TECHNOLOGIES LEADING COLLABORATIVE DISRUPTION

CONNECTIVITY TECHNOLOGIES

Connectivity technology is a crucial technological component that once enabled the awe-inspiring advancements of today. Communication and connectivity revolutionized our modern world, serving as major catalysts and enablers for most of our widespread technologies. For instance, the internet, with its infinite platforms, services, business models, and applications, is part of daily life for billions worldwide — it's no longer the stuff of science fiction and magic realism. At present, we are witnessing another major technological advancement, one that's already directing us to a new horizon: 5G technology will enable unprecedented levels of connectivity characterized by superfast broadband, ultra-reliable low-latency communication, massive machine-type communications, and exceptionally efficient energy usage. Such advancements will lead to real-time communication like never before. In return, and upon the diffusion of 5G, the introduction of a novel generation of technologies will be widely available everywhere.

CLOUD TECHNOLOGIES

The concept of cloud technology has been around since the introduction of Yahoo Mail and Hotmail. These days, technology maturity and affordability have increased. We have IaaS (infrastructure) as a service, HaaS (hardware) as a service, PaaS (platform) as a service, and SaaS (software) as a service. With a full stake of toolchains, Most enterprises, startups, and individuals now have access to affordable, pay-as-you-use, and robust technologies infrastructure that have not been offered before. As new-edge computing capabilities and technology architecture emerge, we are witnessing a paradigm shift in computing. It, the shift, is no longer bound by the need for centralized data centers; rather, edge computing is creating the capability to have thousands of distributed nodes that can be applied to different use cases.

INTERNET OF THINGS

With the increased mass production of sensors and actuators components comes the decrease in their prices. This was first supported by the diffusion of internet connectivity and affordability of computing resources based on the cloud offerings, and then coupled with the introduction of Internet of Things (IoT) digital architecture. The integration of the above elements led to the introduction and diffusion of IoT technologies and solutions that you can find today in most workplaces and many homes. IoT disturbed the normal office and home automation industry through the introduction of a new business model supported by a modern UX and affordable customized offerings.

COGNITIVE TECHNOLOGIES

Cognitive technologies — including Natural Language Processing, Speech Recognition, Semantic Analysis, Image Processing — have matured and advanced at a striking speed in the recent years. These technologies, among many other related ones, are supported by the affordable infrastructures offered by the cloud. Some of the life-altering advancements offered today — popular technologies and solutions — were not affordable just a few years back. Consider the rising impact of Robotic Processing Automation technologies on our day-to-day business process automation, or the possibilities presented by textual semantic analysis for online user-generated content in conjunction with the insights a business can gain into customer feelings, needs, wants, and demands, both collectively and individually.

ARTIFICIAL INTELLIGENCE

As a term, artificial intelligence (AI) was first coined in 1956 by computer and cognitive scientist John McCarthy. But, as a broad area of study, it has existed since antiquity. Many challenges related to affordability of computing power, storage capacity, availability of data sets, more important use cases, and sophistication readiness of the target customers, were slowing down the advancement of the field. In the past few years, though, most of these challenges were resolved, becoming major catalysts for accelerating the advancement and diffusion of AI technologies. As of today, AI technologies are on the top of the technological disruption curve, and AI applications are impacting everyday personal habits and business operations alike. From advertisement recommendation systems that interact with us each time we surf the internet, to call center virtual assistant bots, as well as medical, governmental, and law advisory bots. From weather forecast models to automated parking vehicles and future autonomous vehicles.

E-COMMERCE & DIGITAL MARKETING

E-commerce platforms started to emerge in the early twenty-first century, followed by a wave of diffusion for social network platforms and services. As of late 2020, there are nearly four billion active social media users each month, which is an increase of nine percent from the previous year. Both user-generated content and user-consumed content per day are reaching unexampled levels, with the speed of information, knowledge, and personal opinions locked in acceleration. We are now facing a supernova of content generation and consumption — a phenomenon that is influencing enterprises of all sizes and industries. Positive and negative customer reviews, whether first-person or word-of-mouth, may appear any time and from anywhere, all at the speed of light. Online marketing and sales techniques are becoming more sophisticated each day. Digital marketing and commercialization processes, methods, tools, and technologies are opening new horizons while simultaneously augmenting organizational challenges.

CHATBOTS & VIRTUAL AGENTS

Along with the rising digitalization trend, including e-commerce and the maturity of both cognitive technologies and AI, is that of the diffusion of both chatbots and virtual agents. Surfing the web today means that you have a high probability of interacting with a chatbot. Also, while you're calling your bank or mobile service provider, you may deal with a virtual call center agent. Chatbots and virtual agents are availing new capabilities and potentialities that were not achievable just a few years ago.

VIRTUAL CURRENCY & FINTECH

The rise of virtual currencies and fintech is another disrupting factor. Basic economic formulas are maintained but utilized and managed in different mediums and techniques. The term 'virtual currency' was coined only a decade ago, and the digital form — the invention itself — has existed since the end of the twentieth-century. Today, based on many technological advancements in combination with the readiness of the vast majority of users, virtual currencies are reaching a new diffusion inflection point. Many international banks now support the exchange of virtual currencies, like Bitcoin. Fintech, on the other hand, is posing fresh possibilities while empowering the majority of the crowd to be part of the investment formula. Lending platforms extend the horizons to lenders and beneficiaries, in addition to placing the latest pressures on both the banking sectors and governmental regulatory bodies.

DATA SCIENCE

A tsunami of information is coming from user-generated data, electronic content, sensors-generated content, competition data, and many other diverse sources of digital or digitalized content. Accordingly, the rise of advanced data processing and manipulation techniques was a must to have for achieving value from such data. Techniques and technologies help us understand what happened based on descriptive analytics, why it happened based on diagnostic analytics, and what will happen based on predictive models. The goal, then, is to be achieved by understanding how we can make it happen based on prescriptive analytics and models. As the American author Geoffrey Moore once said, "Without big data analytics, companies are blind and deaf, wandering out like a deer on a freeway." Data is becoming more valuable than gold and petroleum. Organizations that own desired data and have the ability to process and utilize it, hold potential power over competition. It's no wonder how industry giants Google, Apple, and Amazon can go disrupting different industries at the same time. The game is all about data, and those with the ability to process, understand, and act accordingly are most likely to run with the giants. Through the best utilization of data, the digital organizations of today are able to predict the lifetime purchase needs and behavior of its target markets while also accurately forecasting their lifetime share of wallet from such a group. New product development and UX design are supported by epic data science algorithms and advanced analytics.

3D PRINTING

3D printing technologies are maturing faster than anticipated, from accuracy to affordability. Materials science is advancing dramatically, too, with the direct support of 3D printing technologies. In the coming years, 3D printers will not only be observed in industrial factories and small-scale workshops, like fabrication laboratories or 'fab labs,' but also in the homes and hands of everyday consumers. The diffusion of this revolutionary digital technology will reshape many aspects of established manufacturing capabilities and business models, forging a record-breaking era of global human collaboration — not limited to the virtual and digital ones of today, as age-old physical boundaries dissolve. For now, the true impact of such diffusion lies beyond human assessment. Just imagine: you download a CAD design file and pay online, before printing a component on your home 3D printer that will fix your inoperative refrigerator or automobile. Now, imagine a similar scenario when it comes to an R&D collaboration between two entities that are working remotely on the invention of a cutting-edge device or product development. The simple capability of transferring a digital file that will then be replicated physically and materially in just a few hours, calls to mind the futuristic devices and methods of science fiction, like human fantasies of teleportation.

DRONES

Militaries and high-tech industries have employed drone technology since the early-twentieth century. Just like 3D printers, drones are now accessible to an array of professional fields and everyday consumers. Solutions and use cases range from hobbyist photography, film productions, agriculture operations, delivery services, and emergency management to disease control and prevention. With the rising accessibility for drones, many high paying and dangerous jobs in the commercial sector are up for replacement on the basis of safer and more cost-effective solutions for transportation, delivery, and data collection. Regulation is one of the major elements for the diffusion of drones, as current requirements and laws limit the commercial use of autonomous drones worldwide. This challenge is expected to tail off in the coming years.

ROBOTICS

Robots are helping humans complete tasks with greater efficiency and reach. Thanks to advancements in robotic technologies, humanity is also achieving the unthinkable. Most of the technologies of digital disruption discussed in this table are directly impacting the maturity and speed of development within the robotics domain. The scope of this domain is wide, including virtual robots as virtual agents or 'robotic process automation' (RPA) and industrial robotic arms being expanded to humanoid robots. Today, robots are widely used in the mass production of consumer and industrial goods, as well as in scientific studies and experiments, arms manufacturing, surgical procedures, resource extraction, and space exploration. Meanwhile, humanoid robots that look, feel, and act more human than ever before are advancing and maturing rapidly. The commercial diffusion of robots — in every office and home — depends upon achieving the technology maturity, affordability of the cost of ownership, and finally consumer acceptance.

THE
INNOVATIVE
DINOSAUR

WEARABLE ROBOTICS

Exoskeletons are another modern technology that seemingly actualize our sci-fi dreams of expanding and enhancing the human experience. Medical exoskeletons restore a degree of mobility to body parts affected by permanent paralysis, and the military variety assists troops traversing unforgiving terrains. New use cases have emerged out of the rapid improvements in actuator and sensor technology, in turn enabling the engineering of portable systems and the transition from academic research to commercial applications. The number and range of industrial use cases are evolving to make the factory and warehouse experience safer and more streamlined for workers. The integration of mechanical and electronic capabilities with the human body signals mind-blowing potential and possibilities: a lifting of, or transcendence from, our physical limitations as mortal beings, ushering in the age of the 'super worker.' While exoskeletons are costly and thus out of reach for everyday consumers, the price is expected to drop in the coming decade. At that stage, the industrial use model of today will be eclipsed by the widespread everyday use of the future. An ethical dilemma exists upon the diffusion of such technologies with respect to accessibility, equality, and ownership.

CALL FOR BACKERS & CONTRIBUTORS

To be able to achieve the objectives of *The Innovative Dinosaur*, a community of practitioners' needs be established. This is a call for contribution. Each comment and suggestion that we receive will help us to increase the maturity and value of the proposed frameworks, canvases, tools, and methods. Also, we are open to receive frameworks, tools, methods and programs from our community to be available and shared with others. We have tried to design different levels of contributions. Please choose the one which suits your experience, competency, desire, available time, and convenience.

BETA READERS

We are seeking reviews, feedback, suggestions, and improvement proposals for both content and reading experience. All questions, advice, opinions, and critques will help us mature and improve the content and concepts.

RESEARCHERS

Researchers in the field of digital transformation, enterprise innovation management, new product development management, change management, user centric, design thinking, and organization transformation are all welcomed to participate and contribute with thoughts and insights.

THOUGHT LEADERS

Experienced professionals and experts are encouraged to contribute to enriching the content and maturity of the different sections of *The Innovative Dinosaur*. Also, authors of canvases, frameworks, automation tools and book authors specialized in the field are all welcomed to propose sections and content to be added to the current and future versions.

EXPERTS CASE STUDIES

As we are seeking to share best practices and success stories, we are welcoming contributions from Enterprise Professionals, either to share a case study or a success story within the field of digital transformation and innovation management. Both internal and external initiatives are welcomed.

ACADEMIC INSTITUTES & EDUCATORS

Academic institutes, educators, trainers, and instructors who are interested to use *The Innovative Dinosaur* as a whole book, frameworks, tools, methods, or canvases for education purposes are more than welcomed.

BUSINESS ENTERPRISES

Organizations offering services or products that support the implementation and operations of the concepts included in *The Innovative Dinosaur* are welcomed to share and contribute what adds value to the community.

COMMUNITY PARTNERS & AFFILIATES

For community, forums, social networks groups, & pages managers who will promote *The Innovative Dinosaur* through their own communities. Also, community of practice managers are more than welcome to join this category.

PROFESSIONAL BODIES

Professional bodies focusing on the filed of enterprise innovation management, new product development management, change management, user centric, design thinking, and organization transformation who are interested in encouraging their members to participate in one of the different categories are welcomed.

Please share, link, comment and engage
Reviews and Endorsements are welcomed.

LET'S START OUR COLLABORATION

More Information:

🌐 www.theinnovativedinosaur.com
✉ motaz@enterpriseinnovationdesign.com
in www.linkedin.com/in/magamawi

www.ingramcontent.com/pod-product-compliance
Lightning Source LLC
Chambersburg PA
CBHW050041220326
41599CB00045B/7240